SOFT SUBVERSIONS

SEMIOTEXT(E) FOREIGN AGENTS SERIES

Copyright © 2009 Félix Guattari and Semiotext(e)

Published by Semiotext(e)
2007 Wilshire Blvd., Suite 427, Los Angeles, CA 90057
www.semiotexte.com

Special thanks to Jarred Becker, Sande Cohen, John Ebert, Emmanuelle Guattari, Jeanine Herman, Andrea Loselle, Benjamin Meyers, Florence Petri, Gianna Quach, Bernard Schütze, Danielle Sivadon, and Charles Wolfe.

The Index was prepared by Andrew Lopez.

Cover Art: MATRIX XIV, light installation by Erwin Redl,
photo by Max Spitzenberger.
Page 1: Photo by André Smalle, 1980.

Design by Hedi El Kholti

ISBN: 978-1-58435-073-6

Distributed by The MIT Press, Cambridge, Mass. and London, England
Printed in the United States of America

SOFT SUBVERSIONS

TEXTS AND INTERVIEWS 1977–1985

Félix Guattari

Edited by Sylvère Lotringer

Introduction by Charles J. Stivale

Translated by Chet Wiener and Emily Wittman

Contents

Introduction by Charles J. Stivale   9

PART I: GUATTARI BY HIMSELF
   1. I Am an Idea-Thief   21
   2. Institutional Intervention   33
   3. So What   64
   4. Everywhere at Once   81

PART II: WHY ITALY?
   5. An Open Letter to Some Italian Friends   91
   6. New Spaces of Liberty for Minoritarian Desire   94
   7. Minority and Terrorism   102
   8. Like the Echo of a Collective Melancholia   106
   9. A New Alliance Is Possible   113

PART III: MICRO-REVOLUTIONS
   10. The Adolescent Revolution   131
   11. A Liberation of Desire   141
   12. Machinic Junkies   158

PART IV: PSYCHOANALYSIS AND SCHIZOANALYSIS
   13. Lacan Was an Event in My Life   165
   14. Psychoanalysis Should Get a Grip on Life   170
   15. The Unconscious Is Turned Toward the Future   177
   16. The Refrain of Being and Meaning   184
   17. Four Truths for Psychiatry   198
   18. The Schizoanalyses   204

PART V: INTEGRATED WORLD CAPITALISM
   19. Plan for the Planet   229
   20. Capital as the Integral of Power Formations   244
   21. Capitalist Systems, Structures and Processes   265
   22. Microphysics of Power / Micropolitics of Desire   278
   23. Postmodern Deadlock and Post-Media Transition   291
   24. Entering the Post-Media Era   301
   25. Utopia Today   307

Bibliography   309
Notes   313
Index   325

Charles J. Stivale

RETHINKING (WITH) FÉLIX GUATTARI

Félix Guattari continues to fascinate and to intrigue readers despite his renowned supposed "difficulty." In reading him now, sixteen years since his death, one gets a sense, gradually, that it is we who had the difficulties, not him, since we are slowly catching up to a visionary thought that simply came too early for our comprehension. Moreover, his works and those of friends about him just keep on appearing, most notably *Micropolitiques* with Suely Ronik, texts by and interviews with Guattari from his 1982 trip to Brazil (translated as *Molecular Revolution in Brazil*); the collected notes on his first collaboration with Gilles Deleuze, *Écrits pour l'Anti-Oedipe* (translated as *The Anti-Oedipus Papers*); and Franco "Bifo" Berardi's biography of Guattari, *Félix Guattari*.[1] So the logic behind a newly constituted edition of *Soft Subversions* (first published in 1996), like its predecessor *Chaosophy* (1995), is altogether obvious: besides reorganizing diverse texts by and interviews with Guattari in a more systematic fashion, these editions bring forth hitherto unpublished and untranslated texts revealing different facets of his thought.[2]

The revised edition of Soft *Subversions* necessarily has a very new tenor and emphasis. In section I, "Guattari by Himself," we start (with Robert Maggiori's opening question in "I Am an Idea-Thief") by considering Guattari's thoughts on his challenging and often neologistic critical vocabulary. For Guattari, these are "word-tools" that can function as a minor language rather than as universals. In fact, Guattari proclaims himself (modestly?) to be an "idea thief," happily lifting terms from other fields and turning them to his own use. The purpose of this strategy is to forge linkages, i.e., between singularities within a particular field and into a range of components and fields in other conceptual territories, transversally. Assemblages (*agencements*, translated also as arrangements) are an example of such a singular tool, functioning transversally to link concepts and bring them into productively intense interaction. This opening interview reveals a dazzling display of transversality at work, on Freudo-Marxism, global economies, molecular revolutions, and the Freudian unconscious.

The second text, on "Institutional Intervention," is a long unpublished interview with Guattari that overlaps in some ways with the first one. But thanks to much greater biographical detail, we can follow Guattari's intellectual trajectory through his work with Jean Oury at the La Borde clinic, his association with Lacan and the *École freudienne*, and his encounter and work with Gilles Deleuze. Two major points of the lengthy interview concern his work with, and yet distance from, various groups, and then the difficulties that such assemblages (*agencement*, a term he prefers to "groups") have with the forces of power (that is, the dominant social and economic structures) when the assemblages are perceived to oppose the dominant models.

"So What" and "Everywhere at Once" are two parts of a long interview with Michel Butel from 1985. I note this date because in Guattari's biography, this period of the mid 1980s marks the "winter years" of limited possibilities for creation of collective assemblages of enunciation that seemed possible a decade or two earlier.[3] Whereas "So What" is a long essay that retraces Guattari's intellectual trajectory, extending it toward an important new alternative, ecology, "Everywhere at Once" gives Guattari the opportunity to reflect on his pre-Deleuze activism, about the place of May '68 in this trajectory, and also to explain the transformation that occurred through his work with Deleuze.

In the newly constituted second section, five new essays on Italy and minoritarian politics complement two chapters ("Like the Echo of a Collective Melancholia," and "A New Alliance Is Possible") retained from the original edition. Guattari's "Open Letter" reacts to the growing politics of repression in 1977—in this case, openly in support of Antonio Negri. Although Guattari affirms his belief that Negri "did everything he could to prevent terrorist groups inspired by the Red Brigades to expand," his main point is that a strong response to multifaceted forms of institutional repression is necessary. Rather than renounce "on principle all violence; rather, one must develop effective forms of violence that will modify in a revolutionary direction the social relations of power and will set in motion authentic dynamics for liberation" (Open Letter, p. 92 below). But instead of dogmatic groupuscules that become scapegoats for the media, this violence should be that of "of workers, women, and youths who are struggling to change their [social] condition" (Open Letter, p. 92 below). Although Guattari here seems skeptical about the role of groupuscules on the extreme Left, his statements at least hold out the hope that these groups can shake off their sluggishness in order to help the masses realize "clear objectives," notably of "discovering the ways and means for [affecting] irreversible social transformations" (Open Letter, p. 93 below).

An example of this European repression—Giscard d'Estaing's decision to extradite the lawyer Klaus Croissant to German authorities[4]—is the starting point for Guattari's affirmation of "new space of liberty for minoritarian desire against majoritarian consensus."[5] Presented in Berlin in 1978, this address describes in grim terms both the evident forms of totalitarian state repression—in the USSR, Japan, the USA, and Europe alike—and a "repression practiced by the state, a softer, yet also more systematic and deceptive repression," through the infiltration of functionaries in debates on ecology, drugs, women's rights, prostitution, among other issues. In this soft repression, "Power" must recruit members of the intelligentsia to fall in line with "the majoritarian consensus that constitutes the lynchpin [*clé de voute*] of the whole system" (New Spaces, p. 98 below). To fight this, Guattari theorizes a kind of transversal organization and communication, to create modes of exchange between disparate marginal groups and revolutionary movements across Europe (and beyond) through flexible "liaison committees against repression and for new spaces of liberty" (New Spaces, p. 99 below). He cites the September 1977 rally in Bologna as one positive example of "mass international exchange."[6] No "common program" then for marginals and revolutionaries, just "effective action."

The following chapter is part of a long "dialogue" between Guattari and Maria-Antonietta Macchiocchi on minoritarian struggle vis-à-vis Italian "terrorism." Evidence of Guattari's ongoing collaboration with Deleuze emerges in these pages, that is, their attempt in *A Thousand Plateaus* to rethink the minor in a broad socio-semiotic way.[7] Then, in "Like the Echo ...," Guattari focuses on the film *Germany in Autumn* as a way to reflect again on the so-called "terrorist phenomenon" and to contrast German repression to the Italian counterpart.[8] And in the lengthy 1982 interview with Sylvère Lotringer on a possible "New Alliance," Guattari speaks of the "rhizome" of political and conceptual tools and instruments available to continue to struggle in a new political era, that of molecular revolution.[9] While the Italian experience provides an important focal point, Guattari broadens his reflection to France, Poland, the USSR, China, and politics of East-West (under Reagan) vis-à-vis North-South.

The short, revised third section gives three succinct examples of this molecular revolution: difficulties and psycho-social ramifications of youth culture ("The Adolescent Revolution"); an interview on sexual politics and, especially, gay liberation ("A Liberation of Desire"); and a prescient reflection (especially in 1984) on "Machinic Junkies," the production of a "machinic subjectivity" and inherent "doping." Well over a decade before the arrival in France of the Internet and the World Wide Web, Guattari argues that "molecular machinic subjectivity fosters creativity, in no matter what area... Americans are the champions of doping, they have thousands of ways to do it, and invent new ones every day... It is machinic subjectivity that fuels great impetuses like Silicon Valley" (Machinic Junkies, p. 160 below). Yet he also sees the reverse possibility, the search for refuge and not creativity at all. Thus, he concludes: "The visibly doped sectors shouldn't merely be defenses of acquired territories; the residual crystals that constitute machinic dope can penetrate the entire planet, reanimate and relaunch it. A society that has reached the point of being so locked in should open up to this, or it will burst" (Machinic Junkies, p. 161 below). One wonders what Guattari would have made of the "reanimation" (in all kinds of manifestations) unleashed by cyberculture and e-commerce, not to mention the 24/7 new cycle, YouTube, social networking, and real-time gaming.

The revised fourth section offers a range of texts on Guattari's schizoanalytic thinking (with four new texts and four retained from the original volume). While my 1985 interview with Guattari covered diverse topics,[10] one of particular interest was his relationship with Lacan and how the "master's" thought corresponded to the work Guattari had undertaken with Deleuze. Then, in asking psychoanalysis to "get a grip on life," Guattari emphasizes how the collapse both of religions and of their function as mythic references resulted in their replacement, generally, by mass-mediated culture and, specifically, by psychoanalysis and family therapy. Insisting that such subjective formations of reference constitute one's organization of life, Guattari argues that the "social functionality" of mythic references should take precedence over any claims of scientific authority: "The less the shrinks see themselves as scientists, the more they will take heed of their responsibilities... If one refuses to situate a problem in its political and micropolitical context, one ends up sterilizing its impact of truth" (Psychoanalysis Should..., p. 175–176 below). In this sense, social and political life and not claims of scientific authority must ground therapy: "What is important is to determine whether the position [that psychiatrists and health workers] occupy will, or will not, contribute to the overcoming of the realities of segregation, social and psychological mutilation, and whether one will, at least, be able to minimize the damage" (Psychoanalysis Should..., p. 176 below).

Guattari's 1980 interview on the unconscious's turn "toward the future" opens with his self-deprecating description as a "half-wit" and "short-sighted" in terms of a particularly specific vision of molecular mutations as being "the true fabric of long-term historical transformations" (Unconscious is Turned, p. 177 below). To the interviewers' demand for specifics, Guattari points to "the technology of the pill" (Unconscious is Turned, p. 178 below) as a molecular transformation, but also to the way in which the concepts of ideology and of the group have collapsed, to be replaced by new notions. Guattari points not only to his work on schizoanalysis and concepts such as faciality (*visagéité*), but also to the work of artists, like Proust, who "is one of the greatest analysts who ever existed, because he was able to detect modes of communication, major routes between music, painting, social relations, life in the salons, physical sensations, etc. He worked the unconscious as transsemiotic matter" (Unconscious is Turned, pp. 182–183 below) as well as connecting the multiple components held together by the abstract machine of "the refrain," in terms of "being and meaning" through explicit dream analysis. The essay that follows these, from 1985, covers similar ground, Guattari discussing "four truths for psychiatry" and explaining "four levels of intervention" required for the radical conversion of psychiatry. The section's final essay, an interview with a lengthy disquisition by Guattari, addresses the specific means by which he conceptualized schizoanalysis as a viable practice and alternative to the institutional blockages and insufficiencies denounced in his other essays and interviews.

The seven final texts, in section five, all concern Guattari's political vision, particularly on a global scale. Leave it to Guattari to propose nothing less than a "Plan for the Planet" through a detailed analysis over several essays on "Integrated World Capitalism" (published here as "Plan for the Planet," "Capital as the Integral of Power Formation," and "Capitalist Systems, Structures, and Processes").[11] In the context of super-power politics and confrontations in the late 1970s and early 1980s, Guattari dared to sketch an image of the big picture, of the ways in which markets and production were linked globally, rather than separated and divided. While this notion, for us, seems so obvious as to need little discussion, at the time Guattari was suggesting something quite bold, indeed absurd for many ideologues and economists. The "Plan for the Planet" examines, on one hand, the ways in which this world capitalism will succeed in consolidating its hold on means of production globally, and on the other hand, what might be the possibility for the proliferation of marginal groups, minor and autonomous, opposed to the major power formations in nation-states. This mutation is precisely what underlies Guattari's theorizing about Integrated World Capitalism: given that "all productive labor is defined by mechanized labor... Automatized and computerized production no longer draws its consistency from a basic human factor, but from a machinic phylum which traverses, bypasses, disperses, miniaturizes, and co-opts all human activities" (Capital as the Integral, pp. 249–250 below). As

Bifo points out in his introduction to *Piano sul pianeta*, these essays on capital as power formation and capitalist systems are visionary texts that "pointed directly to the long-term trends and prefigured in this way the process that we see developing in the 1990s... [helping] us understand something about what is happening in the planetary economy and psycho-chemistry" (xiii, my translation).

The essay on "Microphysics" of power and desire, delivered at a Milan conference on Foucault in 1985, puts into question Guattari's assertion to me the same year (in the interview that starts section IV) that "I was never influenced by Foucault's work... it was never of great importance." In fact, Guattari does emphasize Foucault's importance, first, for undertaking to "dismantle the false appearance of the individuation of subjectivity" and, second, for proposing a micropolitics that breaks completely "with the analytics of representation issuing from the Kantian tradition," hence constituting a broad "micropolitics of existence and desire": "All the themes we might call Foucauldian existentialism converge on this pivotal point between semiotic representation and the pragmatics of 'existentialization,' and, in this way, places the micropolitics of desire alongside the microphysics of power according to specific procedures" (Microphysics, pp. 289–290 below). Questions of representation also are clearly on Guattari's mind in his brief statement (at the end of the same year) on the "Postmodern Deadlock," responding in part to Jean-François Lyotard's *The Postmodern Condition*.[12] For Guattari, these "postmodern philosophers" represent little more than a "new ethics of disengagement" (Deadlock, p. 296 below), supporting a position that "today's crises in artistic and social practices can no longer result in anything but a total refusal of all collective project-making of any importance. Let's cultivate our garden, and preferably in conformity with the practices and customs of our contemporaries. Don't make waves! Just make fashion, gauged by the art and opinion markets, screened through publicity campaigns and polls" (Deadlock, p. 295

below). To counter this in the "post-media era," Guattari extols the creation of "other 'existential chemistries,' open to all the recompositions and transmutations of these 'singularity salts' whose secret arts and analysis can deliver up" (Entering, p. 306 below). The statement of hope with which this penultimate essay ends resonates for us in a new century as well and gives all the more pertinence to the reorganization and reissue of this volume:

> Analysis again. But where? How? Well, everywhere possible... It can be individual, for those who tend to lead their lives as if it were a work of art; dual in all possible ways, including, why not, a psychoanalytic couch, as long as it has been dusted off; multiple, through group, network, institutional, and collective practices; and finally, micropolitical by virtue of other social practices, other forms of auto-valorizations and militant actions, leading, through a systematic decentering of social desire, to soft subversions and imperceptible revolutions that will eventually change the face of the world, making it happier. Let's face it, it's long overdue. (Entering, p. 306 below)

And given the "plan for the planet" with which this section begins, the "true utopians" for Guattari are conservatives who think things can just go on as always and even want to turn back the clock to some bygone era. In a final optimistic burst about "molecular revolutions," Guattari affirms his belief that "a fabulous expansion [of creativity and machinic vitality] will eventually break down all the conservatisms that 'keep us in place' in this absurd and blind society" (Utopia Today, p. 307 below). Thus, despite the "winter years" that tended to overshadow much of the period covered by these essays, we can find in Guattari's essay great inspiration for reflection and moving forward through activism in our own era.

I
———

GUATTARI BY HIMSELF

1

I AM AN IDEA-THIEF

Robert Maggiore: *Some of your books, like* L'Inconscient machinique [The Machinic Unconscious], *are particularly difficult, because of the extremely abstract nature of the language, the neologisms and the variety of vocabularies borrowed from very different disciplines. Is that an elitist gesture or a necessity dictated by the object of your research?*

Félix Guattari: One thing is sure: it is not a gesture. But it could be a weakness or a necessity. Weakness? I don't think that is the right description for the books I have written with Gilles Deleuze. For my own personal work, let's say it is a chronic deficiency. But it is up to you to be the judge. Obviously, personally, I myself would tend to say that I had to forge my own language in order to confront certain questions, and to forge a language means to invent words, key-terms, carrying-case terms. In the best cases, instrumental word tools are capable of opening up a new set of questions, of carrying them along and articulating various fields. I do not believe in universal literature or philosophy but rather in the virtues of minor languages. So the question becomes rather simple: either a minor language connects to minor issues, producing particular results, or it remains isolated, vegetates, turns back on itself and produces nothing. Therefore I do not think that it is an elitist attitude. I understand that this annoys some people but, in the end, that is not my problem. What bothers me is not being understood when I use a major language, for instance when I want to say something about current politics.

You forge specific tools for specific fields of research. But this creates problems when you communicate that research. Shouldn't the tool be universal?

But I trust neither a universal tool nor the virtues of communication in that area. The most desirable effect that can be anticipated, in the conceptual field, is not in the order of comprehension, but in the form of a certain efficiency. "It works or it doesn't work." Imagine that someone offers you a little calculator to perform arithmetical operations. Is there communication there? A potential usage is transmitted to you. The performances it allows are established as soon as a certain competence relating to its use is acquired. In my view, the same thing happens with theoretical expressions that should function as tools, as machines, with reference neither to an ideology nor to the communication of a particular form of subjectivity. And this is true in every field. Think about May '68. There was no ideological transmission, but rather the repercussion of events. There was a "It doesn't work that way," which was transmitted at machine speed, and not at the speed of ideological intelligibility. In the nineteenth century one thought that the proletariat had to be educated first in order to reach a level of comprehension, like the ability to read certain fundamental texts, then it would translate into practice... But really, things do not work that way!

Let's get back to the way you lift elements of your vocabulary from different, more or less heterogeneous, disciplines.

Lacan accused a third of the members of his Freudian School of being falsifiers. I claim the term *falsifier* for myself, being an idea-thief and shuffler of second hand concepts. Borrowing is not a problem in itself, except on the level of the semantic foundation of a new word. For example, our term "deterritorialization" was based on a concept of territory borrowed from American anthropology. This reference was quickly forgotten and the term integrated into very different disciplines, where it took on syntactic, rhetorical and even stylistic dimensions, which in turn guided us in certain ways.

In the case of Deleuze and Guattari the operation seems to have been successful, because now people borrow terms from you: deterritorialization, rhizome, war machine... But I wonder if, because of the object of your research itself, there wasn't a kind of "necessity" to use all possible concepts, diversifying terms, precisely because "man" is not "something," but a crisscross, an intersection of psychological, biological, socioeconomic, etc. entities, necessitating "multiple takes."

There may be a misunderstanding. What you are saying might suggest that I have to seek out eclectic expressions in order to explore a fundamentally heteroclite field. I don't think so. Instead, I am aware of trying to forge a certain kind of—and here, of course, I am going to use my own jargon—"concrete machine" that traverses different domains. This concrete machine must be capable not of integrating, but of articulating singularities of the field under consideration to join absolutely heterogeneous components. It is not by absorption or eclectic borrowings that this can be achieved; it is by acquiring a certain power, which I call, precisely, "deterritorialization"—a capacity to hook onto deterritorialized fields. I'm not keen on an approximative interdisciplinarity. I'm interested in an "*intra*disciplinarity" that is capable of traversing heterogeneous fields and carrying the strongest charges of "transversality."

Could you give a specific example?

Let's consider Freud's notion, quite enticing really, of the "complex"—it would take too long to enumerate the definitions. But in the beginning people thought this term was weird. Today it is used everywhere. Deleuze and I forged the concept of "arrangement" *[agencement]* that originally belonged to the domain of scientific logic. It's a broader, more all encompassing notion because it doesn't only designate an unconscious formation, but also relates to imaginary representations, to language chains, to economic, political, aesthetic, microsocial, etc., semiotics. Compared to "complex" it is a notion whose comprehension is weaker, but whose extension is greater, enabling categories of diverse origins not to be excluded from the "complex" field, which in turn graft onto other concepts, like "machine." Thus we speak of "machinic arrangements" for an eventual association with "collective arrangements of enunciation."

Why not say "ensemble of machines"?

Because ensemble of machines would give the idea of a spatial disposition in relation to which individuals, subjects, would remain exterior, while arrangement problematizes enunciation and subjectivation: how a subject is fabricated. It points to a conceptual chemistry distinct from any axiomatic idea. I prefer unstable, precarious, transitory chemical formulas to homogeneous axiomatics. The concepts of "arrangement" and "machinic arrangement" have no claims to universality. They are tools. To call them universals would be saying two things: either one expects them to apply to a very large field, or one wants to make them "universals," that is to say foundations, basic principles of a scientific or moral order. But, in my opinion, the analysis of the economy of desire implies a multivalent logic that legitimates the coexistence of discourses that cannot have an axiomatic homogeneity. If you object and say that this is not what I said ten years ago, I answer, "Too bad," or even, "So much the better." Perhaps this is a good sign! Expressions of desire can simultaneously signify formally contradictory things, because they refer to various universes of reference.

But is it due to the subject that expresses the propositions or to the thing about which the judgment is made?

It's both. For example, while delivering a well-constructed speech on women's liberation, I can practically, unknowingly, display phallocratic behaviors. Discourses and realities never cease to interfere with each other. It doesn't do very much good to wave laws or imperatives ordering this or that; I'll still evolve and the world will keep changing rapidly, ever more quickly, much faster than in Heraclitus. How can such fluctuations and contradictions be managed? One day I can say terrible things about *Libération* [the newspaper where this interview appeared],[1] denouncing its positions on such or such a point, and then exclaim, on another occasion, "Oh, where would we be without *Libération!*" This *duplicity* may appear intolerable from a moral, or a moralizing point of view. I believe that concrete situations always confront us with this kind of moral ambiguity, which seems to me specific to schizoanalysis. It has nothing to do with the question "Where are you speaking from?" which broke the eardrums of our generation, but rather, "What is it that begins to speak through you in a given situation or context?" Nor is it a matter of the Lacanian "*it* speaks," but rather of Foucault's questioning of what he calls "utterances": how and why they assembled in a certain way.

How can this be illustrated, for example, in the political realm?

Take the notion of class, or the class struggle. It implies that there are perfectly delimited sociological objects: bourgeoisie, proletariat, aristocracy... But these entities become hazy in the many inter-zones, the intersections of the petite bourgeoisie, the aristocratic bourgeoisie, the aristocracy of the proletariat, the lumpenproletariat, the nonguaranteed elite... The result: an indeterminacy that prevents the social field from being mapped out in a clear and distinct way, and which undermines militant practice. Now the notion of arrangement can be useful here, because it shows that social entities are not made up of bipolar oppositions. Complex arrangements place parameters like race, sex, age, nationality, etc., into relief. Interactive crossings imply other kinds of logic than that of two-by-two class oppositions. Importing this notion of arrangement to the social field isn't just a gratuitous theoretical subtlety. But it might help to configure the situation, to come up with cartographies capable of identifying and eluding certain simplistic conceptions concerning class struggle.

You have considered this arrangement logically within the field of the unconscious and the social field, two areas of research that you have never given up and which have been explored by Freud and Marx. It seems then, that even while criticizing Marx and Freud, you have preserved the questions that both raised—that is to say the edification of a just city and the exploration of the unconscious. Can we do without these questions today?

That wouldn't be easy. But, in order to answer your question, certain changes must be considered. It is impossible to envisage the survival of the human species without considering increasing integration between human work and machinic work, to the point where assemblages of individuals and machines would supply goods, services and new needs, etc. on a massive scale. We are on a dizzying flight forward: we can no longer turn back, return to a state of nature, return to good intentions or small-scale artisanal productions. The ever more world-integrated processes of production authorize—and I think that this is a Marxist intuition that remains valuable—a blossoming of freedom and desire. We have been provided with new means of surpassing medieval, or even Neolithic conceptions of human interaction. In order to constitute and hold human aggregates together, in order to discipline the division of labor, social systems until now have had to use means of organization that, generally, have been catastrophic for individual development. Capitalism can only create the impetus for productive motivations—on personal, local, regional and worldwide scales—by calling upon segregative techniques of incredible cruelty. It only selects and economically valorizes those things that fit its specific needs. Everything else is devalued, polluted, massacred. In this respect, it must be said that Soviet socialism, the socialism of the Gulag, became the supreme form of capitalism. Yet we have inherited one essential thing from it: the understanding that no socialism, no social liberation can rely upon economic reshuffling alone. The alternative is clear: either the revolutionary processes take charge of the ensemble of productive components—and not only the production of markets, but all the productions of life, desire, science, creation, liberty—or they will only retrace previous modes of social domination, which have meanwhile become more and more ruthless. Recently, Paul Virilio spoke here about speed and about a society where only a few people would move about the globe, while all the others would be under a kind of "house arrest." This is the real nature of the problem: how can the restraints inherent in the most integrated and the most sophisticated levels of production, taking into account the electronic revolution, the most advanced technologies, etc., how can they remain compatible with a way of life where people can circulate freely not only in space, but in ideas, emotions, desires, even sexes…

Isn't that a sweet dream...?

I don't know. I'm hyperoptimistic and hyperpessimistic at the same time! I think that we are going to have to face, in the coming years, very difficult trials: an increase in the social control of youth, immigrants treated like cattle, constantly shrinking free space... This is what is in store for us. And, in this respect, I must emphasize the fundamental complicity between East and West, whose displays of disagreement about the menace of a World War cover up a common effort that insures both the subjection of liberation movements and all kinds of potential disturbances. We also cannot forget the background of a demographic trend that will have us go from five billion global inhabitants to eight billion in twenty years and, beyond, to figures that can make your head spin. All this will not make things simpler. That is the catastrophic side. And yet I continue to believe that it is advisable to maintain a sort of calm, since "objective" conditions (although we can hardly use this term anymore) lead one to hope for real revolutions—both molar and molecular—to provide the means to construct a new social order.

What makes you think this?

Neither the "good intentions," nor the "good nature" of a proletariat as the bearer of the hope of the future! But, rather, in what I call *machinic phyla*. Wherever a desire to create or an inclination to really live springs up, wherever something is happening, be it in the sciences or the arts, one encounters a rejection of contemporary systems of organization and hierarchization. Scientific progress and aesthetic or cultural mutations never proceed from authoritative means. As soon as some general headquarters tries to legislate the visual arts, literature, science, etc., research and creation come to a dead halt. If the most complex domains can function perfectly well without bureaucratic and elitist segregation, why should the arrangement of the socius be an exception? The perspective of a real social revolution seems to me as open as the fields of possibility for scientific and esthetic revolutions. Perhaps I am being naïve, but I do not see why the organization of social relations in a way that permits everyone to live and to develop would be more difficult to solve than questions of quantum physics or the manipulation of genes.

It is not a question of "difficulty," but of feasibility. This field of possibility for social revolution that you see emerging in ways of life, in new freedoms and creativity, is not unrelated to or independent from the socioeconomic field of organization, which gives history a bad time: on the contrary, it is conditioned and smothered by it.

In fact, this is what leads me to introduce the notion of "*molecular revolutions,*" which I believe complements rather than opposes traditional notions of social revolution in today's world. Changes do not have to come about from large-scale socioeconomic conditions. All these systems leak from the inside, as systems of defense, but also as systems of mutation. Molecular mutations do not always assert themselves on a large scale, and they must be gauged differently in the short term. But this does not mean that they do not exist. We do not have the same relations to reading, writing, images, space, sex, the body, the night, the sun, pain, as we only had ten years ago. Profound and irreversible mutations are underway in all these areas. In other words, the molecular substratum on which all large social collectivities are inscribed has become a sort of bubbling soup, a "machinic soup," the way a "biological soup" is not "determined" unilaterally by macrosocial conditions.

The question of political intervention on a social global level thus appears to me to have become inseparable from its connections at this molecular level. We don't need to build "ecological niches" or "islands of fresh air" alongside large social collectivities, but, rather, to aim these molecular revolutions (whose aggregative effect is discontinuous, cannot be considered in terms of political programs and often escapes sociological description) towards the construction of new social war machines, which will themselves forge their own support creating a new kind of social praxis. The difference between these kinds of molecular revolutions and earlier forms of revolution is that before everything was centered on ideology or The Program, whereas today the mutational models— even if they involve things which appear to be secondary, like fashion—are immediately transmitted to the entire planet. It is the machinic integration of processes of production, circulation and information that catalyzes this new "deal of the cards." A mutation like that introduced by microprocessors changes the actual sub-stratum of human existence and, in reality, opens up fabulous possibilities for liberation.

I would like very much if, before we wind this up, you would take up the question of the unconscious in relation to Freud.

The "unconscious" is not a very fortunate term. Freud's genius, or perhaps his madness, was to have hit upon the emergence of a subjective continent which philosophy, the history of religions and literatures had only explored from a distance. Then he forged theo-retical instruments, devised analytical techniques and encouraged the creation of schools and international institutions, so that questions that were originally exposed quickly closed up again. For me, it is not a question of "preserving" Freud, but of acquiring the means to explore and exploit the continent he discovered almost by chance. What really happens when one makes a slip of the tongue, when one is dreaming, when one becomes crazed with desire, when one has the feeling that the whole world is lost if the beloved's attention turns in another direction, when one no longer recognizes one's own voice? It is impossible to get rid of these kinds of questions. What psychoanalysts refuse to see is that the molecular texture of the unconscious is constantly being worked on by global society, that is to say, these days, by capitalism, which has cut individuals up into partial machines subjected to its ends, and has excluded or infused guilt into everything that opposed its own functionality. It has fabricated submissive children, "sad Indians," labor reserves, people who have become incapable of speaking, of talking things out, of dancing—in short, of living their desires. Capitalism mobilizes everything to halt the proliferation and the actualization of unconscious potentialities. In other words, the antagonisms that Freud points out, between desire investments and superego investments, have nothing to do with a topic, nor a dynamic, but with politics and micropolitics. This is where the molecular revolution begins: you are a fascist or a revolutionary with yourself first, on the level of your superego, in relation to your body, your emotions, your husband, your wife, your children, your colleagues, in your relation to justice and the State. There is a continuum between these "prepersonal" domains and the infrastructures and strata that "exceed" the individual.

This reminds me of a conversation about informers that I had with Toni Negri, whom I just visited in a far-away Italian prison. We were wondering what the difference is between Pecci, the "repentant" Red Brigade member, and the two hard line leaders, Curcio [primary founder] or Moretti [current leader]. Well, at bottom, nothing. Those who "talk" to the cops and those who play it tough, who commit or finance gross and suicidal acts for the movement, like assassinating or "knee-capping" them, are the same people. Each has invented a militant personality in imaginary symbiosis with the same sort of conception of the world. And when difficulties come up, and when something gets in the way of their plans, everything collapses. These people have constructed themselves around a deep divide between their "militancy" and their lives. This is why they rejected the creativity of Movement 77 [the Italian Autonomists].[2] This is why they have worked for the elimination of movements, like those of Bologna, much more efficiently than all the Cossigas[3] and Berlinguers[4] in the system. Any stratification or segmentation of the movement will always mortally wound it. In contrast, a rhizomic organization can be invented to promote components that lead us through. It is a matter of being able to move from dream to dominant reality, from poetry to science, from the most violent social reality to the most tender daily relations. The field of the unconscious is the site of every possibility, in every domain, of connections and not separations, of stratifications and segmentarities. If there is no fusion between analytical practices concerning the formation of the unconscious, and the political practices of social formations, then the same attitudes, the same dogmatic gregarity, the same hierarchies, the same conditions of exclusion and domination will endlessly recur. Political action should become, in my view, synonymous with the analytical venture—and vice versa!

INSTITUTIONAL INTERVENTION

Your contribution to the movement of institutional analysis is original. On the one hand, you are among those to have first explored this track. On the other hand, you actively participated in various therapy and institutional analysis groups. Indeed, you are still president of CERFI.[1] Can you retrace its history for us, as well as your personal itinerary within this history?

This history is tied to biographical elements related to the functioning of La Borde clinic, to my participation in what, at the time, was referred to as the G.T.Psy (the institutional therapy think tank), and also to an entire political trajectory.[2] It would be quite difficult for me to determine the relative importance of these different elements. In fact, I have never considered myself a theorist of these matters. Not that I consider the theory as secondary; rather, I consider the work of theoretical elaboration that I was led to propose has always been inseparable from certain combinations of circumstances, from necessities of clarification on the occasion of confrontations between groups regarding questions of orientation.

A first series of questions became apparent when I came to work with Jean Oury at La Borde. At that time I was, on the one hand, a political militant in an extreme-left group and, on the other, one of the first participants who was not a doctor to participate in Jacques Lacan's Seminar. An entire preliminary phase of conceptual elaboration constituted for me in trying to establish a bridge between heterogeneous universes, and—I would say today—to try to reconcile the irreconcilable. In my first articles, I put forth the idea of an overcoming of institutional psychotherapy by a technique of institutional analysis. It was then a question of refusing a too restrictive definition of institutional psychotherapy. In my view, we had to study and make use of the link that exists between it and similar practices in other domains: pedagogy, city planning, militantism (especially in the UNEF and the "Mutuelle Nationale des Etudiants de France," with which I was associated.)[3] Besides, I thought that we would be able to advance in this new discipline only to the extent that it would set itself up in connection with larger political problems, for example, the problem of the opposition within the Communist Party (such as it was organized around the newspaper *La Voie Communiste*), the renewal of forms of revolutionary struggle, etc... This attempt lasted until May '68. With a group of militants, we managed to develop an intense multidisciplinary activity within the Federation of Study Groups in Institutional Research (FGERI), and through the first issues of the journal *Recherches*.[4] That gave us the feeling that we had uncovered a problematic that had, until then, escaped the specialists of these different disciplines, their theorists as well as their practitioners; we felt like we had found an undiscovered continent.

The FGERI gathered together psychiatric groups interested in institutional psychotherapy, groups of primary school teachers who came from the Freynet movement,[5] groups of students who took part in the BAPU[6] experience, architects, city planners, sociologists, and also... psycho-sociologists. We considered that a specific analytic process could graft onto two sides of the activity of each of these groups:

—"Research into research itself;" that is, an analysis that takes into account the fact that the researchers cannot reach their goal unless the organizers also put themselves into question with regard to things that don't appear in any way related to the goals of their research. An example: A group of fifteen architects and city planners discussed, for almost two years, not only their projects and their profession, but also many questions concerning their lives, their interpersonal relationships…

—"Transdisciplinary research." To hold onto this same example, these architects and city planners from the FGERI also organized meetings with other groups, among them administrators of the student movement, psychiatrists and psychiatric nurses, teachers, etc… This detour through other disciplines allowed them to clear up false problems (relative, for instance, to the functioning of space: problems concerning volumes, levels, communications, institutional options and micropolitics of promoters and users).

A rather surprising fermentation resulted from these multiple exchanges. People as different as Fernand Deligny, Roland Dubillard, Jacques Besse, François Dolto, Maud Mannoni, Tosquelles, Jean and Fernand Oury, Gentis, Torrubia, Laing and Cooper came into contact with each other. Lacan himself participated in certain meetings. Also found there were numerous militant students who had played a leading role in the movements of May '68. The benefit that each person took from these debates was not merely conceptual; in fact, this interdisciplinary world was supplemented by a collective analytic elaboration whose individual influences were sometimes evident.

It is in this context that the notions of transversality, institutional transfer, and analyzer, were proposed, which were then co-opted in a cruel fashion by psycho-sociologists, as I have already explained elsewhere.

May '68 was an enormous break. From the get go, most of the FGERI groups found themselves in sync with the events. The main leaders of the FGERI were active either in the "Movement of 22 March" in Nanterre, or in other theaters of protest. For instance, the

CET, other groups of primary school teachers, and the members of the FGERI took the initiative of occupying the Institut Pédagogique Nationale. On the other hand, François Tosquelles and several other psychiatrists couldn't relate to this movement in this way, and the break with them was profound. (I remember Tosquelles declaring: "Nothing whatsoever happened in May '68!" That really shocked me.)

It quickly became clear that the new type of microsocial upheavals that manifested themselves from May '68 onwards went much further than we had previously imagined. Personally, I thought that the transformation of institutions, collective equipments, lifestyles, of the media, etc., could no longer be considered independently from a social revolution freed from the restrictive definitions of Marxists. In my view, the time for institutional analysis had also passed. From this point forward, I was concerned with the junction of the "molecular revolutions" that the social struggles had revealed.

In the years following 1968, I pondered the missing links—both theoretical and practical—that prohibited or delayed such a junction. It was clear that in Universities, for example, State powers had demonstrated a real skill for co-opting aspirations for change; people like Edgar Faure, with his project for University reform, perfectly detected the way to immediately get rid of centers of effervescence and creativity by miniaturizing what was at stake in terms of power. In the field of psychiatry, it was enough to get psychiatrists bogged down by sector politics (*la politique de Secteur*) to obtain similar results. Using all the means at their disposal, the established powers sought to dilute the protest movements. Very often, this dilution had the appearance of a process of consultation in order to establish a symbiotic relationship between State power and the aspirations of the protestors. It was a clever trick on the part of the State. It was disturbing to see the extent to which the "Movement," as it was called, was vulnerable to it.[7]

For me, it was thus a kind of period of latency that coincided with a period of intense work with Gilles Deleuze. It was a question of trying to better define how the metabolism of desire in the social field—the collective imaginary—is connected to the structures of power, the State apparatus, the hierarchical pyramid that continuously reconstitutes itself, and which has the power to swallow up and co-opt all embryonic analytic systems. I was led to reexamine, in a critical fashion, my previous ideas about institutional analysis and to reformulate the problematic of the unconscious in an even larger context. (Hence the title of the two principal works that Gilles Deleuze and I then began to undertake: *Capitalism and Schizophrenia*). When I take a look back at the beginnings of institutional analysis, I am tempted to see it as the first approach to what we would later develop. At any rate, I cannot condone its transformation into a university product, or even a commercial one: the courses in institutional pedagogy and institutional analysis—the courses in training… all things that really had nothing to do with our concerns at the time, and even less with my current ones.

How did the expression "institutional analysis" come about? Does it have an author?

I suggested it during a session of the G.T.Psy, because I felt the need for a double demarcation with respect to institutional psychotherapy.

The first demarcation was aimed at the trend represented by Daumézon, Bonafé, le Guillant, etc… (the trend that threw out the expression "institutional psychotherapy" after the liberation of France). There were quite a few of us who hoped that this kind of practice would introduce an analytic dimension and no longer content itself with the references that Tosquelles frequently made to Moréno and Lewin and, secondarily, to Marx and Freud. Except that this analytic dimension, when advocated by some psychiatrists, was still conceived of along the lines of classical analysis. On my end, I slowly evolved toward the idea that analysis could not remain an external supporting force, peacefully coexisting in this field with Marxism, psycho-sociology, group dynamics, social therapy, etc... If the analysis of unconscious subjective formations was to have a role in the social field, it could not be that of the psychoanalysts or psychiatrists, or even that of a group of individuals, but rather that of a complex group of social processes. This first demarcation thus tended to situate institutional analysis in opposition to microsociological institutional psychotherapy, understood in the sense of the old Tosquellian watchword: "It is advisable, above all, to treat the hospital system by disalienating social relationships, by holding sessions with the ill, with the nurses, by energizing the cooperatives, the inter-hospital clubs, etc..." (I wrote an article on this subject for the Mutuelle des Etudiants, in which I tried to define how an analytic group practice could function within systems like the different BAPU, the day hospitals, etc...)[8]

The second demarcation tried to establish that this sort of analytic process could not be a "specialty" of the mental hygiene field, but would also concern pedagogy, the social sciences, etc... In order to denounce this sort of isolated approach to analysis, I remember that we—paraphrasing one of Trotsky's expressions—came up with a funny watchword against psychoanalysis on a single couch, a single clinic or psychiatric hospital... We had to coin an expression capable of responding to this widening of the field.

What was the date of the expression?

Around 1964–1965. That is, a little while before the release of the first issue of the journal *Psychothérapie Institutionelle*.

You are a Psychoanalyst by training?

My training was a total mish mash. I began by studying pharma-cology, which I abandoned after three years. That course of study had been imposed on me from the outside and it didn't suit me at all. Following this, I resumed a degree in philosophy at the Sorbonne, but I felt uncomfortable in the university environment, and I didn't continue my studies beyond this point. I attended lectures by Merleau-Ponty and Bachelard; I still have great admiration for both of them. Moreover, like so many young people of my generation, I was a Sartrean, at least until the encounter, so decisive for me, with Lacan and his work. This encounter led me to undergo analysis with him, followed by courses in analysis. Nevertheless, my training remained inseparable from my activities as a militant in a number of domains…

But the fact is that you were an analyst by profession…

No, I first put my training as an analyst into practice in the psy-chiatric environment, shortly after my friend Jean Oury founded La Borde Clinic.

As an analyst?

No, as a member of the organizing team of the establishment, group meetings, etc… I would almost go as far as saying that I was there in the capacity of a militant bringing a political style into an institution, but not, of course, in the manner of a propagandist of political ideas! Rather, as an individual who had been very actively involved in the Youth Hostel movements, which tried hard to struggle against the ossified structures of various groupuscules, and who then tried to develop a certain style of mass politics in the difficult context of the struggle against the Algerian War. I was somewhat shocked by the manipulative character of the institu-tional interventions of the psychiatrists and psychologists, and I hoped to push along, as far as possible, the game of democracy and collective management in the institutions where I found myself, whatever difficulties might possibly ensue. I became an analyst, all the while continuing to work at La Borde. It was only ten years later that I practiced psychoanalysis in Paris for a dozen years. I suspended my practice following my critical reflection on Freudianism and Lacanism and then took it up again with a renewed approach.

You have never been—this is unusual enough to merit emphasis—an academic. Also, despite the trajectory outlined here, you are also not affiliated with any psychoanalytic school...

Strictly speaking, I have remained a member of the École freudienne, with the title of "Analyst member of the school" (*Analyste membre de l'école*).[9] Despite my criticisms of many aspects of Freudianism and Lacanism, I have been reproached for this loyalty to the EFP by the small group of academics who surround Lacan—a kind of Praetorian Guard which not only intends to assume all rights to the Master's legacy, but also exercises absolute power over the new Lacanian youth movement that they have just founded, known as "Cause freudienne."[10] My position on this is no secret: I have always said that, rightly or wrongly, I hope that out of some analytic trends and through the efforts of mental health workers, something will arise that will radically challenge this kind of elitist technique. I consider both Freudian and Lacanian theory as fundamentally reactionary with regard to everything concerning the connection of questions of desire with the social field. But I don't condemn wholesale all current practical approaches to the analysis, although, all too often, they have become as shamefully reactionary as the theories. Furthermore, I am convinced that the share of true analysis contained in the practices of a number of analysts has nothing to do with their theoretical orientation.

The fate of analysis is not necessarily tied to the existence of all of these camps, to this whole unbearably mannered world that makes up what are known as psychoanalytic societies or schools! After all, it is also in the name of a certain conception of analysis that hundreds of Argentinian psychoanalysts got involved, without hesitation, in the struggle against the dictatorship, and confronted the imprisonments, torture, death…

Can you elaborate on this idea that analytic practical approaches have nothing to do with analytic theories?

From the outside, it's difficult to imagine the weight of the psychoanalytic hierarchy in the selection and promotion of young analysts, the rituals of submission that were coined "control" and "training analysis," "pass," and the fact that money and information are the privilege of those at the top… There would also be a lot to say about teaching of psychoanalysis in the universities, about the role that the new analyst bosses play in the psychiatric hospitals, about the blackmailing into analysis that takes place during the training of specialized educators, and how we are heading in the direction of a much more subtle surveillance system, but also one that is much more rigorous than the traditional ones. Seen from this angle, it is true that theory and practice certainly seem inseparable!

One day, quite a few years ago now, after having patiently suffered through one of my favorite diatribes on this theme, Lacan let out a deep sigh and proceeded to tell me that he was aware of the existence of such "distortions" within l'École freudienne and he added, roughly: "You see, what counts above everything is that through all of this, analysis can continue to exist." I responded that he didn't have to worry himself about this, that analysis would continue to thrive in such conditions, that there would soon be as many analysts as notaries or pharmacists. But I remained sensitive to his concerns. I am also anxious for there "to be analysis"! But not just any sort!

The criticisms of Freudianism and Lacanism that Gilles Deleuze and I developed are not to be taken as a dismissal of analysis as such. There is obviously no question of returning to a Stalinist position of the Politzer sort, or else American-style behaviorism. But I am convinced that analysis will get out of this deadlock only if it ceases to be the exclusive concern of a specialist or psychoanalyst, or even an analytic group, as these cannot avoid constituting themselves as authorities. Analysis must become a process defined by what I have called assemblages of analytic enunciation; it must be founded not only on speech and composed of individuals, but also defined by a specific social, economic, institutional, micropolitical operation, and a non-linguistic semiotics.

As an example of the role analysis plays in the social field, I have occasionally evoked the "Movement of 22 March" in France in 1968, or else that of Radio Alice in Bologna in March, 1977, which was revealing of the situation in Italy during this period.

What is analytic in all of this? All of it was due, not only to the fact that people there spoke up against the reigning ideologies, or that they demanded, both for themselves and for others, more freedom and more creativity...

Through speech, but also through technical and material means, such groups succeeded in modifying what I would call *collective modes of semiotization*. 22 March happened in Nanterre, against the background of a certain kind of city planning, as a particular type of social system, of a clear conception of the relationship to knowledge, of the division between manual and intellectual labor. In Bologna, "Radio Alice" appeared in the context of complex interactions between the "emarginati" (half-student, half-Lumpen), workers from the South migrating toward the industrial North, and the traditional working class (les "garantis") under the influence of the Italian Communist Party and various intellectual trends, etc... The analytic assemblage thus does not exclusively concern individuals, groups and recognized speakers, but also very diverse and heterogeneous socioeconomic, technological, environmental, etc., components.

And your opposition to analytic theories...

It is directed at the theoretical support of this individuation, this specialization, this "elitization" of analysis. The people who work in a CMPP, in a psychiatric service, or else in training programs for social work (*éducateurs*), tell us: "Yes, this is all very good, but what do I do with all of this?[11] I see people who are totally lost. I have to instruct future social workers who are full of goodwill..." And I'm not among those content to say: "Let's wait for a more auspicious time. Let's wait until the revolution creates new conditions..." No way! I repeat again that the processes for elucidating the formation of the unconscious does not correspond to any specific analytic technique. For example, the women's movement in France, in Europe, played a role of the proto-analytic type, not because of this or that leader in the movement who is an analyst, but because the movement introduced—in the manner in which the female condition is felt today in France—something that touched the whole society. This analytic impact concerns elements that are situated "beyond" individuals, elements found in the socius as well as in infrapersonal elements, modes of sensibility, of apperception of time, of the relationship to the cosmos, etc... and defined by what I term abstract machinisms.

This last point seems crucial to me. One of the greatest analysts of contemporary subjectivity, Samuel Beckett, doesn't seem—at first glance—concerned with political and social struggles, the fight for women's liberation, for homosexuals, etc. Nevertheless, his exploration seems to me to be at the heart of the micropolitical mutations of our age. There are fundamental interactions between this type of personal elaboration and the social unconscious. Here we find a view in some sense prospective, and which, on a larger level, calls for the rejection of all dogmatism, all sectarianism, and all disciplinary compartmentalization.

Today, a teacher or social worker who hopes to better understand microsocial relations, emotional relations, the relationship to the world of the children of whom he is in change, is in a potentially analytic position, to the extent that his beliefs are free from pedagogical and psychological dogmas, and he is committed to following the trajectory of singularities with which he is confronted. What seems pathetic to me is that, in the current cultural context, this teacher is often led, by pangs of guilt, to say to himself: "I should first undergo analysis, I have to find a 'supervision group,' I have to know Freud and Lacan by heart..." I know people like this who are institutionally engaged in an authentic analytic micro-process, for whom the prestige of psychoanalytic knowledge, the prestige of analytic societies, has been a factor of inhibition and hang-ups for their practice. I am convinced, in a more general way, that class struggles in developed countries, transformations of daily life—all the problems of "molecular revolution"—won't result in anything unless practices and modes of individual and collective analytic theorization develop alongside these modes of traditional theorization, renew their functioning and their functions, and lead to a collective co-opting of questions about the economy of desire. No one today can propose a theory of reference and, even less, practical protocols in this domain. Nevertheless, the key question remains: as long as there is no new analytic vector of this kind, occupied with the social economy of desire, traversing militant activities, social struggles, mass struggles, institutional struggles, and everyday struggles, we will inevitably fall back into systems of either macro-gulags or micro-ghettos, or else into Giscardian systems of co-option. Only one position—I won't call it duplicitous, but multiplicitous—that consists in attacking these problems with a multivalent logic, will allow us to move forward.

What I mean is that, at the very moment when we are formulating something that we think is right, when we take up a position in the name of its presumed efficacy, it is necessary for us to preserve a kind of "passage to the other," an acceptance of his singularity, and also a calling into question of one's own certainty. "Why are you going in this direction, why did you opt for this kind of formula, what is the investment of power that brought you to do it and, at the same time, what does this imply as far as 'treating' the investments of desire, in particular, the desire of the militants who are following you, or else with regard to the leaders who guide your actions... The same kind of question applies with regards to your colleagues, your children, your spouse, etc..."

These questions, I repeat, cannot be entrusted to specialists. In every militant body that I have known, whether the Communist Party or groupuscules, problems of organization were systematically referred to "permanents." One would always have to deal with such miniature Stalins, modest and hard working. Most members of these groups were in no way aware that organizational issues were as important as the issues that were, strictly speaking, more political, if not more so. They didn't suspect—or else refused to see—the weight of libidinal investments on the manifestations of readership or else in bureaucratic stratifications. In other fields as well (pedagogic, psychiatric, etc...), you find yourself up against the same type of problems. What are the real possibilities for intervention, what degree of freedom do teachers, mental health workers, and social workers really possess? Determining this requires the juxtaposition of different kinds of discourses, not only the discourse of general theorization, but also a "minor theorization," a cartography of affects, on the level of daily relationships, the relationship to space, etc... In this view, analysis consists in connecting and making coexist, neither to homogenize nor to unify—but rather to arrange these different levels of discursivity according to a principle of transversality, and make them communicate transversally.

If you are saying that the people who have to ask the questions are neither the analysts nor the specialists—whatever their specialty— then who are these questioners?

We are crushed under the weight of mass media, by images of power, by a manipulation of the imagination in the service of an oppressive social order, by the fabrication, whatever the cost, of a majority consensus, by the cult of security, by processes of intoxication that scare people about everything and nothing, infantilizing them to the point that they no longer ask themselves questions. Several hundred young people get organized; they piece together transmitters and launch free radio stations. They experiment with a new type of communication; they give people a chance to speak, they go into working-class neighborhoods, produce cassettes together, etc... Then what happens? Repression rains down on them; nevertheless, after some time, they trigger a genuine public reaction. Politicians, although far from being in agreement with the ideological framework supporting these initiatives, still stand up for the young people. François Mitterrand agrees to challenge the law by participating in a free radio broadcast. I would say that, in a way, Mister Mitterrand is "under analysis" by the free radio movement. Maybe he himself doesn't know exactly why he took that step, he who time and time again lays claim to the highest public office. Why did he put himself into an illegal situation and risk finding himself summoned by an examining magistrate? Serious people cried, "He's crazy; what has happened to him?" But what can it mean, if not that he was aware, however unconsciously, of the appearance of a decisive crack in this branch of the media. All of this might not go very far, as he remains hostile to the idea of breaking up the state monopoly. Nevertheless, it seems to me indisputable that this kind of transformation of the relationship to public speech is played out, first and foremost, on the level of the social unconscious.

In order to back up this problematic it is necessary, I think, to create a wider concept of collective equipments, one that would encompass all media and all systems of transportation. The theory of assemblages, as I propose it, no longer allows us to think about collective equipments in the usual way, that is, independently from productive forces, and the training systems of the collective labor force. It implies the existence of a continuum between domains that, until then, had been the privilege either of state apparatuses or of the private sector, or even of private life. I argued that capitalist production not only manufactures commercial goods, but also institutions and infra-individual mechanisms, systems of perception, of behavior, of imaginary representation, of submission to hierarchies and dominant values.[12] Hence the importance today of:

1) Social resources, resources for health, education, leisure, etc…, all of which are the true factories where the labor power and the socius as a whole is manufactured.

2) Mass media, which are tools, not only of communication, but also for the modelization of individuals.

3) Modern means of transportation, which don't serve exclusively to take people to work, but also to transform archaic territorialities, to split up geopolitical space, to permit the mobility of one segment of the population and prohibit that of another.

The modes of "semiotic guiding" operated by collective equipments (in order to give a bottle to her child, a woman listens to Dr. X on the morning radio. In the afternoon she consults a child psychologist at the community clinic, makes him take a test that she cut out of a magazine, etc...) bring about a progressive decline of what I would call territorialities of use. Everyone participates in this tremendous network of collective equipments. Through them, integrated global capitalism carries out vast cross-fertilizations of territories, representations, images, and systems of control. We should tackle this problem and all of its aspects in depth, in order to explore the production of contemporary subjectivity. Unconscious complexes develop less on the familial Oedipus than on this type of equipment of mass media effects and on means of transportation. We can't utter a phrase or make a gesture that isn't immediately inscribed into the network that they constitute. Multiple semiotico-machinic gauges orient, guide, marginalize, or reward us: "That was exactly what needed to be said; that was the right question..." Psychotics and science fiction writers have long anticipated the interpretation of this machinic environment, of these waves, these influences, of these machinic teleguidings... Once again we find ourselves faced with something that is going in the direction of a dissolution of the categories of individual identity, personological poles, family structure, and, finally, social group as such.

You have worked and continue to work in groups. What, for you, is the status of the group? Is it an "intermediary" between the individual and society, or is it part of an organization, an institution?

I no longer have much faith in the specificity of the group, and I would even say that I believe less and less in the existence of the group as an entity. Most of the time, it's no more than a fiction.

Ultimately, aggregates of individuals rarely function as a group; on the other hand, isolated individuals—the "Beckett assemblage," for example—can do group work. I would prefer to start from a much more inclusive, perhaps more vague, notion of assemblage. Who is speaking? Who is intervening? What assemblage of enunciation makes something real? Assemblage is not just speech, subject and signifier; it's the tangling up of a thousand components such that reality and history are what they are, so that it's not exclusively in relation to the economy of micro-groups or macro-groups that we can understand this type of process. Here we are back to a topic that has been with us for a while: we can see the "terminal" of speech, what comes out of the "black box;" we can locate the transmitter and the person, there, in front of us or on the TV, on the microphone, on the telephone; we can easily identify the material origin of the message; we can make out a signature. But for all of that, can we truly say that it (*ça*) is speaking from there? Communication conveys pure redundancies whereas assemblages of semiotization are messengers of many other things, of effects on objective and subjective reality, what I have called diagrammatic effects. Let's return to the example of the free radios: who is speaking in this assemblage? The radio hosts? It's not clear... It perhaps betrays, first of all, a collective sense of being "fed up" with official media... Additionally, technological mutations enter the picture, which has led to the miniaturization of transmitters. And we also have to take into account the evolution of conceptions relating to militantism, etc...

Quite different in this from the category of the group, this notion of assemblage leads us to contemplate problems in their entirety, and to take into account social mutations, subjective transformations, semantic slidings, everything that touches on perceptions, sentiments and ideas. We cannot attribute responsibility for a statement (*énoncé*) to any social transformation, group or individual, in the sense in which we usually understand it. To grasp this type of phenomenon, it is not enough to say, as it still was said a few years ago: "We have to take the context, the implicit, into account..." Power relationships, hierarchies, technological mutations linked to the rise of semiotization machines such as computers, are an intrinsic part of new assemblages of enunciation.

In these conditions, it's the opposition between statement and context, and even between language and referent, which finds itself in question. I have attempted to show that the current trends in pragmatic linguistics continue to separate, in an excessive way, the phonological, syntactic, semantic and rhetorical levels, among others, which, in my view, has the effect of somewhat paralyzing research. The most disparate components can interact in order to "assemble" a statement, a discourse, or a project. This view calls for a case-by-case redefinition of the procedures of pragmatic analysis. It is a question of determining, within each assemblage, the operating components, and the corresponding transference affects, and of finding out which work of semiotic de-outlining (*décernabilisation*) should be brought to bear on each of them.

When confronted with anorexia, an anxiety neurosis, or even the simple stuttering of a child, every specialist shrink will call upon his own theoretical corpus. He will, for example, decree that he is dealing with psychosomatic symptoms, or communication problems better dealt with by family psychotherapy, or of the disturbance of a "matheme" of the unconscious… what else, I don't know. Others will hold the social field responsible, it's the schools that aren't working, OK, so let's change the schools before we devote ourselves to the psychopathological problems of children on an individual basis. Maybe all of this is at stake at the same time, but not in simply any order or to the same degree. What is important to prioritize here is to update the possibilities for intervention, as well as the range of effects that we may expect from them.

If we reexamine in this spirit, for example, the monograph that Freud dedicated to his study of "Little Hans," we cannot fail to question the appropriateness of a number of Freud's interpretations. These interpretations seem more like intrusions likely to confuse the child, and even lead him into neurosis. It hasn't escaped notice that it isn't until the end of a long analytic process, put into place by the father, under the direction of Freud, that phobic symptoms appeared. At the time, Freud was really "in need of" data about infantile sexuality, the importance of which he had just discovered. If we attentively follow the text of his commentary and the account of his father it's possible to locate the stages of a true encirclement of Little Hans's subjectivity. A kind of analytic-familial, panoptic system found itself set up in the heart of domestic territory. His every move, his comings and goings, his dreams and his fantasies, were submitted to an absolutely stupefying observation and control. And we see the child successively abandon the spaces of exterior life that he had conquered up until then—his relationships with girls, his love of long walks, his seductive relationship with his mother, her caresses in the bath—to fall back on highly guilt-laden mastur-bation and, finally, to construct a true bastion of fantasies from which he reclaimed, in a certain way, control over the situation, tor-menting, in turn, his parents, by making them guilty. All of this for the profit of Professor Freud who, at the end of the chain, collects throughout this affair what he finds to be the brilliant confirmation of his gestating theories about the Oedipus and castration complexes. I'm not claiming that we can recreate the true etiology of the neu-rosis from this. There might have been other contributing factors that Freud, despite his ingenuity as an investigator, wasn't able to identify. But I see no reason why we should keep quiet about the clearly pathogenic effect of the situational transfer brought on by the relationship between Freud and the father!

Let's now think about what frequently happens in a number of medical-pedagogical centers or dispensaries of mental hygiene, where they thought that they were doing a good thing by introducing psychoanalytic methods. A specialized therapist with the help, for example, of some modeling clay, explores the past and fantasies of a child, its familial situation. Is he really trying to understand the position of this child in the social networks that are hindering its specific possibilities for development? For an authentic analysis, (a schizoanalysis, a molecular analysis, what we call it isn't important), the first concern won't be interpretation, but *intervention*. What can we do to clear up a situation? In some cases, it would be advisable to concern oneself with the school, in another, the family or, surely, the status of the father in the couple... unless we are up against an economic problem, or issues stemming from sociological inertia. But we also can't leave out physical, biological, physiological, environmental, and other such determinations. There is thus a kind of potential "integral" of all the factors (*instances*) that work together to block an assemblage. Without claiming to elaborate a systemic theory that would account for the interactions of all of these components, we should interrogate the ones that are operative in a given situation. We can now face the question of "institutional transference" in a renewed form. After all, what is the point of defining the elements of transference and counter-transference if it only involves identifying the fantasmatic elements? What's the point of trying to determine the role of the father, the mother, the national education system, Knowledge, Power, the Economy, if we don't offer to intervene in any way and to work through these different components? In persisting to explore and interpret elements on which we won't have anything more than a fictive hold, we run the risk of developing a system of mystification, a new formation of power, capturing and co-opting investments of desire, thereby giving birth to a new system of subjugation potentially even more harmful than those previously in place.

For you, the group is no longer an important or privileged component?

In fact, a group is often nothing more than an illusion. This is quite evident in family therapy. I don't deny the importance, and often even the determining character, of family interactions, in particular in the case of certain psychoses. However, these systematic approaches to the family only serve, in most cases, to hide other components: age group, social environment, socioeconomic conditions and considerations of salary, urban issues, and, above all, individual singularities. Beyond the inventory and an appreciation of the relative importance of these components, let's agree to explore the distinctive feature of an assemblage—what I have called the "machinic," that is, the manner in which it insures communication between passing components, its modes of blocking (*blocage*) and inhibition, its black holes, its catastrophies, etc... I prefer to speak of a "machinic kernel" instead of speaking about structure, system, complex, etc... in order to emphasize that no general formula, no psycho-sociological, structural or systematic recipe, to name but a few, can give us access to this kind of phenomenon. Only the putting into place of an assemblage that is specific and singular in its enunciation, allows for the possibility of a practice that will serve both analysis and change.

Intervention

Let's talk about intervention. What are your professional, social or political practices? On the one hand, you are a prominent figure. On the other, you participate in a group practice: What sort of practice? In the groups that you belong to, do you intervene and, if so, with whom and how?

As I told you before, I think that it's necessary to link this question with the question of interpretation. Sometimes people have told me: "The analysis that you advocate comes down to the work of social assistance or savage psychoanalysis (*psychanalyse sauvage*). Analysis is not at all about that; it's about interpretation and a pure listening (*écoute*) to the unconscious, it's the exact opposite of all intervention."

It seems to me, on the contrary, that these alleged significant interpretations are never neutral. In practice, whether or not we like it, we are, each and every one of us, thrown with all hands into intervention. The people who deny it are either in bad faith or else completely naïve and fooled. "To take into analysis," as is said, a married woman, the mother of a family, doesn't consist in establishing a relationship of pure listening with a transcendent subject. We aren't dealing with autonomous people, but with subsets of complex assemblages that include, for example, the fact that the payment for the course of treatment is connected to the father, one's professional life and salary, medical coverage, etc… Psychoanalysts would have us believe that the money relationship that they establish with a patient remains extrinsic to the field of analysis—except insofar as it relates to anal-sadistic affects. How absurd! Nothing is neutral in analysis. A patient might remain silent for years on the divan: that doesn't mean that his analyst "doesn't intervene"! In reality, it guarantees a certain state of affairs, if only in keeping the idea alive that a pure effect of empty discourse can interact with the unconscious. Something is always supposed to be happening in analysis, even when nothing is happening. Above all when nothing is happening! A minimum of honesty would mean renouncing this kind of bluff! In my view this is one of the essential points of departure of schizoanalysis.

Who can be seen to benefit from this leading to believe in the existence of a secret metabolism at work in the unconscious, when absolutely nothing surfaces in a cure. Neutrality is another illusion: We are ourselves always mixed up in the situation. And we will do better to realize this so that our interventions will be as little alienating as possible. Instead of conducting a politics of subjection, of identification, normalization, social control and setting the people we are dealing with along a semiotic track, it is possible to opt for a micropolitics that at least takes into account our own humble participation in the story; it is possible to work in the direction of dis-alienation, of a liberation of expression, of opening "exit doors," if not "lines of escape," from oppressive social stratifications.

This question of intervention also evokes for me other quarrels of old related to the "directivity" in groups, as well as the entire mythology of a spontaneity which is supposed to permit access to the depths of the unconscious! In fact, the non-directivity, the non-organization of a group can have an effect that is the exact opposite from the anticipated one. The structuring of a group practice can be absolutely necessary in order that those who never manage to speak can do so. In different groups in which I have participated, I frequently ponder these kinds of problems. Collective discourse focuses on certain themes, but maybe other people hope to speak about other things! How can we develop conditions for collective and/or individual expression in a way that will leave room for the most singular modes of semiotization? The act of designating a president or a coordinator for a meeting can free its participants and get them going. Yet this is not a universal panacea. Still, far from being liberating, non-directivism can favor the emergence of phe-nomena of consensus, of oppressive redundancies, and lead to a situation in which participants say exactly what they are expected to say. All of this brings us back to an even older debate, the one that, in the workers' movement, opposes "basism" to centralism.

All of this brings us back to an even older debate, the one that, in the workers' movement, opposes "basism" to centralism. I am convinced that it's necessary to consider these options as tied together into a false alternative. I'll spare you the long history of the criticism of centralism. We know about the havoc wreaked by Leninist forms of organization in the parties, States, intellectual production, etc... This doesn't mean that we should give up on all institutional systems, all organization structure. By failing to map out the traits these struggles share today, even those of a transitional nature, oppressed people would find themselves entirely powerless. And in times of crisis, Spontaneists always end up having recourse to organizations and to traditional leaders. How many times have I seen committees struggling against repression leave it up to one or another groupuscule to organize a common meeting, a demonstration, etc... After which they find themselves the prisoners of watchwords, of a style of action and discourse that completely betrays their initial project. Beyond "basism" and centralism, it's a matter of inventing a new type of organization. Gilles Deleuze and I put forth the term of "rhizome"—the choice of term is of little importance—to index the modes of structuration that authorize an association of differentiated components that do not alter their specificity. In fact, far from being a set back, from the standpoint of efficiency with respect to centralist organizations, I am convinced that this kind of orientation alone will succeed in avoiding the phenomena of bureaucratic inertia and conservatism that currently characterize leftist and extreme leftist groups.

You react strongly to the practice of intervention, to traditional analysis, to contemporary institutional analysis. Can you discuss this type of intervention?

Given the direction in which things are heading, we will soon have ministries of Psychological Intervention and Social Innovation. The Ministry of Health already allocates funds to marginal groups to accommodate drug addicts, psychiatric patients, and children in difficult situations; I happen to know that Simone Weil was planning to challenge the status of psychiatric hospitals. Why not? Marginalized people would be wrong to spit on possible subsidies if they do not infringe on their freedom. Ultimately, I don't see any difference whether a person is paid by the Department of Education, the CNRS, The Ministry of Health, or by the Renault factories. On this point, there are neo-Maoist subtleties that totally escape me! We are all always more or less co-opted! Ultimately, it's about politics and micropolitics, not purity. What can come out of current attempts to co-opt research in the social sciences, to co-opt marginalized people, or indeed, even tomorrow, free radios? (I can easily imagine, tomorrow, a Rocard-Chaban government, proposing a statute for free radios, a supervision of the "Maisons de la Culture" kind. One of two things: either current power relations will evolve irreversibly in the direction of a hierarchization, the establishment of an absolutely terrifying society of social control (not at all like the one that Orwell predicted, which he conceived of on the basis of pre-war fascism, but rather, one emerging from much more sophisticated systems, both hyper-seductive and hyper-repressive and, above all, more miniaturized, spreading through the socius in a much more capillary fashion). In this scenario, the powers that be would have recourse to all available means. We would end up with psycho-sociologists and psychoanalytic divans all the way into the police stations, which would not prevent the police from continuing to beat up people. There will be psychiatrists, as in Germany, who will be able to keep a detainee imprisoned indefinitely, beyond the term of his sentence, for "asocial tendencies." All co-opting will be effective: we will be screwed, or, rather, conditioned like Pavlov's dogs. On the other hand, if we are indeed engaged, as I believe, in a long-term molecular revolution, shaking up, on every level, all the ways of life on this planet, these attempts to co-opt will slide past one another without catching hold of anything in social reality. Marginality and its co-option, as they continue to spread to larger and larger sectors of society, are starting to take on a new character. Today, we are no longer confronted with those categories of marginals traditionally refered to the psychiatric asylum, the prison, reform schools, etc... The new marginal people can be found at Longwy and at Denain, in Corsica and in Brittany, in suburban streets, in public housing (H.L.M.) cellars, in unemployment offices, etc... And that amounts to quite a number of marginal people! These are true social continents that are being marginalized in the context of the said attempts of capitalist restructuration.

In an article that took up old and wild imaginings of Robert Linhart, *Le Monde Diplomatique* thought it wise to circulate, a few months ago, a virulent attack against the CERFI, said to function, apparently, as a "suggestion box" for Giscardisme, all the while praising the "molecular revolution." It's curious to see this sort of literature reappear at a time when searches, interrogations and months in prison are raining down on some members of the CERFI and the CINEL. Certainly a new illustration of the proverb: "He who loves well, punishes well"! Well, it turns out that the CERFI is currently literally boycotted by the official bodies that grant research contracts and that it is denied any legitimate role in the national-ization, or rather, the "CNR-ization" of research. Today, only the journals *Recherches* and *Encres* are left. Believe me, I lament this drying up of our sources for financing. Micro-spaces for freedom, such as the CERFI or La Borde, are becoming increasingly scarce these days; I think that leftist hacks should defend them instead of wildly attacking them.

The co-option of ideas, of techniques, innovations—that's really the false problem par excellence. As of a good while now, there are no longer any "trade secrets" in any domain whatsoever. They all communicate at the speed of the audiovisual. It's useless to try to pit oneself against the general mixing of research and experimentation. Giscard d'Estaing is co-opting institutional analysis. What does it matter? Maybe next year there will be a congress of institutional analysis in Moscow! Wasn't a psychoanalytic symposium held in Tbilisi? The real question is elsewhere; the real question concerns the effective reappro-priation of these ideas, these techniques, and these innovations by collective assemblages of enunciation and by liberation movements.

How do you define yourself within the groups you are presently part of? As a militant individual or a paid professional? Are the groups that you are connected with always ones that you "meet with" by chance? Do groups call on you? How?

I work at La Borde Clinic, where I am salaried. It's already an old experience, and one that doesn't perhaps entirely correspond to what, in my view, it would perhaps be possible to set up today. Be that as it may, despite its unavoidably limited nature, it remains of interest as an "island of fresh air," a place where people can reflect, and where it is possible to try out a certain number of things. But, to tell the truth, La Borde isn't an entirely satisfactory illustration of the views that I've been sharing with you.

The other groups that I am part of are the CERFI and the CINEL. Formally, I am the president of the CERFI, but I am no longer an active participant. I am the director of the journal "Recherches," but I am not involved with it except for when I propose the theme of a special edition myself, or else when the Justice Department tries and picks a quarrel with us.

Can you explain what the CINEL is?

Le Centre d'Initiative pour de Nouveaux Espaces de Liberté is a rather informal organization which raised its voice in response to political problems in Italy (against repression: Bologna 1997, the cases of Negri, Piperno, etc…). In France, it also supported the campaign against the extradition of Klaus Croissant, who participated in the meetings known as the "Tunix" meetings in Berlin in 1978, which were originally "spectacular" initiatives related to the free radios, (for example, the "Anti-noise" (*Antibrouille*) festival of June '78) and which, today, are trying hard to be the impetus for the establishment of "committees of active defense" against repression, not only with regard to "big issues," but also to the rampant micro-fascism whose victims are young people, immigrant workers, "nationalitarian" militants, etc.

At the CINEL, we aren't under the illusion that we are either very active or very effective. We are simply trying to position ourselves against the current "New Philosopher" frame of mind, which consists of renouncing all prospects for militant resistance to the dominant order. This already cost us a number of run-ins with the police and the law: trial for free radios, incarceration of the film-maker François Pain, etc… But even so, I'll say it once again, if we put the quality of its participants to the side, the CINEL is really not such a big deal! It simply shows that, today, public life feeds more on symbols than on tangible realities. In fact, what is interesting about it is perhaps less to be found in its deeds than in the shift of attitude it shows in relation to the customary relations between militants, intellectuals, artists, technico-scientific workers, etc… I feel that these categorizations themselves also need to be rethought. Contrary to appearances, people—I no longer know how to say it: workers, the proletariat, salaried workers…—are much more "intellectual" than is thought! Or, at least, they conceal many more intellectual and artistic aspirations than the media's system of intoxication would have us believe. Here as well, we are in the presence of profound and irreversible molecular mutations.

You have been quite involved with Italian issues.

It's true that, these last years, I have often felt more Italian then French. This is connected to the way in which the Italian problems—the struggle of the "emarginati," the free radios such as "Radio Alice" in Bologna, the "autoreductions," the questioning of relations to labor, etc…—seemed to me to "announce" transformations as yet barely begun in other European countries. To tell the truth, I don't know if the situation in Italy, or else what is now called the "German model," can shed a light on the situation in France. We are clearly caught between two types of possibilities. One is an implacable pyramidal order, the only one compatible with the Global Integrated Capital's big projects of restructuring. The other possibility is for us to erect a new kind of society with more "rhizomatic" modes of sociality, one that would attempt/do its best to articulate the economy of desire and the constraints of the productive economy.

For the moment, we have to concede that it's more the "German social-democrat model" that is gaining influence in Europe. All of those who claim to be challenging this evolution again are subject to particular criticism. Intellectuals and militants who try to tackle these questions are seen as dangerous agitators by those in power, despite the clearly derisory character of their methods of action. I know all too well that the issue of terrorism is poisoning all of the debates and "justifies" all the suspicions. We have, for example, been astonished to learn that police authorities in different European countries got it into their heads that the CINEL was the "French branch" of a vast global terrorist network! Flabbergasting! But that shows the nature of recent police operations and the systematic character of some judicial investigations regarding cases that have no foundation whatsoever. The reigning authorities have absolutely no insight into the escalation of violence and crime in developing countries; therefore, they interpret it in their own way. It's always the same technique that consists of imagining the existence of occult centers and searching out intellectual scapegoats when the investigations, obviously, prove themselves incapable of locating these alleged headquarters (thus the arrests on the 7th of April, 1979 in Italy: those of Toni Negri, Oreste Scalzone and then, one after another, Franco Piperno, Lanfranco Pace, etc..., thus, also, the Graindorge cases in Belgium, etc...). Those in power shoot their mouths off with fantasies, hoping to take out their powerlessness on marginal people and dissidents. Afterwards they can announce, to a scared public, that they are "doing everything in their power to stop the unrest and the violence"! But where are these things coming from? How is it, for example, that the Italian terrorists—whose methods and goals, I repeat, I entirely disapprove of—are not isolated people, but rather develop quite easily among quite diverse social levels of Italian society (marginal people, workers, etc...). This is obviously because active contingents of people in this country no longer expect anything from traditional political formations, without, as yet, having found new forms of expression and intervention.

The development of terrorism in Europe of late seems moreover to belong to the kind of co-opting that I mentioned previously. It is notable that these phenomena are not primarily the result of classical groupuscular systems, and that even when they have adopted traditional modes of theorization and organization, referring to the most ossified kind of Leninism, movements like the R.A.F. and the R.B. have not been able to take root or find an adequate social environment, except in the context of the movements of molecular transformation which I spoke of earlier. It would be necessary to show, in detail, how this "appeal" to terrorism corresponds both to a rejection and to a co-opting of the molecular revolution. Let's say, nevertheless, in defense of the movementists and their potential sphere of influence that, having found no channel through which to efficiently address any issue whatsoever, they knocked up against a dead-end, a situation for which, ultimately, all social elements are responsible in one way or another.

Many more people than is thought are conscious of the current transformations in the social fabric. Power is that much more repressive when it senses that its means of control are dissolving— perhaps first and above all on the level of the social unconscious. It is no longer able to reconstitute a stable society of the sort found in the nineteenth or the first half of the twentieth century. The old right/left dualism, in which the partners divided roles—the right controlling the police, the army, and the businesses; the left holding sway over the unions and the associations—seems a thing of the past. Today we can expect the best just as we can expect the worst. Planetary mutations and an elusive revolution coexist with repressive miasmas that are oozing out all over the place. All of this will perhaps lead to terrible things, worse than the Hitlerian concentration camps (Cambodia, Bangladesh, Central Africa, etc...). The monstrous situation of these billion people mired in physical and moral misery, who don't see themselves reflected in any way in the current social goals and ways of life, who have no connection with these gigantic military machines, these polluting modes of production, which lead to ecological devastations that are more catastrophic by the day, will not evidently find any sort of amelioration, either in capitalist restructuration, or in a return to totalitarianisms of the Nazi kind. Disastrous attempts of the latter kind will likely take place. All the same, I have the sense that a new and broad enterprise of social questioning—and not only among the marginalized in developed Capitalist countries, but also in Third World countries—will transform, bit by bit, our political horizon. It will bring exhilarating "highs," but also catastrophic "lows." The way the situation will evolve in the Soviet and Chinese empires also seems, to me, far from clear. The biggest surprises may still be in store. Current totalitarian systems, whether in their most fascistic forms, or in their most liberal-appearing forms, in fact rest to a large extent on a series of delusions; they are much more fragile than is thought and stay in place only because no force today, if only minimally organized, is in a position to stand up to them.

3

SO WHAT

When I was a child, I was, so to speak, in pieces: really a little schizo around the edges. I spent years trying to put myself back together again. Only my thing was, I would pull along different pieces of realities in doing it.

My relationship to my not-too-terrible but still… petit bourgeois family was lived in a kind of dream world, as were my studies, mostly solitary, except for an experience with gangs that was abruptly and authoritatively put to an end. Then I became interested in poetry, and philosophy. I got involved in social and political activities. I often changed my style, my preoccupations and my character, to the extent that I was called Pierre by my family and Félix in my other worlds.

I ended up—"I ended up," that's saying a lot—I began to put myself together a little only around the age of forty, by working with a friend who was able to take into account all of my dimensions.

For as long as I can remember, I was preoccupied with joining together different layers of things which fascinated me: the philosophy of science, logic, biology, early works in cybernetics, militantism, along with another dimension, which literally had me by the throat: horrible bouts of anxiety and an irrevocable sensation of existential loss.

And then I had some luck; I had some really fortunate encounters. I met Jean Oury, who enabled me to settle into a job and a life—

at the La Borde Clinic—an innovating experience at the crossroads of psychiatry and psychoanalysis. I also met Lacan, who had a friendly and attentive rapport with me during the first years that I knew him. That is until it was ruined, particularly by the appearance of Jacques-Alain Miller, whom I'd rather not characterize more precisely, and of his group at the rue d'Ulm, which established a monstrous symbiosis between Maoism and Lacanism.[1]

I had a lot of luck, then, which saved me from all kinds of sidetracks: neuroses first off, and perhaps psychosis, and psycho-professionalization, from which many intelligent people never recover. Next, the militant path, and finally—this may seem strange—it saved me from the suburbs, the universe of my childhood, kind of wonderful, but which is often, all the same, a cultural dead end.

That's the first descriptive level. The other is the result of a choice. A whole conception of culture, and not only bourgeois culture, implies a sort of castration with regard to the wild dreams of childhood and adolescence. One becomes willing to limit oneself in order to develop a field of competence to the maximum. I understand all this very well, but it's not for me, to such an extent that I managed to define myself as a specialist with a term that I developed, "transversality," to consider the unconscious elements that secretly animate sometimes very heterogeneous specialties.

Currently, for example, I spend a lot of time with ecologists, alternativists, members of the Unified Socialist Party, old-time Maoists and I don't know who else, in order to try and consolidate for the elections of 1986. And I continue my work with schizo-analysis. In between, I travel a lot.

Someone who was more normally put together wouldn't be able to stand this kind of systematic disorganization. But I want it for me, not for other people—for the simple reason that I can only tolerate an idea—more than an idea, what I call a concrete machine—if it crosses different orders. My ideas on psychoanalysis wouldn't interest me if they didn't also help me understand all the garbage one encounters, not only in one's personal life, but also in institutions and groupuscules, that is to say in all kinds of power relations. And, conversely, I think that if you are not capable of understanding someone's personal difficulties in light of the social investments and collective subjectivity involved, none of it can work.

In other words, my problem is to extract elements from one domain in order to transfer them into other fields of application. With the risk, of course, that it may miscarry nine times out of ten, that it may turn out to be a theoretical mess. It may not seem like a big deal, but conceptual transfers from philosophy to psychoanalysis are not so easy. Lacan appears to be a virtuoso in this area, but despite appearances he had some weaknesses in philosophy, with the result that this cost us one more reductionist vision in the field of psychoanalysis.

Without presenting a recipe, I more or less began with my own way of dealing with things which I tried to bend towards my analytic practice. For me interpretation is not the wielding of a signifying key to resolve some "matheme" of the unconscious. It's first of all an effort to determine various systems of reference that belong to the person who is right there, with his or her familial, marital, professional, esthetic or whatever kind of problem. I call it an effort because these systems are there, in front of you, but not in an ordered way. They lack the functional articulations that I call "components of passage," which cause other coordinates of existence to emerge suddenly, allowing for a way out. Lapses, parapraxes and symptoms are like birds tapping at the window. It's not a matter of "interpreting" them, but of tracking their trajectory to see if they can serve as indicators for new universes of reference susceptible of acquiring sufficient consistency to change the direction of the situation.

I'll take a personal example. I consider poetry as one of the most important components of human existence, yet less in terms of value than as a functional element. Poetry should be prescribed like vitamins. "Careful now. Old as you are, you'd feel better if you took some poetry…" Still, however important poetry is for me, it is very rare that I read or write a poem. It's not that I never have opportunities to do so, but that they slip away and then I tell myself I've missed them. The same thing with music: it's fundamental, yet sometimes I can forget about it for weeks. I steer my strategies along these kinds of lines. How, in such or such a context, with such or such a group, can people have a creative rapport with the situation in question, like a musician with his music or a painter with painting? A cure is like constructing a work of art, except that you have to reinvent each time the art anew.

Let's backtrack a little. My analysis with Lacan lasted about seven years. When I became an analyst, a member of the Freudian School in 1969, I gradually discovered the other side of the analytic myth. I found myself with thirty patients pulling at my tails, and I must admit that it was a nightmare. A human cluster with ceaseless demands and problems bound up in dramas before which I was struck dumb. Plus money matters, vacations, bottlenecks between appointments… Whenever I said nothing, it meant, for sure, that I knew a lot more about whatever it was! What a scene! What had I gotten myself into? The "Guru Despite Himself." A stand-up comedy routine. I wanted to scream, "Leave me alone already!" One day I let everyone go and disappeared for a year.

Then I said to myself, it's not because I write books criticizing psychoanalysis that people's problems will be resolved. But maybe it would be worth saving an analytic practice by reinventing it. So I started again from scratch, to arrive at my current position, much more relaxed, with greater freedom, a kind of grace. Today, when someone undertakes analysis with me, I explain that the main thing is that it work: the rule, on both sides, is that it can be ter-minated at any moment. Each session calls the next session into question, because I am completely against the system of the guru condemned to success in therapeutic exploits. What interests me is the collective arrangement of semiotization. And I can say right away that it works, since if it doesn't work, we call it quits.

And the anguish in all this, the anguish that weighed upon me in my youth? Well, I find that I master it pretty much the way other adults do, through the use and abuse of infantile techniques that are even more childish than those of children. Adults are so taken by their business that the closer they come to death the less they see it coming. While children, less armed with all these sys-tems of defense, sometimes maintain a rapport of extreme lucidity in relation to it.

Sometimes I have this image: I see myself walking a plank above an absolute abyss, and I say to myself, "What is this? What does all this mean? How is it that this keeps on happening? Who among us hasn't come up against such evidence?" But immediately one is snatched up, thrown against remote-controlled behavior apparatuses, taken up by emergencies, games and gambles. Even dead tired, one keeps on at the roulette wheel or the poker table with an amazing vitality.

Politicians—it is their infantilism, their childishness that both keeps them alive and sustains their idiotic relation to life. And this shouldn't end! A vacation can be dangerous, or a lover's quarrel, or a toothache.

It is obvious that we are all suspended over the same abyss, even if we use different means in order not to see it. We are all at the mercy of the same stupor that can take you by the throat and liter-ally suffocate you. We are all like Swann, half crazy after his separation from Odette and fleeing, like the plague, any mention that could evoke, even indirectly, her existence.

This is why we each cling to our own semiotic scaffoldings in order to continue walking down the street, waking up each day, and doing what is expected of us. Otherwise everything would stop; people would bang their heads against the wall. The way to have a lust for life, to maintain commitments, to forget oneself is not simple or obvious. "What for?!" has incredible power. It is much stronger than Louis XV and his "*après moi le déluge!*" Is it worth trying to keep everything up, taking up the heritage of generations, keeping the machine running, having kids, doing science, making literature or art? Why not break down, burst and leave it all in the lurch? That's the question. Giving way to it is always only so far away…

The answer of course is at the same time both personal and collective. In life, one can only hold on to momentum. Subjectivity needs movement, directional vectors, *ritournelles*, rhythms and refrains that beat time to carry it along. The most singular and personal factors have to do with social and collective dimensions. It is stupid to imagine a psychogenesis independent of contextual dimensions, but that's what psychologists and psychoanalysts do.

Jean Oury, who got me up on my feet when I was twenty, when I was pretty lost, provides a telling recipe. Many times, and at length, I explained my anxiety crises and attacks to him, without it seeming to move him in any way. Until one day, he answered me with this Zen-style response, "It comes over you at night in your bed, before you fall asleep? Which side do you sleep on? Okay, so all you have to do is try the other side."

Analysis is sometimes like that, a little turnaround is necessary. The humility of the earliest days of the church is what's needed, and to say to oneself, "So what. It doesn't matter. Insha'Allah…" It's really basic. Of course one can't just say this in any old way. One must also have the right semiotic lozenges handy: the precise little indexes that can rock significations, giving them an a-signifying bearing, and working with humor or surprise: the dope fiend with a gun in his hand whom you ask for a light.

This is how the instant fuses with the world. It's in this register that the category of poetic performance, the music of John Cage, the ruptures of Zen—it doesn't matter what you call it—are found. But they're never acquired. Juggling has to be learned, like playing scales. One acquires a relative mastery in certain situations, not in others, and then this can change with age, etc. One of the stupidest things about the psychoanalytic myth is to think that after you have put in your ten years on the couch, you are necessarily stronger than those who haven't. Not at all! There is no relation between the two! Analysis should simply give you a boost of virtuosity, like a pianist, for certain difficulties. It should give you more freedom, more humor, more willingness to jump from one scale of reference to another… Therefore, I would say, in order to continue living, one should circulate in supportive orbits. Shakespeare, we know nothing about him, but we know that he had a "supportive" environment. So, go on, it's now or never, it's time for your last next act, right away. You're depressed? Don't let it get to you: they're waiting…

We're on the edge of a black hole of History today. It doesn't matter whether you are thinking or not. Especially in France, where nobody gives a damn. But what is interesting is that rather than adhering to their most immediate concerns, there are still people who want to change society. Sure, societal issues interest no one, and politics is an illusion, etc. Sure, it all looks pretty dreary. We're really in for it. Because it is not possible that so much stupidity, cowardice, bad faith and malice should have no consequences. Sooner or later, it's unavoidable: everything will crystallize heroically. We can do a lot better than Le Pen,[2] you'll see… Because, watch out, if you think that Le Pen is only a simple resurgence, or some flaky throwback, you're dead wrong! Much more than Poujadism revisited, Le Pen is also a collective passion looking for an outlet, a hateful pleasure machine that fascinates even those that it nauseates. To be content to speak of neo-fascism lends confusion to the matter. Really, one can immediately think of the imagery of the National Front, and forget that Le Pen is also fed by the conservatism of the left, by trade union corporatism, by a beastly refusal to address questions of immigration or the systematic disenfranchisement of the youth, etc. It is not enough to refer to the past, because this kind of fascism strives to find itself in the future. Le Pen is nothing but a homing device, a trial balloon for other, much more potentially frightening formulae.

Let's face it, the economy of collective desire goes both ways, in the direction of transformation and liberation, and in the direction of paranoiac wills to power. From this vantage point it is clear that the left, and the Socialists above all, have understood nothing. Look at what they did with the movement "SOS Racism": they think that they've changed something with their million buttons, but they didn't even consider talking to the people at stake. Has this publicity campaign changed anything in social practice, in the neighborhoods or in the factories? I know some "*beurs*," Algerian-French people who have been rubbed the wrong way by this new kind of paternalism-fraternalism. I don't deny the positive aspects of that campaign, but it's so far off the mark!

The passion for existence is short-circuited by the immersion of individuals into a network of ever more infantile relations of dependence. This corresponds to the way production machines, instruments of the media, social ensembles and public assistance institutions are being used to capitalize human subjectivity so that it disciplines itself and works toward sustaining an old social order, an order composed of hierarchies that are sometimes inherited from the middle ages. It's stupid, but that's how it is!

What's miraculous about this new capitalism, which is as prevalent in the East as in the West, is that these values, these insipid systems of sensibility, these flattened-out conceptions of the world, are internalized, are consciously and unconsciously adopted by most people. This makes for the unpalatable ambiance that spreads over just about everything, and for the massive and loathsome increase in religiousness.

This being the case, the same machinic systems can be turned around and redirected. That's what happens when a creative escape line appears. It can begin at a very molecular level and snowball. From there, one can imagine great world recreations.

Meanwhile, infantilizations of immense proportions are underway. These are really the top priorities, the key enterprises. In a manner which I hope is humoristic, I see the history of human subjectivity as a tremendous succession of collapses. In comparison to ours, Neolithic societies were certainly richer, being extraordinarily capable of perceiving elements of the cosmos and of poetry; the sketch marks of Lascaux, body painting, dance—all amazing.

I'm not preaching the noble savage, but it seems to me that the cruelty of relations within what are called archaic societies at least kept the kind of miasma in which we flounder from covering everything, causing the loss of any theme for creative exaltation. The last great hero in France was De Gaulle. What does that tell us? Better not examine him too closely. There is such a flat-footed side to the character.

And now it gets worse and worse. The new heroes are like Prime Minister Raymond Barre, unbelievably lamentable, or Reagan, an idiot. The Emperor of China also had ritual gestures to keep the cosmos balanced. One false move, and the stars would be thrown off course. Reagan can make as many blunders as he wants, say the most stupid things imaginable: that he's going to push the button, obliterate the Russians, unleash the Apocalypse, no one even laughs…

If one turns away from media representations of politics for a second to look at what happens on the stage of affects which are resistant to any meaning, to look only at gestures, the expressions of the lips, grins—then the majority of the time one would discover that the champions of freedom are as worthless as the other camp, the supporters of conservatism. And when this dance begins at the lowest "grass roots" level, then perhaps one arrives at a possible procedure for validating social molecular practices.

It is like the painter who distances himself from a preliminary vision of things in order to come up with the system of reference that will constitute the real texture of the canvas. It's dark, it's close, it's hot, it's grainy, it recedes into the distance... Politics works the same way. Georges Marchais, the Communist Party leader, what an idiot. Le Pen belongs to the same genre, but more fine-tuned, more finished. But don't they give off the same bristling sensation of infamy and wickedness, and make one's skin crawl?

Just looking at them, one becomes aware of one's own stench. At bottom that's the way we are, and that's the way we can find our own limits. With their berets or their caps and their dirty feet, we suddenly realize how they get under our skin. Who said these people would like to build crematoria? That's much too Wagnerian for them! No, they only want to clean up their little garden paths. "Just give the illegal aliens some money and get them out of here! Let them rot somewhere else, it's not our problem! The Third World? Famine? Bother someone else! All those pictures of kids like wax dolls, that's just propaganda, it's annoying. We don't have time for all that; we already have enough problems of our own. Right?"

There's the "theater of cruelty" for you, the stage where we can learn about everything that is wretched: there, in front of us, and also all around us and even inside us. It is by mapping this genre of subjective formation that we can hope to take our distance from dominant libidinal investments.

And yet, parallel to this impoverishment of content in individuals as producers of subjective singularities, there is an absolutely fantastic expansion of machinic phylums, that is to say, of all the processes of selection, elimination and generation of machines by machines, which never cease producing new, artistic as well as scientific and technical possibilities. Thus, on the one hand there is the infantilization of the production of subjectivity, with the intense binarization of messages, uniformization and unidimensionization of relations to the world and, on the other, expansion of other non-denotative functions of language: the composition of rhythms and the unprecedented production of relations to the world.

I have always been bothered by the din made about the theme of "science without conscience." This is foolish, since it is only because of this very same subjectivity and its ever-accelerating, irreversible degeneration that machinic systems are able to take off the way they do. And isn't it also kind of stupid to hope to improve the condition of the human, one of the most vulgar, mean and aggressive of all species? I am not afraid of machines as long as they enlarge the scope of perception and complexity of human behavior. What bothers me is when people try to bring them down to the level of human stupidity.

I am not a postmodernist. I don't think that scientific and technological progress must necessarily bring about a "schiz" in relation to desire and creativity. On the contrary, I think that machines must be used—and all kinds of machines, whether concrete or abstract, technical, scientific or artistic. Machines do more than revolutionize the world: they completely recreate it.

And what the structuralists say is not true: it is not language and communication that engender subjectivity. At a certain level it is collectively manufactured like energy, electricity and aluminum. Of course an individual results from a biological, metabolistic process involving a mother and a father. But we shouldn't stop there because, in reality, the production of an individual also depends on biological industry and even genetic engineering. And one must admit that if these were not constantly set on responding to the waves of viruses that regularly traverse the planet, human life would quickly be eliminated. For example, the spread of AIDS leads to a kind of hunt for a treasure of immense importance, a race to find the proper "response." From now on industrial production of an immune response will be part of the maintenance of human life on this planet.

Subjectivity works the same way. It is increasingly manufactured on a worldwide scale. I don't only mean to say that representations of sociality and social hierarchy tend toward a general unification. Actually, the fabrication of subjectivity also concerns very varied models of submission to productive processes, like particular relations to abstractions of the economic order. And it goes much further than that. From infancy, the intelligence, sensibility, behavior and fantasy of children are shaped so as to make them productive and compatible to social conditions. And I insist that this takes place not only on representational and emotional levels: a six-month-old put in front of a television will structure his perception, at that stage of development, by fixing his eyes on the television screen. The concentration of attention upon a certain kind of object is part of the production of subjectivity.

Thus we get beyond the simple domain of ideology, of ideological submission. Subjectivity from this point of view has nothing to do with Althusser's notion of the ideological apparatus, because it is produced in its entirety and, particularly, its components involve what I call a-signifying elements, which sustain relations to time, to rhythm, to space, to the body, to colors, to sexuality...

From there all kinds of attitudes are possible. For instance, after 1968, people were filled with nostalgia when Illich's ideas about returning to the smallest units of production, about conviviality, etc., became popular. Or there were those of American neo-liberals, like Milton Friedman & Co., who cynically disagreed: you can say whatever you want, however you want, but the transformations of capitalism are irreversible. While it is true that capitalism has wreaked havoc all over the world, taking into account demographic pressures it would have been much worse without it.

However disgusting these guys are, one can't always cling to the past. I am completely in favor of defending the environment, of course. Only it must be admitted that technico-scientific expansion is irreversible. The real question is to bring about molecular and molar revolutions capable of radically altering its finalities since—and this has to be said again and again—a mutation does not have to be catastrophic. The ever-more artificial processes of subjective production can very well be associated with new social and creative forms. That's where the cursor of molecular revolutions is located.

This whole business of reclaiming cartographic references of individual and collective subjectivity is not just a matter for psychologists, analysts, educators, media or publicity people, etc. It involves fundamental political questions, which are even more urgent today than they were twenty years ago. But our heads are still in the clouds. The hardheadedness that characterized the social critique during the period of the "new culture" seems to have collapsed. The only thing that the culture values is competition—in sports, business and politics.

Perhaps I am a naïve and incorrigible optimist, but I am convinced that one day there will be a return to collective judgment, and these last few years will be considered the most stupid and barbaric in a long time; barbarity of the mind and in representations, but also in reality. What is happening to the Third World and with the environment is truly monstrous, yet people continue to view things through the calm perspectives of actors, journalists and media personalities. Nobody wants to know too much or think too much: "It's going badly, but it's still moving ahead. Progress marches on, so all we have to do is wait. It'll all work out."

It appears to me essential not to let things fizzle out, but to reestablish, as fast as possible, a social practice. A practice—a militant stance, even if that makes people laugh or gnash their teeth—that would not be cut off or specialized, but would establish a continuum between political, social and economic questions, technico-scientific transformations, artistic creations, and the management of everyday problems, with the reinvention of a singular existence. From such a vantage point, the present crisis could be considered a dysfunction in social semiotization. It is obvious that the mechanics of semiotic and institutional management in the flux of production and circulation correspond less and less to the evolution of productive forces and collective investments. Even the most narrow-minded economists are stunned to discover a sort of craziness in these systems and feel the urgent need to find alternatives.

But what? There is no answer if the analysis keeps focusing on dysfunction. Because what prevents the possible elaboration of alternatives—the old idea of a "New International Order"—is not only the "selfishness of oligarchies"—even when this exists—nor even their congenital idiocy. Instead, you come up against another phenomenon, linked precisely to the worldwide production of subjectivity and its ever-greater integration into every human or machinic function: what I call WIC, World Integrated Capitalism.

Let's take the case of Iran. This ancient Third World country had the means to produce a fabulous economic take-off, becoming an international power of the first order. And then a mutation in collective subjectivity occurred which completely upset that system, plunging the country into a complex—at once revolutionary and reactionary—situation, with the return to fundamentalist Shiism and its awesome archaic values. What took precedence there was not the interests of workers, peasants or intellectuals. A passion seized a large portion of the Iranian people, led them to choose to exist through a charismatic leader, through a religious and ethnic difference akin to a collective orgasm.

Today, all political systems, in varying degrees, are confronted with the question of subjective identity. This is what sometimes makes international relations so maddening, since they depend less on arms, on the opposition between East and West, etc., than on these kinds of questions, which seem aberrant. The Palestinian or Irish problems, the national claims of the Basques, Poles or Afghanis actually express the need for human collectivities to reappropriate their own lives, their own destinies through what I call a process of singularization. This emergence of dissident subjectivities calls for a new theory of archaisms. Just one remark on this subject; let's look at the question from a lower point on the ladder. Does infantile regression, in the behavior of an individual, automatically indicate that the person has "returned to childhood"? No. What is really at stake is a different use of pre-existent elements, of behavior or representations, in order to construct *another* life surface, or another affective space, laying out another existential territory. When the Basques, the Irish or the Corsicans fight to reconstruct their land, they have the conviction that they are fighting to defend something inscribed in tradition, they believe that they are relying on historical legitimacy. I think that they reemploy representations, monuments and historical emblems in order to make a new collective subjectivity for themselves. Surely their struggle is facilitated by the staying power of these traditional elements—to the point that they can lead to xenophobic passions. But, in reality, they are pretty much on the same level as the people who live in French industrial or residential suburbs, who also aspire to restore collective ways of life for themselves.

Not everyone has the good luck, or the bad luck, to be Irish, Basque or Corsican. But the problem is comparable: how to reinvent existential coordinates and acceptable social territories? Is it necessary to launch the Liberation Front of Seine-et-Oise [a Parisian suburb], as Godard did in *Weekend*, a new Picardie, a new Belfort territory, and so many Disneylands in metallurgical basins? What else can spring up in our industrial deserts? I say, new territories of reference. And not only in people's minds, also in the workplace, in the possibility of finding their way through social and economic mechanisms. A territory is the ensemble of projects or representations where a whole series of behaviors and investments can pragmatically emerge, in time and in social, cultural, esthetic and cognitive space.

How does one go about producing, on a large scale, a desire to create a collective generosity with the tenacity, the intelligence and the sensibility which are found in the arts and sciences? If you want to invent new molecules in organic chemistry, or new music, it doesn't just happen: they don't fall from the sky. It takes work, research, experiment—as it must with society. Capitalism is not a fair nor a foul weather friend, no more than Marxist determinism or spontaneous anarchy are. The old references are dead, and so much the better. New ones must be invented. Under today's conditions, which are different from those of the nineteenth century, with six or seven billion inhabitants on the globe and the entire technico-scientific revolution, how can human relations be organized without automatically reinforcing hierarchies, segregations, racism, and the erosion of particularities? How to release an inventive, machinic collective passion that would proliferate, as the case in Japan seems to be—without crushing people under an infernal discipline? Oppressed minorities exist in Japan, women continue to be treated as inferiors, childhood is torture. But it is true that the hypermodern cocktail, the *high-tech* current, and the return of archaic structures found there are fascinating! Perhaps not enough attention has been paid to certain theoreticians, like Akira Asada, who perceive that capitalism in Japan does not function on the same bases as it does in the West. Oligarchies do not have the same privileges, class is not delimited in the same way, the work contract is not experienced in the same way...

I say all this to indicate that it is possible to envision different formulas organizing social life, work and culture. Models of political economy are not universal. They can be made to bend, and others can be invented. At the root of all this is life itself and collective desire.

4

EVERYWHERE AT ONCE

Michel Butel: *First there was childhood, then adolescence. After the war there was Lucien Sebag,*[1] *there was* La Voie Communiste,[2] *there was the end of the Algerian War, the break up of "La Voie," there was May '68... all proper nouns. And then the last... Deleuze. "Deleuze," it responded to something you wanted: to work, to create something with someone. You talked about Sebag as if, at a certain moment, you could have worked together. You hoped not to have to continue working alone; I'm not only talking about not continuing with psychoanalysis...*

Félix Guattari: I participated in a myth, the myth of a project, a productive workshop dealing with theory, analysis and politics. It was a particularly exciting time because of the meetings at the FGERI, the Federation of Study Groups in Institutional Research with François Fourquet, Medam... We wouldn't often talk about personal matters and yet they would surface and we could get pretty delirious before switching back to extremely serious matters... Even earlier on, the meetings with Jean Oury were also a kind of collective arrangement of expression...

Now, I'm very hesitant about passing judgment on all of that. I think that there were positive and negative aspects. We were exploring a completely different way of working than what is generally found at universities and research centers. Ideas were germinated that never would have reached fruition, that possibly never would have occurred at all: sudden flashes, projects, institutions, all this through jokes, but also discussions, conflicts, denials, etc.

The FGERI was really quite extraordinary: no funds, no grants, and still there were more than a hundred people, from very different backgrounds, who met on the one hand to reflect on the idea of widening the scope of analysis, getting it beyond the couch, and on the other getting it beyond the kind of psychoanalytic structuralism that was beginning to despotically establish itself around Lacanism. The negative aspect was that "brainstorming" could become an alibi for doing nothing...

But the pre-project work with Deleuze was still very much along these lines. The idea was to discuss things together, to do things together—it was 1969, a period that was still marked by the turmoil of '68. Doing something together meant throwing Deleuze into the stew. In truth, he was already there, he was meeting people, he was doing all kinds of things... It was during the time of the GIP (Group Information on Prisons) that I had gotten Deleuze together with Foucault to embark on what eventually became the CERFI (Center for Study, Research and Institutional Training), by obtaining a research grant for them and their coworkers. In a way then, there really was a moment for this kind of collective work. But as soon as we agreed to work together, Deleuze immediately closed all other doors. I hadn't anticipated that. And the CERFI pursued its path independently of me. This turned out to be a problem for some of the other people involved, like Fourquet, Medam...

At a certain point you were hugely disenchanted, even if you weren't aware of it. There was no political impetus; the Algerian War was over and '68 hadn't happened yet. It was a period of creative suspension... "Am I going to continue with politics? Am I going to continue working?

Am I going to go on being an analyst? Am I going to drop every-thing...?" In the years immediately preceding the encounter with Deleuze, it was as if you were getting ready for something.

Just before '68, I felt like I was riding a powerful wave, connecting all kinds of vectors of collective intelligence: I broke up with "*La Voie Communiste*," with a militant style that was a little too dogmatic, a little backwards... I gradually came to question Lacanism, but less on theoretical grounds than in practice... I questioned a certain style of conjugality, linked to my situation at La Borde... Really, all of that was very promising.

'68 was a very ambiguous move... It's true that there was a very high level of entropy in collective projects; a kind of mediocrity and demagoguery prevailed... I was trying to create instruments of expression, but always with the same gang of people... It was kind of heavy, and power games would always take over, with people like Serge July, Alain Geismar, and the disaster of the Proletarian Left[3]— of which, in my opinion, one will never say enough bad things.

For me, the aftermath of '68 was made up of action commit-tees, psychiatric alternatives, the feminist and gay movements... I was hoping that a collective development could be pursued, but instead a sort of prohibition against thinking set in. Today it's hard to imagine the kind of demagoguery that reigned at Vincennes[4] and in those milieus: "What are you talking about?" "I don't get it." "What does that mean?" "Why use complicated words like that?" Deleuze's course was continually interrupted by unbelievable idiots. A real circus. Such is the price of History...

Then there was the miracle, my meeting Deleuze, which opened the way to a whole series of things. How did it happen? I told him my ideas about group subjectivity, about transversality, etc. I was very pleased. He was very encouraging. And then he said, "Why don't you write all of this down?" To tell the truth, writing always makes me a little uncomfortable; talking with people, discussing things, that's okay, but writing… Then he said, "We can do it together." For a while it wasn't very clear to me. Naïvely I thought "together" must mean "with my friends, the gang." But that didn't last long! I quickly understood that it would only be the two of us. It was a frenzy of work that I hadn't imagined possible until then. Both a careful and scholarly enterprise and a radical and systematic demolition of Lacanism and all my previous references; clarifying concepts I had been "experimenting with" in various fields, but which couldn't reach their full extension because they were too attached to their origins. It was necessary to impose a certain "deterritorialization" of my relations to the social, to La Borde, to the concepts of matrimony and psychoanalysis and to the FGERI, so that concepts like "machine" could be given enough room to develop.

The philosophic shoring up was above all a long-term project with Deleuze, which gave my earlier attempts at theorizing an entirely new energy. It was, if you'll permit the comparison, like the difference between Jean-Jacques Rousseau writing the little melodies of the "Devin du Village" and Bach developing the "Well-Tempered Clavier" from a couple of *ritournelles*…

You say that Deleuze was extremely careful to keep things, day after day, out of collective experimentation. I've always had the impression that, almost physically, there has always been a distance in relation to the triviality of events that makes one expect a kind of take-off from you. At the same time I've always noticed a kind of vigilance that I would personally call Stalinian: your need to understand everything in terms of institutions.

It's true. Deleuze, carefully, with a light touch, broke down a kind of myth about groups that I had had. "Packs" have been roving my mind since childhood. That another "gang" form came about is part of the same social physics; nothing is lost, all the aspects are there, at every crossroad.

Anyway, thank you for the take-off—what others have called my readiness. I believe that I've succeeded to preserve it for almost characterological reasons. Yet it also has its negative sides. Every project I'm involved with has its other side, "Okay, that'll work, that's great, but if it falls apart that won't be bad either, that could even be much better!" In the background there is the refrain of purification: "Drink. Eliminate." I think that perhaps you put too much emphasis on one aspect, my way of pushing everything toward a positive project, a "good cause." You fail to recognize the other dimension of unconscious sabotage, a kind of passion for returning to the zero point.

I also have a kind of capacity in me for detachment, where I become the spectator. There are the people who light up, and then they blink off. And sometimes the light goes out to the extent that I even forget the name of the person in question. Then at other times everything is there, nothing has changed…

There are two ways of looking at this. The positive side corresponds to a dream-like state. For example, one can believe that people one leaves behind can at some point become part of one's life again. The ability to begin again—that is what really works against ordinary horrors. It is also a rule of life that one can't remain dumb-struck forever. One must go on living… So I wonder if it doesn't ultimately mean misunderstanding the capacity for numbness, the incredible breakdowns that take place to people, in life, these blackouts that suddenly make people stop emitting, stop blinking…

I hadn't fully realized the importance of transference, and all the crap it can release in the heart of work relations. I had the freedom to step back, but they didn't always have that. It's easier to understand this in terms of love... Anyway, I think that the problem is not that people stop blinking, but that they blink too much.

Don't we need people who are completely dead, who have no reactions?

I feel closer to what Freud said of children who can't imagine someone else's death. It's like that, switched off. For me most people are dead, they don't exist, never existed. As some sort of an intermediate link, I'm never in the position of defining a finality, an anticipation, a demand. A very passive position.

Coluche.[5] I think he is somewhat of a genius, and I wonder how it was that the tide turned, besides the fact that Mitterand won?

Coluche is an autodidact. In part, he is totally sure of himself, an extraordinary self-assurance, with a facility, an exceptional virtuosity to quickly grasp situations. Like a Buto dancer, he gets a hold of things before they even take shape in people's minds. He is everywhere at once. And at the same time, he is completely fragile, that is to say disarmed by intellectual adversity, by journalists. The intellectual reinforcements we gave him in 1981 were both very valuable and incredibly cumbersome.

All the dangers of being in the public eye were suddenly focused on one individual, like a concentrated ray of sunlight setting one spot ablaze. I think this is what happened to Coluche. As long as he only exposed his clown's mask he was able to manage it, and with great virtuosity. When it was no longer the mask, but his particular fragility, his precariousness, perhaps even a slightly psychotic personality, then... It is great that he has gone back to film.

I have to return to the notion of drawing rare combinations from the deck. The dynamics of singularities always result from a small miracle, encounters that may trigger transformations that are no longer singular, since they can upset the entire planet. Certain events, the lamest as well as the most extraordinary, statistically must occur.

It is foolish to think that '68 came about because of the pressure of the masses—what a joke. It was an amazing chain reaction released by a very unlikely semiotic scaffolding. It was the same for Coluche: a very exceptional coming together. In both cases, the effect imploded, the components were disengaged. Then, in reaction, the whole context rearranged itself in order to preclude recurrence.

I'm sure that there were grand bourgeois, like traditional Gaullists and diplomats whom nothing could excite anymore, who found themselves in total agreement with Coluche.

It eludes programming, because of what I call the production of an endo-reference. Subjectivity is being produced before it is aware of itself. That is what happened in '68: a subjectivity was in the making before anyone had a chance to realize what was going on.

I really like the image of the slumbering beast. A completely dormant mass, totally infantilized by the media. But when some singularity awakens it, it turns into an extremely receptive milieu. Politicians and intellectuals are the last to reach this receptiveness. That stroke of singularity, that arbitrary conglomeration of signs and sounds, is immediately perceived and received by those who crave it. They are already so bored...

II

WHY ITALY?

5

AN OPEN LETTER TO

SOME ITALIAN FRIENDS

More than ever before, it is on the European and global level that political and social problems in Italy and in France are being dealt with. Repression is going international. As happened during the worst days of the Cold War, the U.S.A. is dictating their behavior to Italian politicians. Considering these diverse interferences, retreating behind national borders will lead nowhere [!] Rather than secret dealings, what we need is the largest possible public debate. As far as I am concerned, I would encourage Italian intellectuals to intervene in French political questions. On the other hand, I would be in favor of initiating an international discussion on the development of the situation in Italy. This is the purpose of this letter. It has no other claim than to instigate a kind of "circular" correspondence.

There is another reason that led me to pay attention to the repression which is raining down indiscriminately on the militants and theorists of the Italian Autonomia. Toni Negri is my friend, and I would like to show him my support through the ordeal that he is presently exposed to. I would like to vindicate his claim that he did everything he could to prevent terrorist groups inspired by the Red Brigades to expand. I am convinced that, to a large extent, it was his influence on the revolutionary extreme left in France that spared us a similar phenomenon in France.

Violence in Europe is growing with the social and economic crisis. The first act of violence comes from the capitalist redeployment

that condemns millions of families to misery and disrupts important branches of the economy. The first act of violence comes from
powers that jail hundreds of young workers and students who
rebel against conditions that have been imposed on them while
swindlers of the first magnitude are set free (whatever happened,
for instance, with the Lockheed affair). Today, entire regions of
Italy and France appear emptied, little by little, of their substance.
The major forces on the left, starting with the Italian Communist
Party and the French Communist Party, remain powerless in front
of such an evolution [!] No wonder that thousands of youths are
tempted to launch into desperate actions? The collapse of the
Historical Compromise in Italy and of the French Common Program has, as a consequence, profoundly demoralized the diverse
avant-gardes of the European extreme left. Does this mean that
the hour has come to confront the power of the State with arms in
hand? It is true that we cannot hope to change, exclusively with
pacifistic means, the bourgeois and bureaucratic institutions that
bring about a constant reinforcement of the repression of exploitation and, perhaps, ultimately, will lead to a true catastrophe!
Today, an effective action would necessarily do violence to the
established order. Does this mean that the time has come to form
small clandestine urban guerilla groups? The outcome is known;
such attempts have only had the effect of increasing the strike
force of the reaction and of binding the disoriented masses around
the traditional political parties.

It is thus not a matter of renouncing on principle all violence;
rather, one must develop effective forms of violence that will
modify in a revolutionary direction the social relations of power
and will set in motion authentic dynamics for liberation. Violence
is legitimate when it is the work of workers, women, and youths
who are struggling to change their condition. It is no longer
legitimate when it is only carried out by dogmatic groupuscules

whose principal target, beyond that of a few expiatory victims, is the impact of their action on the media.

Today, police repression and the radio and television's campaign of lies are concentrated on the militants who most clearly denounce the State power-groupuscular terrorism deadlock, who are trying hard to redefine new forms of action. Everyone who is familiar with these questions knows perfectly well that Toni Negri and his comrades have nothing whatsoever to do with the Red Brigades. The police and the legal system know this better than anyone! But, by using them as scapegoats, they hope, magically, to ward off the prevailing social violence. This, the worst of politics, is in every way similar to the politics of terrorism!

Just a few years ago, a great hope for change manifested itself in France and Italy! What did the Communist parties and the extreme left in these countries do with this hope? The former sank even deeper into a politics of demobilizing compromises; the latter were incapable of leaving their ideological and social ghetto. Power, in Italy, will seek to make the most of this situation. Everything leads us to believe that it will try to impose constitutional reforms ostensibly to bring Italy "to the level of Europe," but in fact to liquidate the popular conquests of the last thirty years. Nevertheless, nothing is written in stone. Everything still depends on the left and the extreme left's ability to get out of their sluggishness. It is true that terrorism in Italy is a serious phenomenon and dangerous on many levels. But it is not the real question! Terrorism will disappear the day the masses start to move towards clear objectives. We should permit nothing to distract us from discovering the ways and means for irreversible social transformation, without which we will enter into an escalation of fear and despair on a whole new scale.

— *Félix Guattari*

6

NEW SPACES OF LIBERTY

FOR MINORITARIAN DESIRE

The list of militants of the extreme left imprisoned or pursued in Germany, France, Italy, Greece, Portugal, all across Europe, is getting longer in an impressive way. In Germany, with the execution of the Stammheim prisoners, the death penalty was reinstated, but in a clandestine manner, insofar as the execution seems to have been entrusted to unofficial government police. (There is nothing particularly innovative about this practice since it was already widespread, for example, in France, during the war in Algeria.) In France, in defiance of laws regarding extradition and political asylum, the government handed the lawyer Klauss Croissant over to the German repressive machine and Giscard d'Estaing, in Brussels on the heels of his "feat," proposed setting up a "European legal space."

How high will this wave of repression rise? Does it signal the recrudescence of fascism? Is it a transitory phenomenon that an opposing "upsurge" by the European left can effectively check? Is it exclusively at the instigation of Germano-American capitalism that the current offensives are taking place in Europe? To reassure itself, to justify inconsistent alliances, what we might call the leftist public opinion is too often content with justifying itself through historical analogies. It speaks of fascism, of gulags, and of general leftist alternatives, but it misses the nature of today's true trials of confrontation. In fact, it is no longer possible today to think about international relations in terms of entities that are relatively independent from one another. Nor is it possible to think about national relations in terms of right-wing blocs and left-wing blocs. In all domains new formulas for international dialogue are seeking their path. While the "multinationals" and all manner of lobbies manipulate governments, party headquarters, and unions at their leisure, a new type of internationalism is in the making, brought about, for example, by ecologists, "nationalitarian" movements (Basque, Breton, Irish, etc...) and new political scenes are being put into place that imply objectives, alliances, and strategies that have but little to do with those which have characterized the last decades. The paradox, today, is that most of the important problems currently tend to arise on a global and on a socially microscopic scale, that is, on the level of the individual, the family, the neighborhood, the district... Numerous questions about lifestyle, behavior, that yesterday seemed completely marginal or only of interest to the specialist will, it seems, in the future, become increasingly decisive political concerns; women's liberation, the emancipation of sexual minorities, problems related to drugs, to madness, the relationship to the environment, the body, etc... The organization of the resistance to forms of exploitation of work, forms whose importance was underestimated yesterday, will play an increasingly significant role in social struggles: the work of women, immigrants, young people, part-time work, temp work, "black market" work, etc...

The great political and union formations are far from taking full responsibility with respect to this type of problem, and nothing can currently allow us to think that they will be led to do so. Nevertheless, they are increasingly forced to take them into consideration. At times, they are even subject on the inside to what we have called "molecular revolutions."

The worker's movement which, as of a long time, has organized itself in order to defend the exploited from capitalism, will it be able to associate itself with this new type of social revolution? Does it represent, in its own particular fashion, a new type of conservatism that itself needs to be done away with? Supposing that an alliance was conceivable between traditional formations and the movements that are trying hard to give an organized expression to these new problems, to this new sensibility—in which way will the reciprocal influences work? In the direction of co-opting, of the bureaucratization of the marginal movements? In the direction of putting back into question, in a genuine way, the old political and union machinery. It would be too easy to content ourselves with responding: "Each to his own domain! Economics and politics to the unions and the parties, and daily life and collective desire to the new mass movements!" It is impossible today to distinguish clearly between what belongs to income demands and what belongs to political and micropolitical questions.

It would be thus entirely insufficient to consider that the only driving forces of the current transformations are connected to the consequences of the global crisis, to the evolution of the raw materials market, to the rise of new economic powers in the third world, and to the restructuring of capitalism as it is starting to happen on the international scale. The super-managers of capitalism are, by the way, perfectly conscious of the danger that this new type of social revolution represents and it is as much in response to the economic disorganization linked to the global crisis, as these "molecular revolutions" that are proposed today, in Europe, that the different models of authoritarian democracy in Europe are proposed today and that the wave of current repression has mounted. Which kind of socialism, which kind of Eurocommunism will or will not be compatible with the State machines that are the best integrated to international capitalism? Can communists and socialists, as in the past, be the best defenders of the established order, the best conspiracy agents of the social upheavals that are brewing? Carter, Brezhnev, Schmidt, Andreotti, Giscard D'Estaing, and Mitterand, don't all share exactly the same point of view. At bottom, however, it's really just a matter of nuances of assessment primarily linked to local conditions.

One would have to be terribly myopic to not see that, sooner or later, all of the developed industrial societies—the U.S.S.R., the U.S.A., Japan, and the capitalist societies of old European nations—are heading towards the same type of totalitarian system. Their modes of production, founded on exploitation and segregation; their fundamental aims, that render them incapable of harmonizing the different aspirations expressed in their folds, all lead these societies to give a dominant role to the State in an entire series of essential domains. In this way, the State is led to function concurrently as:

— a local machinery of the true decision-making centers of international capitalism,

— a mediator between the different factions of the local bourgeoisie and bureaucracy,

— a relay of the multiple vectors of subjection of individuals in order to constitute them as atoms well integrated into the collective work force, into existing production relations, social relations, domestic and sexual relations, etc…

In this sort of regime, State power has become quite different from what it was, for example, during the era of Lenin. It is now inseparable from the training and participation systems of the popular masses. We can even consider that today there is a sort of repressive continuum between the State power in the traditional sense and the parties, the workers' unions, the mass media, the social compartmentalization by the school, psychiatry, leisure, sports, and the entirety of collective equipments.

Alongside the modes of subjection by the wage system, by bourgeois legality, by the police, the army, etc… State power relies on systems of alienation. This means that the individual not only leaves it up to different authorities, but also that he personally creates some modes of subjection that become, in one way or another, dominant norms that must be kept watch over, repressed. More and more, the workers movement and the masses are called on to associate with these normalization efforts. (For example, in Italy, the Italian Communist Party calls on the workers to participate in the denunciation of uncontrolled elements. Or, in Germany, televised games lead to a mass denouncement.) In addition to the brutal repression practiced by the state, a softer, yet also more systematic and deceptive repression is thus diffused into all the pores of society. Marginality itself tends to fall under the control of power; in France, for example, civil servants have the task of pursuing questions regarding ecology, drugs, the female condition, prostitution, etc… Of course, the "use of force" continues to exist and even to increase, for example, in prisons, with increasingly frequent use of methods of sensory deprivation and other techniques aimed at liquidating the detained prisoners' personalities, or even just purely and simply liquidating the prisoners, as in Germany. But power hopes only to resort to this—and hence all the more brutally—in extreme cases; that is to say, cases that pass the limit, in particular when dealing with those who no longer live their marginality as a state of fact that they passively submit to, but rather as a social condition, the result of a type of society that they mean to combat.

This is the context in which power appeals to intellectuals, filmmakers, artists, journalists, so that they get involved, unreservedly, in the defense of the social order. The growing importance that the media grants them, in fact imposes on them to integrate themselves, each in his own manner, into the majoritarian consensus that constitutes the lynchpin (*clé de voute*) of the whole system. Let's note that this recruiting is currently carried out very often at the instigation of the leaders of the left (this is particularly significant in Italy).

In this race to integration, what will become of the movements of the revolutionary extreme left? Until now, it seems that the bulk of their actions continues to depend on the traditional left. In France, for example, many of their hopes rest on a possible electoral victory for the Communist Party and the Socialist Party from which they expect the creation of conditions more favorable to social struggles. The least that we can say is that they seem hardly prepared to transform themselves and to adapt themselves to the new forms of struggle that we are evoking here!

It is true that these are still precarious, taking their first fragile steps, often for the preservation of the right of lawyers, of the right to political asylum, etc... and to take on more offensive actions in order to conquer new spaces of liberty (for example, on the question of free radios). It is perhaps becoming possible to envision putting into place a system of liaison, or even coordination systems between them and it presently become advisable to call it "a Movement," not only on a regional and national scale, but international as well.

The mode of operation, in Madrid, in Barcelona, in Burgos, of liaison committees between marginal groups and different revolutionary movements, on the occasion of the struggle against the reactionary law of Social Rehabilitation (*peligrosidad y rehabilitación social*) signals us to a very interesting direction. It is not about—it goes without saying—challenging the indispensable autonomy of women's liberation movements, or of movements of prisoners, homosexuals, drug addicts, squatters, etc... but of extricating minimal objectives, of establishing "transveral" systems of communication—or, if we want to hold onto old formulas, on the level of the base—and of creating a climate of changes favorable to better understanding the different positions of every group.

It is in this spirit that in numerous European countries, liaison committees against repression and for new spaces of liberty are trying to get set up. These liaison committees in no way intend to draft an international program of struggle, or to direct mass actions on the European scale. Their goal is much more modest and much more concrete. They plan:

1) to privilege the liaison between the different collectives that exist on the different national and international levels. (For example, the bringing together of different specialized collectives on free radios with a European Coordination of free radios, an alternative press agency, or even the putting into contact of groups working on behalf of common prisoners).

2) to circulate elements of information and reflection on the development of repression in Europe (for example, on the liaison between the different forms of repression and the evolution of the class struggle, State power's new forms of intervention, etc…)

3) to offer direct support, through assemblies, meetings, study days, national and international gatherings, to the initiatives that lead to an enlargement of information on these questions (without, for all that, leaving out actions of practical solidarity).

4) to bring to the attention of international opinion a certain number of particularly scandalous acts of repression. (Example: the creation of an international commission to investigate them).

In quite difficult local conditions, the meetings of Bologna, in September 1977, successfully demonstrated that mass international exchanges could be organized in a fruitful manner. The meetings in Frankfurt in July 1978 would mark, in my view, a further step with respect to the meetings in Bologna, if they allowed the different components of the Movement to gather, work, and live together, without being leeched on by external interferences. (Here I'm not thinking only of police interventions!) It is only with respect to their own rhythms, their own levels of conscience, their own languages, that a network of exchanges can develop that can release new perspectives on common struggle. It has to be repeated: this is in no way about drafting a "common program" between different marginalities, different minorities and different revolutionary movements! It's simply about putting into gear, about making effective what is possible today in this domain, and nothing more than that.

7

MINORITY AND TERRORISM

Félix Guattari: Whatever the catastrophic situation that was created by the phenomenon of the Red Brigades in Italy, the most important thing to do is to start a much more general debate within the movement. We have to understand that, if there are around two thousand active Red Brigades sympathizers, there are also tens, if not hundreds of thousands of people, young workers and students, who share the same concerns as the Red Brigades.

Maria-Antonietta Macciocchi: *The Red Brigades came into existence through the pressure of facts relating to the "Bolshevik" past, through the powerful influence of an old Stalinist history that has been swept aside. The Red Brigades are ideologically linked to some of the hardest elements in the communist party. That is, for the R.B., there is a "non-Berlinguerian" party within the party's base, and this* base *is susceptible to the old call of Stalinism. Now, what can no longer last in communist parties is the party such as it is, in its old body. In the name of* democratic centralism, *the mystical union of the historic heads of the R.B. is being carried out through the sublimation of the organization of the Party (even when the Party doesn't exist). There is such malaise in the working class, such hopelessness among workers and in factories, that such a crude ideological action can have a big impact. We are witnessing* the crisis, *and we are living the decline of an* old *left. On the other hand, the power that we know* *is indefensible; it is foul. Pasolini was assassinated because he wanted to put Christian Democracy on trial. But the way in which Pasolini wanted to try Christian Democracy did not involve taking Aldo Moro and assassinating him, putting him in the trunk of a car, and bringing his body before the communist party headquarters. The trial he had in mind involved opening, for all the Italian people, the dossiers of the sinister affairs, the pillaging, theft, murders, and all the crimes committed during over thirty years of Christian Democracy. The assassination of a class adversary is not a political project; it's not an alternative to a class society. And "proletarian violence" is no political strategy for a society. In fact, this violence is in the very the process of bringing fascism back to Italy, or else laying the groundwork for a new totalitarianism... I say that everything that we know is indecent, unbearable, from one end of the planet to the other, the issue of the rights of man goes beyond the Eastern borders and is gradually becoming a source of great concern in the West as well. At stake is a new humanism, both theoretical and practical.*

... I don't believe that intellectuals are the guardians of an ethics, and that they should be the first to judge, define, and condemn. It is up to us, above all, to assess, with maximum lucidity, what the solutions are. I have to say that the image of damned expiatory victims belonged to the Red Brigades and the Red Army Faction, and then, by extension, to Schleyer and Moro... Actually, what most bothered and upset us was perhaps less the murders of Schleyer and Moro, than the way in which these murders were used. In particular, the photos that were circulated by these groupuscules were truly abominable. On the other hand, we have to outsmart the trick of trying to exorcise the underlying situation by reducing it to its symptoms, as, ultimately, these are all no more than symptoms: the Red Brigades, The Red Army Faction, the activities of the Black Panthers during another period, in other contexts. I agree with those who denounce this type of action, this type of conception or strategy, but I would still insist that the Red Army Faction and the Red Brigades are indeed part of the movement. Whatever kind of impasse in which they find themselves, they—with perhaps more courage and absurdity—pushed the movement forward. This merits a minimum of solidarity on our part. In order to be able to speak, to have the right to interpellate these people and tell them that they are conducting the worst kind of politics, we cannot adopt the general attitude of universal condemnation, without seeing that this type of violence is practiced everywhere, and on other levels, on much more *molecular* and secret levels. Just look at how immigrant workers and entire segments of the population are treated. Therefore, with regard to this "moral denunciation" that so inflames the media, and on this issue alone, I say: No. It is true that this moral denunciation has to be undertaken, but it must be accompanied by a political and strategic denunciation, and it can neither serve nor justify the reinforcement of current repressive systems. It is for this reason that a number of us said those involved in the Movement 2nd June, in the Red Army Faction, etc., will take part in this gathering, if they so desire, and that dialogue with them will continue. The idea of "isolation" is completely different when considered from the vantage point of the movement, as opposed to that of power and repression. Isolation has to be combated on the plane of both ideas and dialogue. This was the attitude taken by the different branches of the organized autonomy. And it would be totally absurd to think that we can resolve the problem by affirming any solidarity whatsoever with the police, the media, with repression.

For myself, I belong to these large currents of the non-institutionalized Italian left which considered, and still consider, the Red Brigades as outside the Movement—a Movement which, by the way, the Red

Brigades completely despise. What does it mean to leave the door open for dialogue with Stalinists? With the Red Brigades, Marxism comes up once again against the problem of "anti-humanism," the problem of theoretical anti-humanism turning into practical anti-humanism through blind violence.

The question is to understand that this type of violent movement is only just one element, and that there are many more brewing and organizing, on all sorts of levels. It is with these that we must enter into dialogue.

8

LIKE THE ECHO OF A COLLECTIVE

MELANCHOLIA

In many ways the film *Germany in Autumn* will leave its mark on the history of cinema or, rather, of "engaged" cinema. First, because it is a collective work that presents not a juxtaposition of sequences made by different filmmakers but rather the fruit of discussions and elaborations in common. Next, because it was made in the heat of the moment, immediately after the events of Autumn 1977, which allowed for the creation of a remarkably authentic atmosphere. One feels, even when the sequences are acted out, that the actors and directors (who sometimes play themselves) are still under the sway of these events in such a way that a truth passes directly, with no visible break between the elements of reporting, fiction, and documentary.

This attempt, call it "analytic," to go beyond auteur cinema suggests to me a new possibility for grasping collective emotional elements through film. This kind of "analysis" occurs around two poles.

The first involves the manipulation of events by the mass media. Schleyer's death, the skyjacking to Mogadishu, and the deaths of the inmates of Stammheim prison have been transformed into an emotional charge placed entirely at the disposal of social control and repression. The reference to Sophocles' *Antigone* becomes a key to the film, the events in Germany that autumn taking on the proportions of ancient drama. In this light, the deaths of Hans Martin Schleyer and of the RAF prisoners would function as an outlet or an exorcism in two acts, a double sacrifice meant to internalize a collective guilt that goes back to Nazism and beyond that in a violence supposedly essential to the German mentality.

The other pole of the film consists in the authors' attempts to counteract this collective intoxication by the media, to obstruct the "infernal machine" of guilt inducement—to paraphrase here Jean Cocteau on Oedipus. It is essentially a matter of getting out of the RAF-West Germany confrontation, of the repression-reprisals cycle, of the quasi-symmetrical simplification of ideologies in opposition. For the most part, the filmmakers manage to keep their own reactions on the most immediate level: on the level of what they felt and what they saw camera in hand; they film their squabbles with their peers, they stage their own fantasies. On such a serious topic, in such a dramatic context, that takes guts. And yet the result is no less serious and, no doubt, much more truthful than any other means of inquiry or reporting, or propaganda film. Through each sequence, we are witnessing the proliferation of the escape routes, sometimes minor, laughable, or bizarre, that personally enabled the authors to become disengaged, to a certain extent, from this Manicheaen drama. The very personal behavior which in any event defies current political classifications—Fassbinder embracing a friend, a young woman professor starting out with a shovel over a frozen field, a child watching in astonishment the burial of the Stammheim prisoners, a young man remaining seated near the gravediggers and the police after the procession's departure, a young woman and her little daughter on the road home—constitutes so many elements of life, elements of survival, so many flashes, escapes from the so called "tragic destiny" of the German people. This in no way implies that the problematic of repressive power is left aside, nor that of social control, of the media's role in daily fascism. In this respect, the film is quite explicit in its descriptions and denunciations. But its main objective lies elsewhere. On these points, opinions are already crystallized, and one explanation more or less will hardly make a noticeable difference. What is questioned here is the collective emotional context in which these opinions take shape, that is, one of the essential components in the massive foundation of any opinion that becomes law.

In this domain, the real consequence of "terrorist" actions of the RAF/Red Brigades type does not at all seem to have been taken into account by the leaders of these movements. Schematically, two positions come face to face on this question of armed struggle, in the heart of the European far left. The first, close to that of the RAF, considering that current social struggles go beyond the national and onto the international scale, and especially those between German-American imperialism and the Third World, deems it appropriate to destabilize the bastions of capitalism by all available means, beginning with armed underground warfare, and to reveal the intrinsically fascist nature of their democratic bourgeois regimes, while waiting for the avant garde of the working classes, together with the oppressed masses of the Third World, once more to grasp hold of the old torch of the struggle for socialist revolution. The second position, which can be compared to that of the so-called "spontaneist" tendency, represented in the film by Horst Mahler, former "terrorist" practicing his self criticism, consists on the contrary in denouncing, and rightly so, a "politics of the worst" which would only lead away from its initial objectives.

But this second view quickly plunges one into social-democratic, humanist reappropriation and ends by condemning all violent acts in the name of a morality that accommodates itself to even greater acts of violence perpetrated in its own name. It promotes the idea that the only means of social transformation are those sanctioned by the law.

In its own way, each of these two positions seems to mask the true meaning of the new forms of underground action which are developing all over Europe and which seemingly are becoming one of the specific features of the blocked political situation characteristic of capitalist regimes.

What a film like *Germany in Autumn* brings to light, in an original way, is that the intense emotional charge associated with the "terrorist phenomenon" has become a fundamental given of current political strategies. Like it or not, politics today has become inseparable from the collective affects molded and transmitted by the media, which constitutes a means of subjection crossing over classes and nations, and at the heart of which it is very difficult to separate the manipulated fantasies from socioeconomic realities.

All formations of power, at whatever level, are the object and/or agent of this manipulation of the media "material." Thus when young men and women rush headlong down the road of "terrorism," they don't do so only because of ideological systems, but also as delegates or sacrificial offerings of a subjective movement that surpasses them on all sides. Their actions, their feelings are "in touch" with those who approve of them, but also with all those layers of militants, of young revolutionaries, who have found no end to the struggles they have led for fifteen years. Furthermore, it is the passivity of the "swine," of the meek that comprise public opinion, which is worked on from within by their spectacular and desperate gestures. They, in return, manipulate the information and images transmitted by the media, and use their prestige to force the hand of those with whom they rub elbows.

In my view, what should be questioned is not the principle of armed struggle, nor its methods that are a part of all revolutionary movements, but, at the heart of each specific situation, its real influence on the totality of anticapitalist struggles. Clearly, the liquidation of a leader like Schleyer could never derail the functioning of the system. Instead, by providing power with the opportunity to fully deploy its police brigades and its media arsenals, it helped to further ensnare millions among the exploited. In other words, the real drama is not that a man was killed, but that these actions were conducted in a way that simply does not break free of the repressive bourgeois system, fascist assassinations, or kidnappings carried out by unofficial police gangs, and that in the final account, their only result will have been to echo the collective melancholy that has present-day Germany in its grip. As far as I am concerned, I know of nothing more sinister or odious than those photos of Schleyer or Moro,[1] with their little placards on their chests. While I refuse to judge whether or not their executions were well-founded—to judge their judges—I cannot stand this type of operation; for it is this sort of image, propelled across the media, which leads to a legitimate feeling of pity for those who are its objects and of disgust and revulsion toward those who are its authors.

Capitalism has only managed to consolidate those very bastions that the RAF and the Red Brigades claim to shake, insofar as it has managed to develop a majority consensus founded on social ultra-conservatism, the protection of acquired advantages and the systematic misinterpretation of anything that falls outside of corporate or national interests. And whatever works toward the isolation of individuals, whatever reinforces their feelings of impotence, whatever makes them feel guilty and dependent on the state, on collective agencies and their extensions—which the unions and traditional leftist parties are fast becoming—feeds this consensus. To claim to lead a revolutionary movement without attacking these phenomena of mass manipulation is an absurdity.

While the secret war conducted by the industrial powers along the north-south axis to keep the Third World in tow is indeed the main issue, it should not make us forget that there is another north-south axis which encircles the globe and along which conflicts of an equally essential nature are played out, involving the powers of the state and oppressed nationalities, immigrant workers, the unemployed, the "marginals," the "nonguaranteed"[2] and the "standardized" wage earners, the people of the cities and of the barrios, of the favellas, the ghettoes, the shanty-towns, engaging the opposition of races, sexes, classes, age-groups, etc. To conduct this other war, to insure its social and mental control over this whole everyday, desiring world, capitalism mobilizes tremendous forces. To ignore this kind of opposition or to consider it of secondary importance is to condemn all other forms of social struggle led by the traditional Workers' Movement to impotence or reappropriation. Like it or not, in today's world, violence and the media work hand in glove. And when a revolutionary group plays the game of the most reactionary media, the game of collective guilt, then it has been mistaken: mistaken in its target, mistaken in its method, mistaken in its strategy, mistaken in its theory, mistaken in its dreams...

To express complete solidarity with the victims of capitalist repression—with all of the victims—in no way implies exonerating the aberrations that led to the unconscionable spectacles of the skyjacking to Mogadishu or the supposed People's Courts that deliberated in a cellar! The inane reproduction of the state's model of "justice" and repression, the revolting use of the media, the narrow-minded sectarianism, the manipulation of the "fellow travelers" are not questions of secondary importance. The merit of a film like *Germany in Autumn* is that it helps us to see these problems in their entirety. It not only gives us a virulent critique of German society, but also initiates an examination of underground armed struggle on its own terms. In this last matter, its criticisms still remain too timid and unfocused. Again one feels the weight of the event and the fear of reappropriation by the powers that be. But it does touch on the main point, which is the morbid dramatization spawned by the altogether absurd confrontation between a monstrous state power and pitiful politico-military machines. The authors of this film are not shooting with a P.38, but with a most singular expression of desire, the right to an unrestrained word, regardless of the pressures, regardless of the dramatic, or rather tragic, character of the situation today. It is an essential prerequisite of any effective revolutionary advance.

9

A NEW ALLIANCE IS POSSIBLE

Sylvère Lotringer: *There's a lot of talk nowadays about the "end of politics" and the "end of the social." But obviously the social has not evaporated, and politics continue each day to produce its effects. Yet there is a visible and growing disaffection with what until now has constituted the major political and ideological issue: the confrontation between the Eastern and Western blocs. The antagonism is once again hardening up, but it's becoming increasingly clear that politics, in its best acceptation, no longer happens at that level. At what level, then, does it happen? And how can one reformulate political action in a time of decline for Marxism as an instrument of analysis, and in a time of bankruptcy for "real" socialism, as opposed to what some continue to call (optimistically perhaps) "possible" socialism?*

Félix Guattari: I have never taken seriously the notion that we have outgrown Marxism and that we are now on the verge of a new political era. I have never considered ideas, theories or ideologies as anything but instruments or tools. Whence this expression, which has had a certain success and has since been used by Michel Foucault, that ideas and concepts are all part of a "tool box." As tools they can be changed, borrowed, stolen, or used for another purpose. So what does it mean, "the end of Marxism?" Nothing, or only that certain Marxist tools are no longer working, that others are in need of review, that others continue to be perfectly valid. Hence it would be stupid to junk them all. All the more so in that reevaluating these concepts means reexamining them—exactly as a reevaluation of Einstein's theories includes a reexamination of Newton's. One can't say that Newtonianism is totally dead. We are dealing here with a "rhizome" of instruments; certain branches of the rhizome collapse, little sprouts begin to proliferate, etc. For me, Marxism in general has never existed. I have sometimes borrowed or adapted some Marxist concepts I could put to good use. Moreover, I like reading Marx. He's a great writer. As an author he's unbeatable.

And is politics unbeatable?

I've never confused politics with "politicking." So a certain bankruptcy of politicians' politics doesn't upset in any way what I had tried to designate by the concept of "micropolitics." Politics as I understand it, simply cannot be inscribed on the same surface at all. It concerns the relationship of large social groups to what surrounds them, to their own economic set-up, but it also concerns attitudes that run through the individual's life, through family life, through the life of the unconscious, of artistic creation, etc.

The "post-political" era, then, is not the end of politics but rather its inscription on new surfaces.

It obviously does not mean that there's no more politics. In the same way when Jean Baudrillard says that there is an "implosion" of the social, I don't even know what he's talking about. Let's simply say that the social no longer expresses itself in the usual configuration of forces.

The confrontation no longer involves left and right, or the struggle for power between the workers' movement and the bourgeoisie...

Let's not even talk about the workers' movement! The situation has become much too complex to conceive of it in these terms. We now have to deal with immense masses of people who have nothing to do with any definition of the working class. I don't mean that there are no more relationships of force, simply that the powers of the state, capitalism and Soviet bureaucracy can no longer handle the situation. We are currently in a phase of considerable turmoil, a phase one could call pre-revolutionary, although I'd rather define it as a "molecular" revolution, where virtually no one can control anything anymore.

What exactly do you mean by "molecular revolution"?

Let's take as an example the period of the end of the *Ancien Régime* in France and in Europe. It's very difficult to get a clear picture of the situation. The fall of the Bastille is just the tip of the iceberg. The *Ancien Régime* was, and had been for several decades, a society well along the road to total collapse. A certain way of conceiving the law, religion, the body, filiation, the family, time, literature—all that was moving, changing, bursting at the seams. It took some time for the bourgeoisie to pull themselves together and redefine what could be their new grounds. And it took even more time for the workers' movement to find something around which to gather and to establish itself in a relationship of force.

Now that the bipolar class relationships have ceased for the most part to be operative, and with them a good deal of the Marxist analysis of society, how does one go about recognizing the ways in which the molecular revolution takes form in our society?

First of all we must stop claiming that there is no more "social," that it no longer exists and that nobody gives a damn. We should at least try to recognize the nature of the phenomena we're dealing with, try to recenter the focus where politics has migrated, where the situation has become critical, difficult to get a grasp on, to attach a meaning to. Secondly, we should put into question all of the so-called political instruments at our disposal, and that goes for the forces of world capitalism as well as for the forces of contestation still striving to establish another kind of society or purpose for life on this planet. What is complicated in all this, it seems to me, is that a sort of complementarity or symmetry has been established between a current of dogmatic Marxists and ossified social-democrats who are incapable of recognizing the radical change in the conditions of contemporary life, and a current that derives largely from the positions of Milton Friedman and others, and which tends to say, with the total fatalism of Voltaire's *Candide*, that things being as they are, they cannot be otherwise, and that in any case capitalism is a better world—an analysis that can be disastrous in its applications, as we have seen in Chile. As analysis, however, it is not without merit since it implies a reexamination of questions one had thought resolved, to wit that the way the capitalist market works, in spite of all its trash and its honors, is less catastrophic than certain centralist planifications which lead to total failure. We have seen rich agricultural countries collapse into total famine. As far as I am concerned that doesn't mean that we must choose between the two, but that capital itself doesn't go to the end of its potential. It's obviously not a question of making capitalism even more capitalistic but of diverting and orienting in another way the powers of deterritorialization borne by capitalism. I am in favor of a market economy, but not one geared only on profit and its valorization of status, hierarchy and power. I am in favor of an institutional market economy, one founded on another mode of valorization. Instead of being more capitalistic, we want to make an anticapitalism within capitalism. Thirdly, we should be ready to connect anything that could initiate a new sequence of events: snowballing sequences, little glimpses of events which right away slap you in the face, like May '68 in France. Since no revolutionary war machine is at present available, and there is no way to get a good grip on reality, then the collective subjectivity is, so to speak, "tripping": from time to time it has "flashes." It sees things, and then it stops. There was the "autonomist" movement in Italy. Today, there is the collective vision of the threat of war facing Europe, of nuclear devastation. And then there is Poland—and we pass on to other things. But it's all going to come back. All these flashes don't mean that there is a total incoherence in this subjectivity, but simply that an effort is being made to perceive something which is not yet registered, inscribed, identified. I believe that the forces which in Europe now rally around the peace movement are the same which, in other phases, will rally around the ecological movement, around regionalist movements, around X number of components of what I call the molecular revolution. What I mean by that expression is not a cult of spontaneity or whatever, only the effort to not miss anything that could help rebuild a new kind of struggle, a new kind of society.

Was the Italian experience only a "flash"?

The Italian experience is linked to the fact that the structure of power in Italy was largely behind the times in relation to the other European nations. The economic integration has become so marked in Europe or in the world that the discrepancy with Italy became more and more striking. With the absence of a state economic policy, and the widespread embezzlement among Italian society, marginal sectors of the economy have paradoxically come to play a considerable role in the economic mechanism, including in the Italian balance of trade. Thus a kind of "society without a State," to use Pierre Clastres' formula, established itself in the middle of structures otherwise controlled from the point of view of state power. On top of that, while the left has slowly withered away in other European countries since the Second World War, a very powerful configuration of forces in favor of the left has maintained itself in Italy—although it has proven incapable of being anything else than an adjacent accomplice of the Christian Democrats.

In the meantime Italy has known an unprecedented cultural effervescence characterized by an immense collective work of publication, of translations—which now make the Italians the most intellectual people on earth. It will take decades before we realize that our Age of Enlightenment is happening not in France nor in the United States or in Germany, but in Italy. And those people have a double edged intelligence, both theoretical and practical, which consists of trying to grasp the seeds of mutation at work in this society. Instead of considering their situation from a negative point of view, as a step backwards, as a lack to be remedied in the wave of modernization, through the integration of up-to-date industrial techniques, the Italians understood that what used to be considered a social deficiency could become one of the most positive characteristics for the future. After all, why not consider that a certain kind of discipline, of separation between work and leisure, between intellectual and manual work, etc.—has become pointless? Why not envision instead another form of valorization, which they call "auto-valorization"?[1] Of course, they collided immediately headlong with all of the conservative forces, beginning with the most conservative of them all: the Italian Communist Party.

The Italian experience has been rapidly sabotaged by the dogmatic one-upmanship of armed groups. It became easy for the Italian State to eradicate the Autonomia movement by accusing it of having been the "brains" behind the Red Brigades.

These schemes of armed struggle have had a disastrous effect on the movement. They furnished the powers-that-be with a perfect pretext for eliminating those mass structures of somewhat vague outline which constituted "internal colonies" capable of surviving by practicing passive active modes of resistance such as the "auto-reductions."

Do you think that the autonomist "flash" can resurface elsewhere?

It is bound to, for the need to reformulate the political stakes is felt not only within developed capitalist countries, but everywhere. In France, we've already benefited in small ways from the Italian experience: our fight for free radios took off directly from them. Union leaders in France learned from them that certain demands were no longer in tune with the present struggles… That the Italian Autonomy was wiped out proves nothing at all. From time to time, a kind of social chemistry provides us with a glimpse of what could be another type of organization, much less molecular, much less atomic, which would result in another type of equilibrium, very different from previous models.

We also see this social chemistry at work in much more ambiguous situations, like in Poland, where paradoxically religion has become a motor for change.

In Poland we are witnessing a violent rejection of bureaucratic society. People cling to religious ideologies—does that make it a religious phenomenon as such? Yes, but we should enlarge the definition somewhat. In other countries like Iran or the Middle East, such phenomena are expressed in other ways. For the moment, there is no common semantic feature through which these movements could recognize and support each other. I believe, however, that we should dare draw an "integral" for these various subjective movements inasmuch as the live forces of society are incapable of having a hold on the inner springs of change.

For the moment, then, there are lots of molecules, but no revolution. And when a revolution occurs, as in Iran, it's once again somewhat "archaic" motives that mobilize the people.

Solidarity isn't an archaic phenomenon, it's a new form of struggle. There aren't many countries where suddenly 10 million unionists arise out of the blue.

Paradoxically, Polish unionism surges up in the East at the very moment the trade union movement in the West is losing steam.

It's not because Solidarity is called a union that it actually is one. It may be an altogether new structure, more apt to take into account everyday problems. If Solidarity had been a regular union Walesa could've worked out a compromise and avoided the mess. But it's a kind of union that cannot be manipulated. The people don't follow. That doesn't mean that it's an anarchistic organization either.

It's a form of unionism that immediately asserted itself on the political level.

On the global level, yes, but also on a micropolitical level. Solidarity takes care of what's happening in the street, in the food lines, etc.

And the other elements of the Polish situation, the self-help aspect for example: doesn't that tie in with certain intuitions of the Italians?

I certainly think so. But, from another angle, that ties in also with those weaknesses adjacent to all such intuitions. There's a lesson to be learned from the events in Iran as well as in Italy or in Poland, if one paradoxically tries to nail down the synchronic traits of these three situations: there won't be any lasting change so long as this type of struggle doesn't go beyond national boundaries. It may prove to be very hard and painful, but I always considered preposterous the idea that the kind of revolution that occurred in Italy could have drastically altered the power situation there.

In a sense, the level of these struggles is always above or below that of national structures—in internal colonies and alternative networks, as in Germany,[2] or bigger, transnational crystallizations.

Yes, I agree.

How do you think these extremes could connect?

I'm afraid they won't until more drastic situations develop. I'm fairly optimistic about the prospects for political and social action: I find recent revolutionary crises much more mature and promising, much richer in possibilities of expression everywhere. I fear, however, we still have to go through catastrophic crises before we get there. I believe that both the East and the West are going to experience military dictatorships and very hard fascist regimes.

Do you agree with Paul Virilio that we're now confronted with a tremendous growth in military power and a reinforcement of the scientific-military complex at the expense of civil society?

Let's take a closer look at what this analysis seems to imply considering the deep crisis Russia's going through right now. Does it mean, however, that power in Russia is on the verge of falling into a kind of Bonapartism? Does it imply that the disarray of political structures in the USSR is bound to give the military establishment total control over Soviet society? The hypothesis could well be cor-roborated by spectacular events in Poland, but they are misleading. We're not presently witnessing a takeover by the military establish-ment, but a whole series of social forces and antagonisms that involve the Church and bureaucracies of all kinds.

Russia has renounced developing its internal consumption for the sake of a protracted arms race—both in conventional and nuclear weapons.

It may well be that the military establishment in the Soviet Union forms a backbone strong enough to withstand current crisis. China presented the same phenomenon with the Lin-Piao line. This line represented the minimal consistency of Chinese society at a time when Maoism was verging on total collapse. So it's true that every-where, in Africa as well as in Latin America, the role of military establishments has substantially increased. Nevertheless, I don't believe that a mutation in the major developed countries (either capitalism or bureaucratic socialism) will put them simply and squarely under the aegis of military "machines." And therefore I don't believe that international relations will be wholly defined by this antagonism.

But isn't Reagan himself busy dismantling the edifice of the "welfare" state while dramatically reinforcing the American military potential?

In the USA, one thing is for sure: the Kissinger-style conception which envisioned relationships of power in international affairs as a function of local situations, contradictions and specific socio-historical "singularities," is progressively becoming outmoded. It's as if one sort of diplomacy was being phased out to make room for a purely strategic frame-reference—with a peculiar Manicheanism inherent to the cowboy mentality of Reagan and his cronies.

This Manicheanism actually seems to serve everyone.

Exactly. One could conclude that a true symmetry does exist between the two superpowers and that we are presently witnessing a profound change in the international situation. But I don't think so. At present, the movements of social transformation indeed lack coherent and collective political representation, but so does capitalism. International capitalism is undergoing a real trauma as well. It has a hard time coping with the consequences of its own structural crisis. On strictly economic grounds (monetary, oil, etc.) it somehow manages to come up with solutions, however difficult or dangerous they may be, but on the political level, it offers absolutely no perspective. In the final analysis, it has no policy whatsoever concerning the development of Third World countries, in Asia, in Africa, or Latin America. Countless disasters—human, ecological, etc.—now affecting entire countries do not really go in the direction of, nor benefit, an Integrated World Capitalism. International capitalism has not been able to manage the violent crisis which involves whole populations, masses, working classes, farmers, Third and Fourth World countries. As a result I don't believe that the current phase of American capitalism and Soviet antagonisms is anything else but transitory. On the contrary, I foresee in time (in a rather long time) a revival of the American-Soviet complicity and the rise of an international police force.

Do you think that we'll soon witness the negotiation of a new Yalta?

We'll end up with a new distribution of zones of influence, meant to force the planet into a North-South axis and soften the East-West tensions. American capitalism and Soviet bureaucracy have too much to gain by getting along and by compromising. That was also, incidentally, Schmidt's intuition which he shared with the social-democratic tendencies in Europe.

Politics is also a way of avoiding war, or of pursuing war by other means. Human intervention and decision-making power, however, seem more and more incapable of preventing a nuclear holocaust or a generalized conflict.

I love science fiction and *Dr. Strangelove* schemes, but I don't believe at all in the script of a nuclear war. There's going to be a war, yes, but what war? The same war that we've known for thirty years. When you consider the wars in Chad, or in El Salvador, or in Guatemala, from the point of view of human suffering—wounds, torture, deaths from starvation—what is all that but war? Can we hope for a worse outcome? There's going to be wars like these, but everywhere. Fragmented wars, always ambiguous because they deal with local problems while serving the cause of an international police force. The example of Vietnam is spectacular. This interminable war which continues somewhere in Cambodia, at the outset it was a popular war, a war for the liberation of South Vietnam. But like all popular wars, it soon became the arena for the superpowers, and it was China and the Soviet Union who finally profited from it. The final outcome—the Pol Pot experiment, monstrous, disastrous results for the populations—nowadays these wars are always won by the superpowers.

There are wars that cannot be won, even by superpowers. And that's a new phenomenon that shouldn't be ignored in spite of the increasing number of fragmented wars.

Obviously there is a risk, and the unconscious collective sensibility that permeates peace movements does perceive the danger. But these movements today are quite different from pacifism as it developed during that magnificent period which preceded the First World War. Socialists then advocated the demoralization of the army—of their own army. If such an idea were to spread now, it could work wonders.

We should not underestimate the—so to speak—"positive" effects of the nuclear threat. To begin with, the new movement isn't just backed up by the socialists or even the left. And it's not only fear—the great bourgeois fear—which is being called upon. In Germany the movement is already pulling together many heterogeneous and often conflicting elements—citizen's initiatives, leftists, Christians, ecologists, conservatives and conservationists. I perceive in it the loose contours of an original form of political action expressing in the collective unconscious a still undefineable, but very real, demand for another type of society. Also crucial is the fact that the peace movement, like the ecology movement, can snowball in no time, bypassing purely national boundaries. It took only a few months for the anti-nuclear movement in the USA to reach nationwide stature. The doomsday vision probably ties in to a profound change in the political sentiment of the population at a time when all the avenues of the future appear blocked by the maneuverings of the superpowers and by the muddle of the ideological options we used to depend upon. It's been quite some time since we've witnessed such a mobilization of energies.

I also see emerging there an idea that, if it were to materialize, could yield enormous power—the idea that American missiles don't really protect us against Soviet missiles, and vice-versa. Politicians keep telling us: if you're not protected by the American nuclear umbrella, the Russians will come. Let them come! They are already in such a mess in Poland, not to mention Afghanistan, that the extra of Germany, France or Italy would prove fatal. Fantasies keep piling up, and then one says: "Enough is enough."

For the moment, we have very few ways of putting pressure on the USSR. After all, dissidents there are being persecuted, and peaceniks prosecuted. In the Western camp, however, paths of action are not altogether lacking. In spite of appearances, and the policies of the Reagan administration,

Europe may not be first on the firing line. Moreover it's not certain that it is in Europe that the peace movement can exert the most effective pressure. If the movement were to gather momentum in the USA—where the military-scientific complex is much more in the open and information on nuclear weapons circulates more freely than anywhere else—if a real political intelligence were to shape up among the American peace movement, that could prove to be of paramount importance.

I entirely agree. That would become possible when people would begin to realize that they have allies in Russia, in Africa, everywhere and that a new alliance is possible because they have common enemies. It's that, I think, which is behind your proposal.

The pacifist movement is actually a mosaic, a collage of many colors that doesn't fit into the traditional political mold, which doesn't follow the logic of partisan politics. That corresponds roughly to what you said about molecular revolutions, even if the modalities are somewhat different. This mosaic in formation keeps moving—elements form in one place, migrate elsewhere, reappear in strange new forms, contradictory forms even.

Let's do a little science fiction also, just for fun. Imagine Russia is in a mess even ten times weaker than in Poland. The relationship of power would change entirely if everyone felt that the political and military-industrial structures of the Soviet Union were beginning to crumble down. Imagine they have two more Polands and two more Afghanistans on their hands…

Do you think this is likely to happen?

The Russians have got themselves stuck in the same wasp's nest as the Americans in Vietnam. It's going to go bad for them. Further, it's not out of the question that an armed conflict erupts in Poland. No Eastern bloc country has yet been exposed to armed resistance. This is a crucial point.

Solidarity always opposed armed resistance. Paradoxically the Church assumes a moderating role with regard to the deep aspirations of the population.

Armed resistance may eventually flare up, and with it a lot of problems. I'm not saying that it's the solution, but we're getting close to the point where the crisis in the Soviet Union will become practically unavoidable.

III

MICRO-REVOLUTIONS

10

THE ADOLESCENT REVOLUTION

Christian Poslianec: How would you describe adolescence?

Félix Guattari: In my opinion it's something in adults' minds, something that exists for them on all sorts of levels, as a fantasy, as a segregative social practice, as a collective assemblage, etc. But adolescence as a lived experience can't be defined in terms of age groups. I prefer looking at it as made up of different sorts of "becomings": becoming-child, becoming-woman, becoming-sexual… These becomings can occur at any time, not necessarily at a fixed age. It is well known that one can become a child again, at the age of seventy-five. One can also never become a child. A twelve- year-old can be an old dotard. One can become a woman; one can become a potted plant. One can become all kinds of things, but I don't think it depends on genetic programming.

So you eliminate all possible reference points from the person you have in front of you. You don't put people into little boxes…

I still have to take them into account because that's what most people do. The little boxes begin in nursery school when the little girl jumping rope has to arrange her body in a certain way and progressively submits to all kinds of behaviors and images. The boxes are everywhere. But on the level of what I call the economy of desire, obviously, there are no boxes. And so, trying to stay close to your question and not be too evasive, I think that adolescence, as far as I can recognize it, constitutes a real microrevolution, involving multiple components, some of which threaten the world of adults. It is the entrance into a sort of extremely troubled interzone where all kinds of possibilities, conflicts and sometimes extremely difficult and even dramatic clashes suddenly appear. A whole new world opens up when one emerges from the relative equilibrium, the homeostasis or autoregulation of childhood (a category that should be handled with tweezers). But, almost immediately, everything closes up, and a whole series of institutionalized social controls and the internalization of repressive fantasies march in to capture and neutralize the new virtualities.

So, what would a microrevolution be? Some obvious, and some not so obvious things. First of all, of course, there is the puberty factor, whose onset breaks up and disorganizes the previous physiological, biological and behavioral *status quo*. This kind of transformation brings about profound modifications, not only on what happens inside of people's heads, on reflexive and conceptual levels, but also on the perceptive level...

And emotional...

Emotional, of course; but I would like to emphasize the perceptive mutations which relate to space, to the body, to time. Proust explored these transformations, which involve synaesthesia, in depth. All of this can lead to a complete toppling of behavioral structures, as Merleau-Ponty put it.

And all this occurs during puberty?

No, I am not speaking of a specific phase. You can also have an "adolescent revolution" without considerations of sexual-genital components. What counts in archaic societies are their collective arrangements that serve to integrate the individual into structures of initiation and allow for entry into society. Obviously, such initiations do not result automatically from the onset of puberty. Perhaps, conversely, it is the release of the components of puberty that, to some extent, results from the initiation into an age group. Today's social "molting periods" no longer take such collective and spectacular forms. They are much less easy to pinpoint because they are no longer ritualized in the same way. But they are just as important.

I have mainly worked with young adults or adolescents between the ages of seventeen and twenty-two, and I am tempted by the idea of a "second puberty." Ways of apprehending the world change, particularly through a powerful desire for autonomy in every area: emotional, sexual, financial, intellectual, etc. As if there were a whole internal revolution taking place without the "rich outward signs" which take place during puberty, although I can't exactly say what happens. Does this correspond to something more specific for you than it does for me?

Perhaps you have had experiences that I haven't had. The young men and women with whom I deal are generally much less autonomous than those you describe as going through this "second puberty." It is perhaps even the opposite for psychotics who often lose their autonomy when they enter puberty, which frequently coincides with the onset of pathologies.

I often have the impression that during adolescent periods, "imprint phenomena," to take up a term from ethology, are activated. An entire zone of psychic and behavioral disturbances, sometimes of tumultuous richness, expose many adolescents to formidable trials—from which some never escape unharmed. All of this leads to normalization, to characterological difficulties, to neuroses or to all sorts of traumas. It is true that few people preserve an authentic memory of their adolescence. Writers who know how to describe it, like Andre Gide, are rare.

For girls, the ravages are perhaps worse. The capacity for recuperation from the bludgeoning of normative systems frequently takes on frightening forms. Not only because of exterior interventions of explicit repressive attitudes, but also because of internalized systems of punishment that even develop from what seem to be liberating practices. Compare them, for example, to certain groups of homosexuals who elicit mixed reactions in me since their supposed dimension of emancipation appears above all to be linked to nearly explicit activities of normalization and psychological confinement. In any case, this first adolescent revolution is of the greatest importance in the crystallization of personality. It is no accident that this is where Kraepelin located the origin of *dementia praecox*. It's true that "infantile psychosis" was invented later on, but I'm not sure it's an improvement. In actual terms, clinical descriptions always come back to the period of puberty. Certainly it could be said that a maturation of psychosis may occur before that period, with the revelation, "after the fact," of childhood disorders. But I find these conceptions perplexing. I find it dangerous to speak of psychosis before puberty, because nothing is really crystallized until that point. Imposing an entire etiological program in infantile stages has its risks. Start with the Oedipus complex or much before that according to Melanie Klein—and then an entire chain of distortions and imaginary identifications are inferred… And you know the rest. Really, I must repeat that serious madness, like serious vocations, comes into being during the *adolescent revolution*.

I thought that everything was already happening in a child at age six! That is what many contemporary pedagogues say…

Yes, I know, but that's really not too sharp. With an idea like that, every kind of passivity, every kind of resignation can be justified. Nothing really starts or ends before or after the age of six. Such schemas of causality should be eliminated. What counts is how people deal with insertion into family, social, sexual, athletic, military, etc., situations. Every such moment concurrently produces both a rupture and possibilities for new beginnings, taking into account sociological, institutional, environmental, collective infrastructural conditions, the mass media… Paradoxically, entry into the workplace occurs later and later, while the entry into adult semiotics occurs earlier and earlier. In my opinion this results in ever more precocious forms of sexuality and, at the same time, a chronic immaturity in that same sexuality. I'm not against it—but is this what sexual freedom means? It is not at all clear. Because entry into semiotic life means having a job, entering production, the production of models, the production of subjectivity. During the whole of adolescence, there is considerable anxiety concerning the coming of "normal adulthood."

In this issue[1] we have interviewed two "youths" from technical schools who are about to enter into the system of production. As a matter of fact, the anxiety that equates "entering life" to getting a job, to getting shut in, to being productive, to the end of whatever dreams they still may have had, is clearly manifest.

It's where everything ties together. You get your technical diploma, or whatever; you develop your linguistic and performance competencies in the race to get ahead, in areas that depend not only on education or professional training, but also on sexuality. Have you passed your puberty certificate? Are you sure that you're normal? The jury in this kind of competition is often the merciless opinion of your closest buddies, your sweet girlfriend... It's a dirty deal. And this unhealthy interest is becoming more widespread, not only among psychologists, educators, daycare workers, mothers and all the Ruth Westheimers of the media.

Infantile, adolescent and adult sexuality never cease to be confronted by tests like, "Do you come too soon? Or too late?" "And your orgasm, is it too clitoral?" What an idiotic mess. And see how seriously babies concentrate on the television screen. "That's hard work, poor things." A modeling of perceptive systems also occurs during the stages of infancy. It is clear that this type of childhood has little to do with the rural or proto-capitalistic urban societies of 50 years ago. Now, a kind of psychological seriousness is conveyed by the media, through educational games... "Does my baby suckle at the right time? Does he masturbate when he should? There is something wrong, Doctor: he doesn't masturbate yet. What do you prescribe?" A widespread anxiety accompanies every incident in the development of the child. And it's getting out of hand. For the most part it results from psychoanalytical drivel concerning psychogenesis, all these nameless stupidities that not only postulate stages of intellectual development, but also stages of behavior, and emotional stages. Now isn't this too much already!

Half a century ago youths, in rural areas at least, were freer than those in urban areas. They were not watched over, they were not always under the eyes of adults. This is no longer the case. Now when they leave school they have to return home right away—there are no more haystacks, quiet hideaways, places where one can go in secret. They move from the gaze of adult-teachers to that of adult-parents, to the gaze of the TV. And they are always closed off that way, whereas in the city, it was the opposite not too long ago. Freedom could be found in basements, in parking lots, in everything that was underground; that is, in the unconscious of the city, where a certain sexuality in relation to the forbidden, including its unfortunate sexist and violent aspects, would take place. There was something really wild about it. Now it is disappearing because of the control of children's free time.

I would add that it is not only children and adolescents who are under control. The entire society finds itself infantilized, puerilized, under the "panoptic" regime described by Michel Foucault. Because everything you have just described can just as well be applied to the father, to the mother, etc. We are all turned into children by mass media society and the various apparatuses producing subjectivity. And maybe "adolescents" are less affected than others; perhaps they are even the most resilient to it. At least up until the moment when they fall apart during an agonizing crisis, unless they make a massive transfer onto a partner, hang on to conjugal life, join the usual circuit.

What you were just saying about that force, the violence that occurs at a given moment—which can be one of the possible definitions of adolescence—could it be considered a political force (in the etymological sense) that can change something, a "hope" even, as the adolescents interviewed say that they put no trust in society, in politics, or even perhaps in any collective organization of any sort at all? They also say that they experience their sexuality in couples: that their sexual life exists as a couple. For me, all these words interfere with each other: security, integration, revolt, etc. Is it clearer for you?

I'm not at all convinced that one can speak so quickly about a return to the couple. A new micropolitics of the couple surely exists, but not necessarily a return. There's another definition, at least in many cases, since, obviously, conservatism is also on the rise and is causing much damage. Whatever it is, I think that the manner in which relations between men and women take place today is very different from what it was two or three generations ago. A careful study would be welcome. This doesn't only happen on the level of daily life, doing the dishes and things like that, or the manifestations of possessiveness or jealousy, etc., but also on the sexual level. It is no longer the same sexuality, because women take charge of their bodies with relatively less dependence on their partner.

And yet there have always been couples. And why not? The myths of sexual communities, with their sometimes half-delirious leaders, to my knowledge, have pretty much fallen apart. But this does not necessarily imply a return to the traditional couple. And I don't see any reason for condemning couples. What matters is how they work. What becomes of the individuals of whom they are composed? What happens to their lives, their emotions, their desires? Analysis presents a similar problem. The question is not whether or not it is necessary to be "two," or alone, or ten, in order to conduct analysis, but to determine what must be done.

A symmetrical answer: it is not true that politics is dead from a social implosion.[2] No doubt, a certain kind of politics and a certain social implosion have occurred. But I believe that there is a collective, unformed search, from above and below, for another kind of politics. This is what I call "micropolitics," and "molecular revolution." It begins with very immediate, daily, individual preoccupations, yet remains connected to what happens at the social level, and even, why not, at the cosmic level. An ecological sensitivity also means a preference for a vision that is at the same time molecular and worldwide in scope. Obviously it is something quite different from the radical socialism of our fathers and grandfathers. But if it is not political, what is it? It is true that its subjects, its objects and its means are no longer the same. Instead of individual subjects, of abstract citizens, there are collective arrangements. It can't be done according to sexual criteria, as a political group, or as an age group. That is what I call a complex multidimensional arrangement. Groups like this, covetous of their autonomy and their singularity, can change the nature of human relationships on a large scale if they can manage to rid themselves of narrow segregationist attitudes. Its objectives are also of another kind. It can't be said that they are ambiguous, but they have multiple facets. They may derive from an immediate pleasure, for example from being together, as well as from more political and social preoccupations that have little to do with everyday wheeling and dealing. So the objects become the whole world, animals, plants, shapes, sounds, humanity…

De Gaulle was completely demoralized in May '68 because he saw that no one even held a grudge against him. It was what he represented that was rejected, and he could remain in power because no credible political alternative was available. He saw that he governed a population of zombies. Perhaps a new kind of '68, of a completely different style, is developing behind the scenes. Your students, your youths, your rockers—their preoccupations are literally imperceptible to "normal" people. Some might say, "People like that don't even know what they want. What they want doesn't make any sense." And since nothing registers in these people's minds, they consider them completely crazy. Except that, from time to time, something does register. Once in a while, from inside the establishment, it turns into Watergate. And on other occasions, from the populace, completely unexpected things come about, like revolts against work, or alarming statistics concerning the fact that people couldn't care less about dying for their country.

When this happens, those in charge ask themselves, "Where did that come from? Who are their ringleaders? Who is putting such ideas into the heads of our youth?" But the way such political situations work is not traditional either. It doesn't happen through social communication, through discourse, programs, *explication de texte* or reference to Great Authors. It has gone over to the side of reflexes, to collective sensibility, to systems of nonverbal expression. Children and adolescents are not aware of their becoming, at least not predominantly in terms of meaningful discourse. They use what I call "a-signifying systems": music, clothing, the body, behaviors as signs of mutual recognition, as well as machinic systems of all kinds. For example, my son is into politics. Not so much through discourse, but with his soldering iron: he sets up "free radios," where technical discourse is hooked right into politics. There is no need to explain the opportunity and the political rationale of free-radio broadcasting; he got it right away. It is the intervention of machinisms—and not only those of communication as means, as political media, which seem fundamental to me. I have confidence in all the technico-scientific categories to which this new political field gives rise.

11

A LIBERATION OF DESIRE

George Stambolian: *In 1970 the authorities forbade the sale to minors of Pierre Guyotat's novel,* Eden, Eden, Eden. *More recently, they outlawed and seized the special issue of the magazine* Recherches *("Encyclopedia of Homosexualities") to which you had made important contributions. You were even taken to court on the matter. How would you explain these reactions by the French government?*

Félix Guattari: They were rather old-fashioned reactions. I do not think that the present government would behave the same way because there is, on the surface at least, a certain nonchalance regarding the literary and cinematographic expression of sexuality. But I don't have to tell you that this is an even more subtle, cunning, and repressive policy. During the trial the judges were completely ill at ease with what they were being asked to do.

Wasn't it because this issue of Recherches *treated homosexuality, and not just sexuality?*

I'm not sure, because among the things that most shocked the judges was one of the most original parts of this work—a discussion of masturbation. I think that a work devoted to homosexuality in a more or less traditional manner would have had no difficulty. What shocked perhaps was the expression of sexuality going in all directions. And then there were the illustrations—they were what set it off.

In your opinion, what is the best way to arrive at a true sexual liberation, and what dangers confront this liberation?

The problem, as I see it, is not a sexual liberation but a liberation of desire. Once desire is specified as sexuality, it enters into forms of particularized power, into the stratification of castes, of styles, of sexual classes. The sexual liberation —for example, of homosexuals, of transvestites, of sadomasochists—belongs to a series of other liberation problems among which there is an a priori and evident solidarity, the need to participate in a necessary fight. But I don't consider that to be a liberation as such of desire, since in each of these groups and movements one finds repressive systems.

What do you mean by "desire"?

For Gilles Deleuze and me desire is everything that exists *before* the opposition between subject and object, *before* representation and production. It's everything whereby the world and affects constitute us outside of ourselves, in spite of ourselves. It's everything that overflows from us. That's why we define it as flow. Within this context we were led to forge a new notion in order to specify in what way this kind of desire is not some sort of undifferentiated magma, and thereby dangerous, suspicious, or incestuous. So we speak of machines, of "desiring-machines," in order to indicate that there is as yet no question here of "structure"—that is, of any subjective position, objective redundancy, or coordinates of reference. Machines arrange and connect flows. They do not recognize distinctions between persons, organs, material flows, and semiotic flows.

Your remarks on sexuality reveal a similar rejection of established distinctions. You have said, for example, that all forms of sexual activity are minority forms and reveal themselves as being irreducible to homo-hetero oppositions. You have also said that these forms are nevertheless closer to homosexuality and to what you call a "becoming-woman." Would you develop this idea, in particular by defining what you mean by "feminine"?

Yes, that was a very ambiguous formulation. What I mean is that the relation to the body, what I call the semiotics of the body, is something specifically repressed by the capitalist-socialist-bureaucratic system. So I would say that each time the body is emphasized in a situation—by dancers, by homosexuals, etc.—something breaks with the dominant semiotics that crush these semiotics of the body. In heterosexual relations as well, when a man becomes body, he becomes feminine. In a way, a successful heterosexual relation becomes homosexual and feminine. This does not at all mean that I am speaking of women as such: that's where the ambiguity lies, because the feminine relation itself can lose the semiotics of the body and become phallocentric. So it is only by provocation that I say feminine, because I would say first that there is only one sexuality, it is homosexual; there is only one sexuality, it is feminine. But I would add finally: there is only one sexuality, it is neither masculine, nor feminine, nor infantile; it is something that is ultimately flow, body. It seems to me that in true love there is always a moment when the man is no longer a man. This does not mean that he becomes a woman. But because of her alienation, woman is relatively closer to the situation of desire. And in a sense, perhaps from the point of view of representation, to accede to desire implies for a man first a position of homosexuality as such, and second a feminine becoming. But I would add as well a becoming-animal, or a becoming-plant, a becoming-cosmos, etc. That's why this formulation is very tentative and ambiguous.

Isn't your formulation based in part on the fact that our civilization has associated body and woman?

No, it's because woman has preserved the surfaces of the body, a bodily *jouissance* and pleasure much greater than that of man. He has concentrated his libido on—one can't even say his penis—on domination, on the rupture of ejaculation: "I possessed you" "I had you." Look at all the expressions like these used by men: "I screwed you," "I made her." It's no longer the totality of the body's surface that counts, it's just this sign of power: "I dominated you," "I marked you." This obsession with power is such that man ultimately denies himself all sexuality. On the other hand, in order to exist as body he is obliged to beg his sexual partners to transform him a bit into a woman or a homosexual. I don't know if homosexuals can easily accept what I'm saying, because I don't mean to say that homosexuals are women. That would be a misunderstanding. But I think that in a way there is a kind of interaction between the situation of male homosexuals, of transvestites, and of women. There is a kind of common struggle in their relation to the body.

"Interaction," "transformation," "becoming," "flow"—these words suggest a recognition of our sexual or psychic multiplicity and fluidity which, as I understand it, is an essential aspect of what you call schizoanalysis and psychoanalysis which, I believe, you have completely abandoned?

I was Lacan's student. I was analyzed by Lacan and I practiced psychoanalysis for twelve years; and now, I've broken with that practice. Psychoanalysis transforms and deforms the unconscious by forcing it to pass through the grid of its system of inscription and representation. For psychoanalysis the unconscious is always already there, genetically programmed, structured, and finalized on objectives of conformity to social norms. For schizoanalysis it's a question of constructing an unconscious, not only with phrases but with all possible semiotic means, and not only with individuals or relations between individuals, but also with groups, with physiological and perceptual systems, with machines, struggles, and arrangements of every nature. There's no question here of transfer, interpretation, or delegation of power to a specialist.

Do you believe that psychoanalysis has deformed not only the unconscious but the interpretation of life in general and perhaps of literature as well?

Yes, but even beyond what one imagines, in the sense that it's not simply a question of psychoanalysts or even of psychoanalytical ideas as they are propagated in the commercial press or in the universities, but of interpretative and representational attitudes toward desire that one finds in persons who don't know psychoanalysis, but who put themselves in the position of interpreters, of gurus, and who generalize the technique of transfer.

With Gilles Deleuze, you have just finished a schizoanalysis of Kafka's work. Why this method to analyze and to comprehend literature?

It's not a question of method or of doctrine. It's simply that I've been living with Kafka for a very long time. I therefore tried, together with Deleuze, to put into our work the part of me that was, in a way, a becoming-Kafka. In a sense the book is a schizo-analysis of our relation to Kafka's work, but also of the period of Vienna in 1920 and of a certain bureaucratic Eros which crystallized in that period, and which fascinated Kafka.

In a long note you speak of Kafka's joy, and you suggest that psycho-analysis has found only Kafka's sadness or his tragic aspect.

In his *Diaries* Kafka gives us a glimpse of the diabolic pleasure he found in his writing. He says that it was a kind of demonic world he entered at night to work. I think that everything that produces the violence, richness, and incredible humor of Kafka's work belongs to this world of his.

Aren't you really proposing that creation is something joyful, and that this joy can't be reduced to a psychosis?

Absolutely—or to a lack.

In the same book on Kafka you say that a "minor literature," which is produced by a minority in a major language, always "deterritorializes" that language, connects the individual to politics, and gives everything a collective value. These are for you, in fact, the revolutionary qualities of any literature within the established one. Does homosexuality necessarily produce a literature having these three qualities?

Unfortunately, no. There are certainly homosexual writers who conduct their writing in the form of an Oedipal homosexuality. Even very great writers—I think of Gide. Apart from a few works, Gide always transcribed his homosexuality and in a sense betrayed it.

Despite the fact that he tried to prove the value of homosexuality in works such as Corydon?

Yes, but I wonder if he did it in just one part of his work and if the rest of his writing isn't different.

In Anti-Oedipus *you and Deleuze note that Proust described two types of homosexuality—one that is Oedipal and therefore exclusive, global, and neurotic, and one that is a-Oedipal or inclusive, partial, and localized. In fact, the latter is for you an expression of what you call "transsexuality." So if there are two Gides, aren't there also two Prousts, or at least the possibility of two different readings of his work?*

I can't answer for Proust the man, but it seems to me that his work does present the two aspects, and one can justify the two readings because both things in effect exist.

You spoke of the demonic in Kafka. Well, Gide, Proust, and Genet have been accused of being fascinated by the demonic aspect of homosexuality. Would you agree?

To a point. I wonder sometimes, not specifically concerning the three names you mention, if it isn't a matter of persons who were more fascinated by the demonic than by homosexuality. Isn't homosexuality a means of access to the demonic? That is, they are the heirs of Goethe in a certain way, and what Goethe called the demonic was in itself a dimension of mystery.

But the fact remains that in our civilization homosexuality is often associated with the demonic.

Yes, but so is crime. There's a whole genre of crime literature that contains a similar demonic aspect. The demonic or the mysterious is really a residue of desire in the social world. There are so few places for mystery that one looks for it everywhere, in anything that escapes or becomes marginal. For example, there's something demonic in the life of a movie star. That's why it's used by the sensationalist press.

Doesn't that tell us that we are hungry for the demonic, that we are hungry for things that aren't "natural," that we have exploited movie stars and homosexuals to satisfy our need for the demonic?

I'm not against that because I'm not at all for nature. Therefore artifice, the artificially demonic, is something that rather charms me. Only it is one thing to live it in a relationship of immediate desire, and another thing to transform it into a repressive machine.

Let's go back to the homosexual writers. I'd like to quote here a remark of yours that struck me. It's the last paragraph of your interview published in the August 1975 issue of La Quinzaine littéraire. *You say: "Everything that breaks something, everything that breaks with the established order, has something to do with homosexuality, or with a becoming-animal, a becoming-woman, etc. Any break in semiotization implies a break in sexuality. It is therefore not necessary, in my opinion, to raise the question of homosexual writers, but rather to look for what is homosexual, in any case, in a great writer, even if he is in other respects heterosexual." Doesn't this idea contain a new way to approach or perhaps to go beyond a question that has so obsessed certain Freudian critics and psychoanalysts—namely, the connection between homosexuality, or all sexuality, and creativity?*

Yes, of course. For me, a literary machine starts itself, or can start itself, when writing connects with other machines of desire. I'd like to talk about Virginia Woolf in her relation to a becoming-man that is itself a becoming-woman, because the paradox is complete. I'm thinking about a book I like very much, *Orlando*. You have this character who follows the course of the story as a man, and in the second part of the novel he becomes a woman. Well, Virginia Woolf herself was a woman, but one sees that in order to become a woman writer, she had to follow a certain trajectory of a becoming-woman, and for that she had to begin by being a man. One could certainly find in George Sand things perhaps more remarkable than this. So my question is whether writing as such, the signifier as such, relates to nothing, only to itself, or to power. Writing begins to function in something else, as for example for the Beat Generation in the relation with drugs; for Kerouac in the relation with travel, or with mountains, with yoga. Then something begins to vibrate, begins to function. Rhythms appear, a need, a desire to speak. Where is it possible for a writer to start this literary machine if it isn't precisely outside of writing and of the field of literature? A break in sexuality—therefore homosexuality, a becoming-woman, addict, missionary, who knows? It's a factory, the means of transmitting energy to a writing machine.

Can a break in semiotization precede a break in sexuality?

It's not a break in semiotization, but a semiotic connection. I'll give you a more familiar example. Take what are called mad people from a poor background from the point of view of intellectual formation—peasants who never read anything, who only went to grade school. Well, when they have an attack of dissociation, a psychotic attack, it happens sometimes that they begin to write, to paint, to express extraordinary things, extraordinarily beautiful and poetic! And then when they are "cured," they return to the fields, to the sugar-beets and asparagus, and they stop writing altogether. You have something of a psychotic attack in Rimbaud. When he became normal, he went into commerce: all that stopped. It's always a question of a connection. Something that was a little scholastic writing machine, really without any quality, connects with fabulously perceptive semiotics that start in psychosis, or in drugs, or in war, and that can animate this little writing machine and produce extraordinary things. You have a group of disconnected machines, and at a given moment there is a transmission among them, and everything begins not only to function but to produce an acceleration of operations. So you see, I'm not talking about sexuality. Sexuality is already specified as sex, caste, forms of sexual practice, sexual ritual. But creativity and desire are for me the same thing, the same formula.

I'd still like to ask you the following question. Could you begin the search for what is homosexual in a heterosexual writer with a great writer like, for example, Beckett, whose work offers us a "homosexuality" which seems at times to be the product of extraordinary semiotic connections, and which, in any case, confounds all previous representations and goes beyond them?

I think of those characters who travel by twos and who have no sexual practice because they live completely outside of sexuality, but who nevertheless represent a kind of collective set-up of enunciation, a collective way of perceiving everything that happens. And so many things are happening that it's necessary to select, to narrow down, in order to receive and distill each element, as if one were using a microscope to capture each of the intensities. Indeed, there is perhaps in Beckett a movement outside of the sexes, but then there is the absolutely fabulous relation to objects, a sexual relation to objects. I'm thinking of the sucking stones in *Molloy*.

Then how does one explain the elements of homosexuality, of sado-masochism, in his work?

But that's theater, because if there's a constant in Beckett's work, it's that even when he writes novels, he creates theater, in the sense of a *mise en scène*, an acting out, of giving something to be seen. So then inevitably, he gathers up representations, but he articulates them to create literature. What's more, Beckett is someone, I think, who was very interested in the insane, in psychopathology, and therefore he picked up a lot of representations. The use he makes of them is essentially literary, of course, but what he uses them for is not a translation, it's a collage, it's like a dance. He plays with these representations, or rather: he makes them play.

You said in your article on the cinema[1] *that any representation expresses a certain position with respect to power. But I wonder if Beckett hasn't succeeded in writing a politically "innocent" text.*

I no more believe in innocence than I do in nature. One thing should be made clear—if one finds innocence, there's reason to worry, there's reason to look not for guilt, of course—that's the same thing as innocence, its symmetry—but for what is politically in germination, for a politics in dotted lines. Take Kafka again. Although his text isn't innocent, the supremely innocent character is K., and yet he is neither innocent nor guilty. He's waiting to enter a political scene. That's not fiction; it's not Borges, because he did enter a political scene in Prague, where one of the biggest political dramas was played around Kafka's work. So, innocence is always the anticipation of a political problem.

Everything that's written is therefore linked in one way or another to a political position?

Yes, with two fundamental axes: everything that's written in refusing the connection with the referent, with reality, implies a politics of individuation of the subject and of the object, of a turning of writing on itself, and by that puts itself in the service of all hierarchies, of all centralized systems of power, and of what Gilles Deleuze and I call all "arborescences," the regime of unifiable multiplicities. The second axis, in opposition to arborescence, is that of the "rhizome," the regime of pure multiplicities. It's what even innocent texts, even gratuitous games like those of the Dadaists, even collages, cut-ups, perhaps especially these things, will make it possible one day to reveal the pattern of similar breaks in reality, in the social field, and in the field of economic, cosmic, and other flows.

So sexual liberation is not going to rid us of political connections.

Sexual liberation is a mystification. I believe in, and will fight for, the taking of power by other castes and sexual systems, but I believe that liberation will occur when sexuality becomes desire, and desire is the freedom to be sexual, that is, to be something else at the same time.

How does one escape from this dilemma in which one caste replaces another?

What these liberation movements will reveal by their failures and difficulties is that there really aren't any castes. There's the possibility that society will reform itself through other types of subjective arrangements that are not based on individuals in constellation or on relations of power that communication institutes between speaker and listener. There will be arrangements, I don't know what, based neither on families, nor on communes, nor on groups, where the goals of life, politics, and work will always be conjugated with the analysis of unconscious relations, of relations of micropower, of microfascism. On the day when these movements fix as their goals not only the liberation of homosexuals, women, and children, but also the struggle against themselves in their constant power relations, in their relations of alienation, of repression against their bodies, their thoughts, their ways of speaking, then indeed, we will see another kind of struggle appear, another kind of possibility. The microfascist elements in all our relations with others must be found, because when we fight on the molecular level, we'll have a much better chance of preventing a truly fascist, a macrofascist formation on the molar level.

You and Deleuze often speak of Artaud, who wanted to rid us of masterpieces and perhaps even of written texts. Can one say that the written text already contains a form of microfascism?

No, because a written text can be lengthened. Graffiti in the street can be erased or added to. A written text can be contradictory, can be made into a palimpsest. It can be something extremely alive. What is much less alive is an *oeuvre* and Artaud himself did not write a work or a book. But then, one never writes a book. One picks up on books that have been written; one places oneself in a phylum. To write a book that wants to be an eternal and universal manual, yes, you're right; but to write after one thing and before another, that means participating in a chain, in a chain of love as well.

I'd like to return for a moment to what you said about desire and the problems of liberation. I think of people who might profit from that kind of formulation in order to circumvent the question of homosexuality and the specificity of this struggle, by saying that all that is just sexuality and that sexuality alone matters.

I'm very sympathetic to what you say. It's a bit like what they say to us regarding the struggle of the working class. I understand that, but I'd still like to give the same answer: it's up to the homosexuals. I'm not a worker or a homosexual. I'm a homosexual in my own way, but I'm not a homosexual in the world of reality or of the group.

Yes, but the theories one proposes on homosexuality are always important, and they are never innocent. Before writing Corydon, *Gide read theories. Before writing* La Recherche, *Proust was totally aware of the psychological thought of his time. Even Genet was influenced after the fact by the theories of Sartre. Obviously, it's often writers themselves who are the first to see things that others transform into theories. I'm thinking of Dostoevsky, Proust, and, of course, Kafka. You've already begun to use your own theories to study the literature of the past, and they are related perhaps to what may someday be called a "literature of desire." Writers, critics, and homosexuals have the choice of accepting or rejecting these theories, or of playing with them. But they can neither forget them nor ignore the words of moralists, psychoanalysts, and philosophers, certainly not today, and certainly not in France.*

Right, I completely agree. It's truly a pollution. But in any case, what do you think of the few theoretical propositions I've advanced here? It's my turn to question you.

Judging your position by what you've said here and by what you've written, I think that you and Deleuze have seriously questioned Freud's system. You have turned our attention away from the individual and toward the group, and you have shown to what extent the whole Oedipal structure reflects our society's paranoia and has become an instrument for interiorizing social and political oppression. Also, I'd like to quote the following passage from Anti-Oedipus: *"We are heterosexuals statistically or in molar terms, but homosexuals personally, whether we know it or not, and finally transsexuals elementarily, molecularly." I can't claim to understand fully this or other aspects of your theory, but you do show that the time has come to address ourselves to the question of sexuality in another way, and that's a kind of liberation.*

Well, I want to tell those people who say "all that is sexuality" that they must go farther and try to see what in fact is the sexuality not only of the homosexual, but also of the sadomasochist, the transvestite, the prostitute, even the murderer, anyone for that matter, in order not to go in the direction of reassurance. They must see what a terrible world of repression they will enter.

Despite the passage from your work I just quoted, when you speak you often cite groups that are always outside the dominant field of heterosexuality.

For me desire is always "outside"; it always belongs to a minority. For me there is no heterosexual sexuality. Once there's heterosexuality, in fact, once there's marriage, there's no more desire, no more sexuality. In all my twenty-five years of work in this field I've never seen a heterosexual married couple that worked along a line of desire. Never. They don't exist. So don't say that I'm marginalizing sexuality with homosexuals, etc., because for me there is no heterosexuality possible.

Following the same logic there is no homosexuality possible.

In a sense yes, because in a sense homosexuality is counterdependent on heterosexuality. Part of the problem is the reduction of the body. It's the impossibility of becoming a totally sexed body. The sexed body is something that includes all perceptions, everything that occurs in the mind. The problem is how to sexualize the body, how to make bodies desire, vibrate—all aspects of the body.

There are still the fantasies each of us brings. That's often what's interesting in some homosexual writing—this expression of fantasies that are very specialized, very specific.

I don't think it's in terms of fantasies that things are played but in terms of representations. There are fantasies of representations. In desire there are semiotic flows of a totally different nature, including verbal flows. It's not fantasies; it's words, speech, rhythms, poetry. A phantasmal representation in poetry is never the essential thing, no more than is the content. Fantasy is always related to content.

What counts is expression, the way expression connects with the body. For example, poetry is a rhythm that transmits itself to the body, to perception. A fantasy when it operates does not do so as a fantasy that represents a content, but as something that puts us in motion, that brings out something that carries us away, that thaws us, that locks us onto something

Aren't there fantasies of form as well?

Fantasies of form, fantasies of expression, become in effect micro-fascistic crystallizations. This implies, for example, in scenes of power of a sadomasochistic character: "Put yourself in exactly this position. Follow this scenario so that it will produce in me such an effect." That becomes a kind of fantasy of form, but what counts there is not the application of the fantasy, it's the relation to the other person, it's complicity! Desire escapes from formal redundancies, escapes from power formations. Desire is not informed, informing; it's not information or content. Desire is not something that deforms but that disconnects, changes, modifies, organizes other forms, and then abandons them.

So, a literary text escapes all categorization as well as any sexuality that can be called one thing or another?

Take any literary work you love very much. Well, you will see that you love it because it is for you a particular form of sexuality or desire: I leave the term up to you. The first time I made love with Joyce while reading *Ulysses* was absolutely unforgettable. It was extraordinary. I made love with Kafka, and I think one can say that, truly.

Proust said it: "To love Balzac; to love Baudelaire." And he was speaking of a love that could not be reduced to any one definition.

Absolutely. And one doesn't make love in the same way with Joyce as with Kafka. If one began to make love in the same way, there would be reason to worry—one might be becoming a professor of literature.

Perhaps! Then literature can be a liberation of desire, and the text is a way of multiplying the sexes.

Certain texts, texts that work. Nothing can be done about those that don't work. But those that do function multiply our functioning. They turn us into madmen; they make us vibrate.

12

MACHINIC JUNKIES

We must begin by enlarging the definition of drugs. In my view, all the mechanisms producing a "machinic" subjectivity, everything that contributes to provide a sensation of belonging to something, of being somewhere, along with the sensation of forgetting oneself, are "drugs." The existential aspects of what I call the experience of machinic drugs are not easy to detect. Only the surfaces are visible, in activities like cross-country skiing, piloting ultra-light motorized vehicles, rock music, music videos—all these sorts of things. But the subjective dimension of such influences is not necessarily in an immediate relation to the practice in question. It is how it all works together that is important.

The example of Japan, considered on a large scale, is significant. The Japanese make the best of an archaic, or let's say a pseudo-archaic structure. This is the counterpart to their being on machinic dope, and in this way the society does not dissolve into dust. They have remade a feudal territoriality out of their traditions, by perpetuating the alienated conditions of women, by absorption into repetitive work on machines... These are also conduits for subjective positioning—well, not really "for," but that is the result: it works! The Japanese structure their universe and order their emotions within the proliferation and disorder of machines, while hanging on to their archaic references. But, above all, they are crazy for machines, for a machinic kind of buzz. For example, did you know that the majority of people who have climbed the Himalayas are Japanese?

"Doping" and drugs, is this a simple analogy? It seems, according to the most recent work in the area, that it is not at all a metaphor. Repeated pain and certain very "engaging" activities incite the brain to secrete hormones, endorphins, which are much "harder" drugs than morphine. Is this not then some sort of self intoxification? At the La Borde clinic,[1] I observed the extent to which anorexics resemble drug addicts. The same bad faith, the same ways of fooling you by promising to stop... Anorexia is a major form of "doping." So is sado-masochism, as is any other exclusive passion that induces bursts of endorphins. One "turns oneself on" with the sound of rock-and-roll, with fatigue, with lack of sleep like Kafka, or one knocks one's head against the floor like an autistic child. One can use excitement, cold, repetitive movements, strenuous work, sports, fear. Skiing down a practically vertical slope will transform your notions of personality for you. It is a way of making yourself *be*, of personally incarnating yourself, while the ground of the existential image is blurred.

Again, the result of "dopings" and their social representations have every chance of being out of phase with each other: an intense buzz involves processes that radically elude individual consciousness, bringing about biological transformations whose need is experienced only vaguely, although intensely. A "drug machine" can generate collective euphoria or oppressive gregariousness, but it is nonetheless the response of individual urges. The same thing occurs with minor buzzes. The person who comes home exhausted, spent after a draining day, who automatically turns on his television, evidences another personal reterritorialization by totally artificial means.

I find these phenomena of contemporary doping ambiguous. There are two means of access: repetition, stupidly, like the mono-mania of pinball and video game addiction, and the intervention of "machinic" processes that are never futile, and never innocent. There is a machinic Eros. Yes, overdriven Japanese youths commit suicide upon completing high school; yes, millions of guys practice their golf swings in unison in concrete parking lots at 6 AM; yes, young workers live in dormitories and give up their vacations... They are machine-nuts. And yet, in Japan, there is a kind of democracy of desire that extends into business. A balance... to doping's advantage?

For us, machinic dope works more in favor of a return to the individual, but it seems nevertheless as indispensable to the subjective stabilization of industrial societies, above all at times of stiff competition. If you don't have at least that pay-off, you really have nothing. Molecular machinic subjectivity fosters creativity, in no matter what area. Believe it. Having been politically destructured after the collapse of opposition movements, this is all that young Italians do—as an "individualist" way of getting by. In a society that can't tolerate, that can't manage its intensity, doping loses its dynamism, or is out of the picture. For better or for worse, it must even and above all integrate the apparent disorder of doping with what seem to be unproductive outlets. Americans are the champions of doping, they have thousands of ways to do it, and invent new ones every day. It is pretty successful for them. (The Russians on the other hand, don't even have the old dope of Bolshevism.) It is machinic subjectivity that fuels great impetuses like Silicon Valley.

And France? French society isn't necessarily "out of it." French people are not stupider than others, or more impoverished libidinally. But they are not "cool." Let's just say that the social superstructures are more "molar." For us, there are hardly any institutions that leave space for processes of machinic proliferation. France, as people constantly say, is traditional. And while the whole planet is currently undergoing fantastic changes, France makes faces at the great machinic dope. It is the anti-dope.

France seems to have had a pretty bad start. Europe too. Perhaps machinic processes call for large spaces, large markets or great old royal powers. Also, as Braudel suggests, a concentration of semiological, monetary, intellectual means—knowledge capital—

like New York, Chicago, California, with all of America behind them. Or Amsterdam in the seventeenth century. Only this can allow for manageable entities: Megamachines.

In France, doping belongs to a more or less private club, as a refuge. People subjectivize themselves, and remake their existential territories with dopings, but complementarity between machines and refuge values is not guaranteed. If the buzz aborts, if it fails, the whole thing will implode. There is a critical threshold. If it doesn't bring out a social project, like Japanese enterprise or American mobility, one can die from it. Look at Van Gogh or Artaud. They could not get out of the machinic process and it destroyed them. Like true addicts. My existence carried away into a process of singularization? Perfect. But if it stops short ("Stop, time's up, turn in your papers!"), catastrophe is immanent for lack of perspective and a micropolitical outlet. It is necessary to make oneself exist "within" the process. Repetition in a doped void is horrible: '60s counterculture. There are plenty of buzzes that have caused much pain when their outmodedness became apparent: Third Worldism, Marxist-Leninism or Rock-and-Roll…

It's either miserable prostration or the creation of an unprecedented universe. Subjective formations concocted by dopings can either get things moving again, or kill them slowly over a low flame. Behind all this there are possibilities for creation, changes of life and scientific, economic and even aesthetic revolutions. New horizons or nothing. I'm not talking about the old story of spontaneousness as a creative factor. That is absurd. But within the grasp of the immense undertakings to stratify and serialize our societies, there are subjective formations roaming about that are capable of getting the power of the process going again and promoting mutant singularities and new minorities. The visibly doped sectors shouldn't merely be defenses of acquired territories; the residual crystals that constitute machinic dope can penetrate the entire planet, reanimate it and relaunch it. A society that has reached the point of being so locked in should open up to this, or it will burst.

IV

PSYCHOANALYSIS

AND SCHIZOANALYSIS

13

LACAN WAS AN EVENT IN MY LIFE

Charles J. Stivale: *Regarding the current intellectual scene, in a recent issue of* Magazine littéraire, *D.A. Grisoni claimed that* A Thousand Plateaus *proves that "the desiring vein" has disappeared ...*

Félix Guattari: Yeah, I saw that! (Laughter)

... and he called Deleuze "dried up."[1] *What do you think of this? What is your conception of the schizoanalytic enterprise right now, and what aspects of the two volumes of* Capitalism and Schizophrenia *appear to you as the most valid?*

They're not valid at all! Me, I don't know, I don't care! It's not my problem! It's however you want it, whatever use you want to make of it. Right now, I'm working, Deleuze is working a lot. I'm working with a group of friends on the possible directions of schizo-analysis; yes, I'm theorizing in my own way. If people don't care about it, that's their business; but I don't care either, so that works out well.

That's precisely what Deleuze said yesterday evening: I understand quite well that people don't care about my work because I don't care about theirs either.

Right, so there's no problem. You see, we didn't even discuss it, but we had the same answer! (Laughter)

Deleuze and I spoke briefly about the book by Jean Paul Aron, Les Modernes.[2] *What astounded me was that despite his way of presenting things, he really liked* Anti-Oedipus. *What particularly struck me in his statement about it was that "despite a few bites, the doctor (Lacan) is the sacred precursor of schizoanalysis and of the hyper-sophisticated industry of desiring-machines" (285). A question that one asks in reading* Anti-Oedipus *is what is the place of Lacanian psychoanalysis in the schizoanalytic project. One gets the impression that you distance yourselves from most of the thinkers presented, but that Lacan has a rather privileged place to the extent that there is no rupture.*

In my opinion, what you are saying is not completely accurate because it's true in the beginning of *Anti-Oedipus*, and then if you look, en route, it's less and less true because, obviously, we didn't write at the end the same way as we did in the beginning, and then it's not true at all throughout *A Thousand Plateaus*, there, it's all over. This means the following: Deleuze never took Lacan seriously at all, but for me, that was very important. It's true that I've gone through a whole process of clarification, which didn't occur quickly, and I haven't finally measured, dare I say it, the superficial character of Lacan. That will seem funny, but in the end, I think that's how Deleuze and Foucault... I remember certain conversations of that period, and I realize that they considered all that as rather simplistic, superficial. That seems funny because it's such a sophisticated, complicated language.

So, I'm nearly forced to make personal confidences about this because, if I don't, this won't be clear. What was important for me with Lacan is that it was an event in my life, an event to meet this totally bizarre, extraordinary guy with extraordinary, crazy even, acting talent, with an astounding cultural background. I was a student at the Sorbonne, I was bored shitless in courses with Lagache, Szazo, I don't remember who, and then I went to Lacan's seminar. I have to say that it represented an entirely unforeseen richness and inventiveness in the university. That's what Lacan was; he was above all a guy with guts; you can say all you want about Lacan, but you can't say the contrary, he had no lack of guts. He possessed a depth of freedom that he inherited from a rather blessed period, I have to say, the period before the war, the period of surrealism, a period with a kind of gratuitous violence. One thinks of Gide's Lafcadio. He had a dadaist humor, a violence at the same time, a cruelty; he was a very cruel guy, Lacan, very harsh.

As for Deleuze, it wasn't the same because he acquired this freedom vis-à-vis concepts, this kind of sovereign distance in his work. Deleuze was never a follower of anyone, it seems to me, or of nearly anyone. I wasn't in the same kind of work, and it was important for me to have a model of rupture, if I can call it that, all the more so since I was involved in extreme leftist organizations, but still traditionalist from many perspectives. There was all the weight of Sartre's thought, of Marxist thought, creating a whole environment that it wasn't easy to eliminate. So, I think that's what Lacan was. Moreover, it's certain that his reading of Freud opened possibilities for me to cross through and into different ways of thinking. Its only recently that I have discovered to what extent he read Freud entirely in bad faith. In other words, he really just made anything he wanted out of Freud because, if one really reads Freud, one realizes that it has very little to do with Lacanism. (Laughter)

Could you specify in which writings or essays Lacan seems to read this way?

The whole Lacanian extrapolation about the signifier, in my opinion, is absolutely un-Freudian, because Freud's way of constructing categories relating to the primary processes was also a way of making their cartography that, in my opinion, was much closer to schizoanalysis, i.e. much closer to a sometimes nearly delirious development—why not?—in order to account for how the dream and how phobia function, etc. There is a Freudian creativity that is much closer to theater, to myth, to the dream, and which has little to do with this structuralist, systemic, mathematizing, I don't know how to say it, this mathemic thought of Lacan. First of all, the greatest difference, there as well, is at the level of the enunciation considered in its globality. Freud and his Freudian contemporaries wrote something, wrote monographies. Then, in the history of psychoanalysis, and notably in this kind of structuralist vacillation, there are no monographies. It's a meta-meta-meta-theorization; they speak about textual exegesis in the nth degree, and one always returns to the original monography, little Hans, Schreber, the Wolf Man, the Rat Man.[3] So all that is ridiculous. It's as if we had the Bible, the Bible according to Schreber, the Bible according to Dora. This is interesting, this comparison could be pushed quite far. I think that there is the invention of the modelization of subjectivity, an order of this invention of subjectivity that was that of the apostles: it comes, it goes, but I mean that it's moving much more quickly now than at that time, i.e. we won't have to wait two thousand years to put that religion in question, it seems to me.

It also seems to me that there are many more apostles who have betrayed their master than apostles who betrayed Jesus.

I was thinking more of the apostles, I see them more as Freud's first psychoanalyses; then, it's the Church fathers who are the traitors. Understand, with the apostles, there is something magnificent in

Freud, he's like a guy who has fallen hopelessly in love with his patients, without realizing it, more or less; a guy who introduced some very heterodoxical practices, nearly incestuous when you think of what was the spirit of medicine at that period. So, he had an emotion, there was a Freudian event of creation, an entirely original Freudian scene, and all that has been completely buried by exegesis, by the Freudian religions.

A few minutes ago, you mentioned Foucault. I asked Deleuze this question about Foucault yesterday evening: what are your thoughts on Foucault nearly a year after his death? How do you react to this absence, and can we yet judge the importance of Foucault's work?

It's difficult for me to respond because, quite the contrary to Deleuze, I was never influenced by Foucault's work. It interested me, of course, but it was never of great importance. I can't judge it. Quite possibly, it will have a great impact in different fields.[4]

Deleuze told me something very interesting: he said that Foucault's presence kept imbeciles from speaking too loudly, and that if Foucault didn't exactly block all aberrations, he nonetheless blocked imbeciles, and now the imbeciles will be unleashed. And, in terms of Aron's book, Les Modernes, *he said that this book wouldn't have been possible while Foucault was alive, that no one would have dared publish it.*

Oh, you think so?

I really don't know, but in any case, when it's a matter of machinations on the right …

It's certain that Foucault had a very important authority and impact.

14

PSYCHOANALYSIS SHOULD GET

A GRIP ON LIFE

Anti-Oedipus managed to stir things up a bit with its severe criticism of the "familialism" of psychoanalysis. After about ten years, however, this has now become a banal issue. Nearly everyone realized that that criticism had the ring of truth. I duly respect Freud, for what he represents; he was incredibly creative. His strokes of both genius and folly were rejected as he remained marginalized, kept at the peripheries of the scientific and medical arenas, over a rather long period of his life, and it was during this period of marginalization that he managed to draw attention to subjective facts which had been, until then, totally mistaken. His successors, however, in particular those of the Lacanian structuralist strain, have transformed psychoanalysis into a cult, turning psychoanalytic theory into a kind of theology celebrated by affected and pretentious sects which are still proliferating. At the time of my studies at the École freudienne, I was struck by the schism that inserted itself between the sophistication of the theoretical propositions taught there and the attitude people had developed vis-à-vis the clinical domain. Those with discourses that were not particularly brilliant and short on razzle-dazzle, still managed to hold down a fairly reasonable practice while, inversely, those known for distinguished and elegant discourses employed in their monkey-see-monkey-do mimicking of the *Master*, often behaved outright irresponsibly in therapy. To take charge of someone's life and direct its outcome, all the while running the risk of perhaps having all efforts lead one down a blind alley, is a matter of no little significance! There are people who come to you in total disarray, who are very vulnerable and very responsive to your suggestions, so much so that if the transference gets off on a bad footing the peril of alienating the person becomes a real threat. This phenomenon is not peculiar to the domain of psychoanalysis. Most of us are certainly aware of other examples of grand theories that have been employed for religious and perverted purposes and have had dreadful consequences (I can think of the Pol Pot regime in Cambodia or of certain Marxist-Leninist groups in South America...).

In short, this method of furthering the cause of psychoanalysis no longer holds much water; others continue to do it with great talent—for example, Robert Castel.[1] On the other hand, one must admit that it is also important not to tip the scale and sink into reductionist, neobehaviorist or systemist perspectives so typical of the Anglo-Saxon tradition which are currently conveyed by trends in family therapy.

Should one wish to go beyond this critical point to envision possibilities for the reconstruction of analysis on a different basis, I feel it is important to restate the question in terms of its status as a *myth of reference*. In order to live one's life—one's madness as well as one's neurosis, desire, melancholy, or even one's quotidian "normality"—each individual is bound to refer to a certain number of public or private myths. In ancient societies these myths had social consistency sufficient to allow for a system of reference with respect to morals, religion, sex, etc., in a manner that was much less dogmatic compared to what we have today; hence, in the case of a sacrificial exploration, the collectivity sought out ways to locate the kind of spirit dwelling within the sick person and to uncover the cultural, social, mythical and affective nature of the transgression. If a practical ritual no longer worked, one oriented oneself in another direction without pretending that one had come up against a resistance. These people probed subjectivity with an indisputable pragmatism and with an appeal to codes of conduct shared by the whole social body that provided the *testing grounds* for the effects of these codes. This is far from being the case with our psychological and psychoanalytic methods!

In societies where human faculties are highly integrated, the mythical systems of reference, at the very beginning, were taken over by great monotheistic religions that strived to respond to the cultural demand of castes, national groups and social classes. In time, all this collapsed with the deterritorialization of the ancient forms of filiation, of the clan, the community, the chiefs, etc. Consequently, the great monotheistic religions in their turn declined and lost a major portion of the direct sway they once held over collective subjective realities. (Aside from certain paradoxical situations today like those of Poland or Iran where religious ideologies have recovered their structural function for a whole nation. I draw on these two examples for their symmetric and, at the same time, antinomic nature: the latter leaning towards fascism, the former towards social liberation.) Generally speaking, however, reference to sin, confession, and prayer no longer carry the same weight as they once did; nor can they intervene any longer in the same manner in the problems of individuals held in the grip of psychotic intensity, neurosis or whatever form of mental distress. To make up for this loss, we can often see spectacular and daring ventures to bring back onto the modern scene animistic religions and traditional approaches to medicine in countries like Brazil with the *candomblé*, Macumba and Voodoo, etc.

To compensate for the relapse of these religions, great devices of subjectivation have emerged as conduits of modern myths: from the bourgeois novel of Jean-Jacques Rousseau to James Joyce, from the star-system of cinema to hit songs and sports and, generally speaking, the whole array of what we recognize today as mass-mediated culture. Only here we are talking of ruptured family myths. Psychoanalysis and family therapy constitute in their own right a kind of background reference, providing a body and a serious demeanor for this profane subjectivation. To restate my point, it seems to me that nobody can possibly organize their life independently of these subjective formations of reference. When one is through with one of them—whether it has lost its motivating force, or whether it is reduced to the level of banality—one sees that in spite of its degeneration and impoverishment, it continues to survive. This is perhaps the case with Freudianism and Marxism. Unless they are replaced in their role as collective myths, they will never wither away! They have, in fact, become a kind of chronic collective delirium. Take the end of the Hitlerian paradigm, for example: the matter was already lost in 1941 and 1942; but it was seen through to the end, to total disaster, and it has managed to linger well after its end. As Kuhn pointed out so well with reference to scientific paradigms, a body of explication that loses its consistency is never simply replaced by a more credible alternative. It retains its place and hangs on like an ailing patient.

Under these conditions it is useless even to attempt to demonstrate in a rational way the absurdity of most psychoanalytic hypotheses. One has to drain one's own cup to the last drop! And this probably applies just as well to the systematization of family therapy. Psychologists and social workers today display a certain avidity for rediscovering frames of reference. The university is poised as a resource to supply them with scientific bases. In most of the cases, however, all we are dealing with are reductionist theories that position themselves side-by-side with real problems—a metonymic scientificity, in a manner of speaking. In fact, when the *users* go to see a shrink, they know very well that they are not dealing with real scientists, but with people who present themselves as *servers* in a particular problematic order. In the past, when people went to see a priest, the servant of God, they were to some extent familiar with his methods of proceeding, his intimate ties with his maid, with the neighbors, and had some idea of his way of thinking. Psychoanalysts are, no doubt, people held in high esteem! However, they are far more isolated and, in my opinion, will not continue to carry on with their business much longer by referring to deflated myths.

Once the necessity, or dare I say even the legitimacy, of mythic references is understood, the question is no longer aimed at their scientific validity but is redirected towards their *social functionality*. This is the true site of theoretical research in this domain. One can theorize a production of subjectivity in a given context, within a particular group or with respect to a neurosis or psychosis, without having to resort to the authority of science in the matter and refer instead to something that would imply a formalization of a sense of the universal in order to affirm itself as a universal truth. I feel a strong urge to underline that we are not talking about ways to create a general theory for the human sciences—not even for the social and juridical sciences—since theorization, in all the matters it may encompass, cannot amount to more than what I call a descriptive or functional *cartography*. In my estimation, this would involve an invitation to all parties and groups concerned, in accordance with the appropriate modalities, to participate in the activity of creating models that touch on their lives. Furthermore, it is precisely the study of these modalities that I perceive as being the essence of analytic theorizing. I read in the papers quite recently that twenty million Brazilians are on the brink of dying of hunger in the northeast part of the country, which may lead to the engendering of a race of *autistic dwarfs*. In order to understand and help this population, references to symbolic castration, the signifier or the Name of the Father would hardly amount to more than a paltry form of support!

On the other hand, people who need to confront these types of challenges would make unmistakable gains were they able to create a certain number of social instruments and functional concepts to deal with the situation. The political dimension of the production of subjectivity is clearly evident in such a case. Yet it goes beyond that under the auspices of other modalities and into different contexts. I repeat, therefore, the less the shrinks see themselves as scientists, the more they will take heed of their responsibilities; we are not talking about an air of guilt-ridden responsibility displayed by those who pretend to be speaking in the name of truth or history. I belong to a generation who witnessed the attacks on J.P. Sartre, where some people imagined, in the age of *La Nausée*, that they knew for certain the reasons behind suicide and delinquency among the youth of that period, and held him responsible for all of it. Intellectuals who labor on the building of theories sometimes caution us against states of affairs they disapprove of and will even take some responsibility for the consequences that follow from the theory. This, however, only seldom amounts to a direct assuming of responsibility. On the other hand, they often frequently exert an inhibiting function by treading, unwarranted, on a terrain where they constrain the emergence of certain problems that could be looked at from more constructive angles.

I always find myself politically involved in various ways and degrees. I have been participating in social movements since my childhood and, moreover, I became a psychoanalyst. This has led me to reject any tight compartmentalization between the individual and society. In my view, the singular and collective dimensions always tend to merge. If one refuses to situate a problem in its political and micropolitical context, one ends up sterilizing its impact of truth. To intervene with one's intelligence and one's means, as feeble as they may be, or as simple as they may appear, nevertheless, remains quite essential. And this is an integral part of any propaedeutic, of any conceivable didactic process.

After 1968, psychologists, psychiatrists, caretakers on mental wards, were all seen as cops. This we have to admit! But where does this begin, where does this end? What is important is to determine whether the position one occupies will, or will not, contribute to the overcoming of the realities of segregation, social and psychological mutilation, and whether one will, at least, be able to minimize the damage.

15

THE UNCONSCIOUS IS TURNED

TOWARD THE FUTURE

Recherches: *As a psychoanalyst, a writer, but also a militant, you occupy a special position in the political scene. Most intellectuals disappointed by Marxism are concerned exclusively with human rights and the defense of a number of humanist ideals, but you maintain an offensive attitude toward Western social structures, that of a revolutionary intellectual. How do you manage to sustain this dual activity?*

Félix Guattari: I believe I am neither an intellectual nor a revolutionary. I'm just pursuing something I started long ago, perhaps with a certain imperviousness to hazards of the present situation. And sometimes, in the eyes of influential people, I even feel like a "half-wit," someone kind of backward. It's true that I have a rather particular vision of things, which perhaps comes from the fact that I am very short-sighted. I have a tendency to stick a bit too closely to a text as well as to an event. That is perhaps why I got interested in analysis at a very young age and why I forged parallel visions for myself, a naïve vision, and to compensate for it, politically and philosophically, an "armed" vision. The passage from this molecular vision, sticking closely to texts and events, to a more theoretical dimension is never easy for me to make. But I remain convinced that molecular transformations are the true fabric of long-term historical transformations.

People often object to your penchant for abstraction, shock formulas. For once could you be more concrete about what you mean by molecular transformations?

Let's take an example: the technology of the pill. Here's something that deeply transformed relations to the sexual body, to conjugality and the family. It's only a little gesture, an evening ritual, a monthly purchase at the pharmacy, but it radically alters the socius. Another example: the relationship to justice. The creation of a very "politically committed" association of magistrates like the "Union of Magistrates" refers to an invisible transformation of the relationship to the thing judged, to the judicial institution, to legal texts, etc. Whether these transformations are positive or negative, this isn't the place to debate that. The same holds true in a multitude of domains that have to do with neighborhood, information, or even movement, speed, the kind of translations Paul Virilio talks about. All these mutations, which I have termed molecular, are what I wanted to bring to bear upon a different conception of the unconscious and also of history.

This conception only widens the gulf that separates daily life from traditional conceptions concerning the transformation of society. It is an incentive to redefine the role of organizations, groups, in short, the political snuggle. Don't parties, trade unions, leftist groups have anything left to say in your opinion?

Let me state it very clearly: I do not believe in either the death of politics or in social implosion, dear to our friend Baudrillard. On the other hand, two notions seem to have collapsed: that of ideology and that of group.

Reference to ideology masks the connections between different "machines" at work in the social process. It might have to do with machines of a scientific nature, an aesthetic, institutional nature, but also technical machines, logical machines that intertwine their effects in order to trigger off an event, something historically important, as well as a microscopic, almost imperceptible decision-making process. Reference to ideologies do not account for such events. For example, the eruption of what one could call "the Khomeini effect." One could ask: who are the Shiites? Should we interpret this movement in terms of religious fanaticism? One invokes paranoia: but where does this paranoia originate? In Freud? In Bleuler? In ethology? Carter's advisors are tearing their hair out trying to grasp the possible causes of such a phenomenon, which never have the systemic or structural character of ideologies. It is always due to the interaction of very heterogeneous factors stemming from different logics, or from a multivalent logic, that results in the coexistence of systems— I prefer to say machines—plugged into the real. Unlike Althusser, I do not rigidly oppose ideological discourse to scientific discourse. I would approach scientific or aesthetic discursivity in the same way.

Another notion in crisis is that of the group. There are social aggregates that have no specificity of group action whatsoever, and, conversely, there are isolated individuals who shape the socius "from within," so to speak; writers like Beckett, like Proust, have effected direct transformations on the social unconscious. It does not specifically involve effects of communication occurring within a group; the group is only the medium through which a multiplicity of components circulate.

At one time I came up with the idea of the "subject-group." I contrasted these with "subjected groups" in an attempt to define modes of intervention which I described as micropolitical. I've changed my mind: there are no subject-groups, but arrangements of enunciation, of subjectivization, pragmatic arrangements that do not coincide with circumscribed groups. These arrangements can involve individuals, but also ways of seeing the world, emotional systems, conceptual machines, memory devices, economic, social components, elements of all kinds.

In your last book, L'Inconscient machinique *[The Machinic Unconscious],[1] there is a long passage on "schizoanalysis." Is this a new technique of treatment, a sort of super-psychoanalysis that therapists seduced by your proposal should attempt to use by drawing up "maps of the unconscious"? Or is it just a pretext to refine the criticism of psychoanalysis and enrich your conception of the unconscious?*

Your question brings us back to the debate between technology and ideology. In my opinion this opposition does not hold up. Yet this question is very present in current, internal debates at the Réseau Alternatif à la Psychiatrie.[2] Should one reject everything that exists in the technical domain and merely wage war on the political front, in such a way as to bring together political struggle and the transformation of psychiatry? Should one, on the contrary, try to salvage existing techniques and put them to the best use? I answer: neither. Ideological battles cannot be dissociated from technologies (for example, technologies of information or of group manipulation). Moreover, when one tries to be a strict technician, and believes to be merely applying the principles of psychoanalysis, or family therapy, or psycho-pharmacology, one is not freed from micropolitical fields for all that. Under these conditions, it is impossible to circumscribe a legitimate technical object. The schizoanalytical aphorisms I set forth in my book have no other goal than to suggest intellectual tools, a conceptual machine, that can be transformed according to each person's liking. It is not a super-psychoanalysis, or a univocal reading of the political.

By turning to animal ethology, particularly the study of birds, aren't you outlining a sort of human ethology, an individual surrounded by "visagéité" (faceness), obsessed by "refrains," in short, an "alienated" individual who no longer has anything human about him?

Rather than the unfortunate term "alienation," which no longer means much of anything, I prefer turning to the notion of "subjection" which I contrast with that of "subjugation": subjection deals with people, power relations, and subjugation with machinic relations and power relations. It is at an extrapersonal level that relations of subjugation are established. What happens to an individual in his machinic environment is always below or beyond his person. Beside affective, perceptive, intellectual and discursive components, there exists ethological components which psychologists and anthropologists have not taken sufficiently into account. Research in human ethology demonstrates the existence of nonverbal systems of communication and specific territorializations. In particular, I have in mind "greeting behaviors," automatic, subliminal smiles, which can only be detected in slow motion film and which one finds again in all cultural areas. The way these features of visagéité work cannot be explained by analyses such as those by Spitz, concerning interhuman relations at the infant stage (identification with the mother, etc.). It happens at a level of expression that cannot be mechanically explained by an intrafamilial system. It does not imply the existence of a univocal determinist causality. It is interesting to study how individuals and groups juggle with these precoded features of visagéité, with these expressive refrains, a bit like a pianist arrives at mastering reflexes that, in the beginning, seemed completely mechanical. The work of actors—those Georges Aperghis directs in the field of musical theater, for example—heads in this direction. Distinctions between the innate, the acquired, learning, the imprint, are being called into question by this current research. There is a continuum between these domains that, in my opinion, could be illuminated by the concept of arrangement I mentioned earlier. How can one otherwise understand that systems of genetic encoding manage to "pick up" new information, new behaviors, new morphological systems? The formation of the biosphere, and of what I have called the *mechanosphere*, does not result from chance, but from modes of concatenation by blocks of semiotic sequences and chains of highly differentiated encodings.

The work of Proust gives you opportunity to demonstrate the methods evoked above. How can Remembrance of Things Past *constitute a type of "scientific work," as you assert?*

I have always been exasperated, as many people have, by psychoanalytical readings of literary works. "Beneath" the purely literary work one seeks to discover the real man, his inhibitions, his anxieties, his affective problems, familial problems, etc. Here again, this raises the question of methodology. If one believes the unconscious is something buried in the past, crystallized in the form of signifying chains, certain keys should be enough to find the complexions or "mathemes" that compose it. But if one starts from the transsemiotic unconscious, which is not solely structured by signifiers, and no longer turned toward the past but toward the future, an unconscious that bears the capacity to "engineer" new objects, new realities, then everything changes. To make a comparison, if you want to study computer science, it's better to go into research departments or workshops where new computers with the greatest technological capabilities are being built rather than limit yourself to standard models that were built fifteen years ago. Well, this is the same thing. If you want to analyze your unconscious, rather than going to Freud and Lacan, refer to the richest authors—Proust, Beckett, Joyce, Faulkner, Kafka or Artaud—because scarcely anything better has been done since. Interpret Freud, Jung and the others through Proust and not vice versa. The unconscious has to be built, invented. Proust is one of the greatest analysts who ever existed, because he was able to detect modes of communication, major routes between music, painting, social relations, life in the salons, physical sensations, etc. He worked the unconscious as transsemiotic matter.

In this analysis of Proust's work, you set forth the idea that music and in particular "Vinteuil's little phrase" constitutes not only "the national hymn of Swann's love," but structures the whole of the novel, the shape of the sentences, the outline of the plot, etc.

Yes, a certain system of refrain structures (I prefer to say "machinates") both Vinteuil's little phrase—the novel never stops presenting it and then withdrawing it—and the story of Vinteuil and his daughter; and beyond, the whole strategy of the novel (the fact, for example, that a character who has drifted off is replicated or disappears). A certain kind of music is linked to the "Baron de Charlus" construction, another to the branch of the "young girls" and to a different conception of homosexuality that merges into a vector of becoming-woman ("enriched" and multidimensional homosexuality). When I say that the unconscious is made of multiple components, turned toward the future, etc., one might well wonder what holds all these components together. For the time being, I reply: "abstract machines" carried by this sort of refrain, a notion close to René Thom's "logos," but different in that these machines do not lend themselves to a mathematical or structuralist reduction. Nor do they come down to an undifferentiated whole, to a muddle of interactions. An abstract machine can be adjacent to a technological mutation, it can result from extraordinary marriages such as that of Khomeini-Kissinger: an ayatollah in his monastery dreams of killing the Shah; a brilliant manipulator dreams of salvaging the fortune of this same Shah: the result is fabulous… But one could very well have imagined other, much quieter marriages such as that of Sadat-Carter… and thus, other refrains, another international music.

16

THE REFRAIN OF BEING AND MEANING:

ANALYSIS OF A DREAM ABOUT A.D.

That dream "nonsense" might be meaningful relates back to the oldest forms of subjectivation. Breaks in syntax, semantic proliferation, pragmatic inductions: all dream realms play a role of bifurcation in relation to meanings and norms prevalent during a state of wakefulness. The subject of this paper is to show that, in order to reach consciousness, it is not necessary to oppose the basic logic of latent contents to that of repression. It is possible to use a model in which the unconscious is open to the future and able to integrate any heterogeneous, semiotic components that may interfere. Then, meaningful distortions no longer arise from an interpretation of underlying contents. Instead, they become part of a machinic set-up entirely on the text's surface. Rather than be mutilated by symbolic castration, recurring incomplete goals act instead as autonomous purveyors of subjectivation. The rupture, the breach of meaning, is nothing else than the manifestation of subjectivation in its earliest stage. It is the necessary and adequate fractalization which enables something to appear where the access before was blocked. It is the deterritorializing opening. To illustrate this problematic, I have chosen one of my own dreams containing numerous over-determinations, presented as a hologram, which have been recurrent themes throughout all major turning-points in my life.[1]

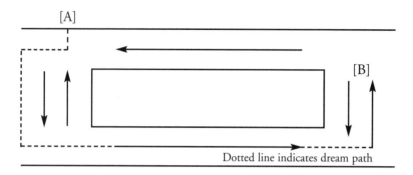

Dotted line indicates dream path

Dream Text

In the company of Yasha David and his wife, I come out of house [A], which is next to a large, rectangular-shaped town square, which seems to belong to a large, provincial town, rather than to a big city. The streets running along the two longer sides of the town square are one-way in opposite directions, whereas those along the shorter sides are two-way. All together, this constitutes the circuit along which I travel for about three quarters of the dream.

We are on the verge of separating and I tell myself that I do not remember exactly where I parked my car. I suggest, first of all, looking around the town square. Yasha believes he remembers where the car is. He and his wife help me look for it. We arrive at point [B], located at the right of the town square. Then, I have an urge to congratulate Yasha on the success of our joint venture. However, I refrain from saying what I was about to say, since I realize that I would have called him Gilles [Deleuze]. I speak of the risks we shared; we were at the edge of an abyss. "Let me start over," it was as if we were hanging onto the wall of an abyss. But, eventually, we made it out all right. Feeling an outburst of affection, I want to kiss them both. Again, I refrain from acting on my first impulse since I remember hearing that Yasha is very jealous over his wife. So, I settle for hugging them both.

Associative Remarks And Narrative Developments

Yasha David: A Czechoslovakian intellectual and refugee living in France, with whom I worked for over a year on several large exhibits commemorating the centennial of Kafka's birth. Those in charge at the Pompidou Center made it so difficult that, on several occasions, we thought we would have to abandon the project.

Yasha David's wife: I do not know her very well, since we have crossed paths only two or three times. In transcribing this dream, I realized that the woman in my dream was not her but the wife of another friend, Helena Gallard (who, in reality, writes her first name "Alena"). Alena is also Czechoslovakian and also worked on the Kafka exhibit, though only in the preparatory stages. I have confused Yasha David's wife and Alena several times in the past. Alena, her husband Jean Gallard and I have met several times in the past in Mexico City, Paris and Amsterdam. I like this couple very much, perhaps even bordering on fascination. However, I have a feeling that there are problems in the relationship of which I know nothing.

The Rectangular Shaped Town Square

I am reminded first of all of the main town square in the eastern province of an old Mexican city, whose name I know well but cannot remember when writing the dream. I finally find it by cross-checking, Michoacan. The name of the city must be Pascuaro. I stayed overnight in a hotel next to the town square. I was very much impressed by its provincial charm and the fact that it seemed destined to remain the same throughout the centuries. I remember thinking, "This is where I would like to end my life." In the background of this Mexican memory is the echo of another very old one, of a large, shadowy public square in the town of Louviers in Normandy. I lived with my maternal grandmother on Rooster

Street ("rue au coq") which runs into the town square. Several days after writing down this dream, I realized with surprise—I was overwhelmed by the new evidence—that the square in my dream had to be the main square of Mer. Mer is a small village on the Loire river, close to where I currently spend half of the week. Nevertheless, my dream is not about the Mer of today, but that of over forty years ago during what was called "the exodus," when millions of French people prepared to flee the 1940 German invasion. I do not know how, but my parents had managed to rent a small house right at point [A] of the town square as I depicted it from my dream. We anticipated staying through the war, ready to move south of the Loire, if need be. I was literally thrilled with this possibility (I must say that I lived through this entire period of upheaval as if it were an extraordinary adventure). However, at dawn the very next day, we had to leave immediately since we heard that all bridges on the Loire in the Germans' path were to be blown up.

The Direction Of Traffic Around The Town Square

The existence of a vectorial element superimposed over the figural dream representation refers to two formative components: (1) A dream, going back about a year, that I named "the wooden floor dance dream," in which my second son, a very young child, moved away from me in an emotionally charged atmosphere. We were at a ball; I ended up exiting through the door on the right side of the large quadrilateral-shaped room. Then, after returning through the door on the left, I proceeded to weave my way back through the dancers from the left to the right side. (2) A graph, also quadrilateral, depicting a new definition of the Unconscious by transforming four basic entities: the Flows, the Machinic Phylum, the Existential Territories, the Intangible Universe. But one question evoked by this graph (which, by the way, had already inspired the formal composition of the "wooden floor dance dream") remained unanswered. It was about the symmetry, which was too conspicuous for my taste, of inter-entity transformations along the abscissas and the ordinates of my diagram. In the dream exposed here, an area—the upper part of the trajectory—can be perceived as, if not impassable, then at least as requiring a detour and consequently a break in symmetry. The hesitations, doubts, inhibitions, forgetfulness and slips of the tongue which make up the texture of this dream all seem to gravitate towards this very area which, only recently, I had described as "vacuolic."[2]

The Forgotten Car

I forgot two aspects of my car: its place within the dream context and its name. While writing the dream, the initials BMW appeared under my pen instead of Renault. This substitution of a car that I owned twenty years ago for one that I currently own also refers back to another dream. At this point, we can already consider that we are dealing with a dream intersection rather than a meaningful, self-contained entity. This type of dream activity is much more frequent than is commonly believed.[3] In this other dream, I had also forgotten my car, the BMW I owned before. However, the setting was in the troubled years during which I owned it, more precisely, those around 1968. I was walking down Gay-Lussac Street—a name that I often block-out—looking for my car. Eventually, I went on my way by bicycle. On the other side of Boulevard Saint Michel,[4] I discovered I was in a Socialist Party meeting; the French ecologists were being expelled by numerous guards led by Lionel Jospin in person.[5] Considering that the current issues arise from the act of forgetting the Renault:

    — A hole is created in space by the missing car; this spatial "gap" of a familiar object, which in some way is a part of my ego, enters together with the opening of the door to the house [A]. This parenthesis of an element of the ego does not affect the dream car's basic character, meaning that it remains a Renault;

— I feel that going from the word "Renault," written out, to "BMW," an acronym, has a certain quality of meaning;

— I experience some hesitation regarding the sequence of events between forgetting the car's location and the near slip of Yasha David's name. This hesitation echoes my confusion when Yasha David states that he might remember where I left the car;

— Finally, I cannot refrain from mentioning the mechanical association, however stupid it may be, which consists of prolonging the question of that which is forgotten, in the form of a: where is the car...? type of analysis. It is true that recently I reread the Freud-Fliess correspondence and I wondered about the strange, disguised, homosexual relationship on which Freud built the text of his self-analysis.

The Slip Of The Tongue In The Dream

Gilles Deleuze's name came to mind instead of Yasha David's in this duplicated deeper consciousness that I created in my dream. This substitution will function as a matrix of enunciation which will generate dialogical polyphonic progressions, as defined by Mikhail Bakhtin,[6] using essentially feminine characters—Adelaide, Arlette Donati, Alena Gallard, Micheline Kao, my mother, my grandmother, etc.—harmonic constellations in the heterogenous texts that we will examine later.

The Abyss

There are three associative orientations:

— a speleological reference that I cannot seem to identify;

— a text by Samuel Beckett, which I believe is entitled "Le Dépeupleur," where an entire population survives by hanging on to a circular wall;

— a test that I invented as a youth and pompously baptized "The sociological-existential integration test," in which the initial rules are progressively cancelled as the game is being played.

Inhibition When Confronted With Jealousy

I was robbed recently, and a good twenty years of my notes were stolen. A friend offered to help reconstruct my "memories" by interviewing both my friends and me on my past. When she said that she would interview Arlette Donati, with whom I lived for seven years during this period in the '60s, I thought it likely that she would describe some of my jealous behavior towards her—that I prefer to forget. Here, however, the classical logic of Freudian denial comes into play: "I am not jealous, since it is Yasha David who is jealous."

Polyphonic Analysis Of Manifest Lines Of Subjectivation

Here, one must identify lines of parallel and intercrossed meaning in the same manner as Bakhtin's dialogism. Only later will we seek to qualify the meaning synapses that, from a deterritorializing and fractalizing rupture, will act as a catalyst for the function of setting up a Constellation Reference Universe. Initially, we will distinguish the manifest phylum of discursive meaning, as they appear in the written text of the dream, and the latent phylum, as they develop during the oral clarification in an "associative" perspective.

There are five principal manifest phylum:

1) around the town, the town square, and the closed circuit of streets which encircle it;

2) the forgotten car;

3) Yasha David and the slip of the tongue in the dream which he incurs regarding Gilles Deleuze;

4) an abyss;

5) the inhibition when faced with jealousy.

The third manifest phylum, the only one that puts forth proper names, is distinct from the others due to its function as a synaptic operator. Also worthy of note is that these components are heterogenous.

The first one appears as a visual iconic representation that we will classify under Existential territory (Et).

The second one evokes an absent vehicle, a potentiality that may or may not exist, which we will classify under Discursive Phylum. The third one is a psychopathological mental process of daily life that we will classify under Synapses.

The fourth one is a significant text that becomes an iconic statement during the associative developments. In this respect, it is the opposite of Existential territory: it is a chaotic black hole. The fifth one is a "Coarté effect" (using Rorschach's definition) that we will put with the non-discursive Reference Universes.

Analysis Of Latent Lines Of Subjectivation

Development of the first component. The dream place reference was immediately identified from an iconic point of view, however, it took me several days to find the proper name of the town in question. It was the town of Mer. The other references—Pascuaro in Mexico, Louvier in Normandy—remain in the background of the first one, despite the fact that, initially, they are mentioned before Mer. (It is as if I had to break through successive levels of resistance.) One should avoid leaping too quickly to the conclusion that the phonetic structure "mère" (mother in French) arises from the lexeme "Mer." Mer is a proper name to which I more readily associate my father, who made the decision, at the time of the exodus, for us to find lodgings in this town and exactly at the town square. For me, the fact that the last "e" and the accent of the word "mère" are missing from Mer is significant. It is the "mère," or mother, less a few things; the mother freed of responsibilities and restrictions. It is the "père," or father, who is much freer of movement and also much more distant.

The town square of Louviers (which is roughly adjacent to a park where I believe my mother took me in a baby carriage), however, represents solely a maternal background.

After examining the works of the dream's central synapse, we will then return to the third dimension of the constellation—the Mexican town square of Pascuaro with its connotation of sweet death. All that we can retain for now is that the door of the house at [A] leads to a composite father/mother existential territory.

Development of the second component. What actually happened following the cultural exhibit at the Georges Pompidou Center in which Gilles Deleuze participated, was that I offered to drive Yasha David home. We walked together to the parking lot underneath the Pompidou Center. I realized that I had forgotten where I left the car. We went in circles for a long time among the different levels, before I remembered to my embarrassment that I came on foot. That was what really happened. However, I have dreamed very often of forgetting my car.

The same is true here; I cannot approach the turnoff on rue Gay-Lussac,[7] the ecologists, the Socialist party, etc., without first working through the synapse; in the meantime, it is important to note that the car theme, for me, is that of a desiring-machine. My life changed dramatically after I got my driver's license—very late, since I was already 35. An indirect consequence is that I became more independent, which eventually led, among other things, to a divorce. It was my father who, on his deathbed, insisted quite adamantly that I obtain my license. He felt isolated, too dependent on my mother. He wanted me to come and see him more often. I also remember that he had given me a fifty-franc bill so that I would register for the driver's test. That made a big impression on me because he was completely unaware of the fact that fifty francs was no longer worth very much.

Analysis Of The Synaptic Component

The deterritorializing and fractalizing dream agent is an abstract tool that appears thanks to two elements:
— the act of forgetting (the car);
— the slip of the tongue (concerning Yasha David's name).
These two elements can be expressed within one single structure written in three parts:

	Renault	Mer	Yasha David
I am looking for my	_____ in	_____ with	_____
	BMW	Gay-Lussac	Gilles Deleuze
	(forgotten)	Street	(slip of tongue)

It must be noted that the first articulation is already organized in a complex manner. I dream that I have forgotten my car, but, at the same time, I forget the type of car, substituting it with another—the BMW.

Twenty years ago, during the events of 1968, I owned a BMW. I have memories of driving through very violent demonstrations at the wheel of this car. I lived with Arlette Donati at the time and my collaboration with Gilles Deleuze started shortly thereafter. Thus, a Renault, from the Yasha David period in the present, exists with a more prestigious BMW, from the 1968, Arlette Donati,[8] Gilles

Deleuze period in the past. Yet, the way the past period represses the present one is not according to simple dynamic opposition. It contains a dialectic dimension that produces machinic gains which will operate in other ways of subjectivation. This is essentially a deterritorializing movement appearing in the passage from the whole word Renault to the acronym BMW. Afterwards, we will see that this "acronym-ization" will spread over to the neighboring proper names, thus, allowing the first, abstract, machine core to develop. At the time of this dream, I was having a very problematic relationship with an Italian woman named Adelaide, whom I called A.D.

Thus, the following transformation can be diagrammed:

1984	Renault	A.D.	Yasha David
1968	BMW	Arlette Donati	Gilles Deleuze

It is as if the acronymization of 1968 moved up to 1984 transforming Arlette Donati into A.D. (Adelaide).

Harmonic Constellation Analysis Of Text Levels

Polyphonic lines developed according to their own spaces of meaning as a function of their respective machinic propositions—which are themselves set in extrinsic, rhizomatic coordinates. So, the town square developed into the town of Mer, Louviers, Pascuaro, and then into the father/mother, etc. Currently, the point is to determine core deterritorialized texts expressed in the dream as well as in reality, since from the point of view of producing subjectivity—which is the one I adopt here—there is no longer any reason to keep the latent unconscious contents separate from consciously expressed texts. These "assigning" or "interpreting" agents, as defined by C. S. Peirce, are non-discursive inasmuch as they make up deterritorialized universes, which give rise to the organization of heterogenous means of semiotization.

An example of this type of heterogenous component, which generates discontinuous structure fragments, is the transformation of Renault into the acronym BMW, or the name Arlette Donati slipping into A.D. In addition, in the last exam pie, the deterritorialization of the abbreviation is correlative to a phonological reterritorialization since this is the level on which A.D. operates within the name Adelaide.

It is important to note also that these sources of partial texts cannot, as such, be designated through syntagmatic links and paradigmatic axes. Here, they are merely linked to proper names, summoned by three women whom I loved successively: Micheline Kao, Arlette Donati and A.D. It is as if code names or inchoative verbs acted as agents of this very same non-significant rupture, opening the door to the beginning of a stated existential function. Instead of being prisoner to a significant quadrature, the synaptic semiotic link here is in a position to generate a fractal proliferation which will explore the resolution of a problematic in limbo; that of the relationship with birth and death inasmuch as it can generate inhibition.

An initial partial harmonic core revolves around dream components I and IV (i.e., that of the father/mother territory and of the abyss) attracting him to the components of a spoken field, in relation to their intrinsic coordinates. One must remember that the predominant form of expression of component I is essentially visual. After leaving [A], I enter the superimposed background world of mother (*mère*) Louviers—Pascuaro. This iconic component is, however, duplicated and even disturbed by a certain phonological syncretism which becomes evident at two points:

— the transformation of Mer to *mère*;[9]

— the transformation of Michoacan to Micheline Kao who, in a way, was my first wife, even though we were not officially married. These superimposed background worlds make up a sort of glass palace at the bottom of which I perceive an abyss-zone at point [B], through the doubts, the missing items; the caesure relating to the act of forgetting the car.

The Existential territory of Mer remains closed like a bicycle circuit. Nevertheless, it is cracked: an abyss lives tangentially in it. I can only apprehend this abyss from the exterior, metaphorically or metonymically, through proper names that are stuck onto it associatively.

It is the second harmonic core that will enable me to define it better. It results from the application of the synapse constituted by component III as the second machinic component and the fifth emotive component. The Renault-BMW passage causes me to transit a regressive/mortiferous world towards a type of initiation course. I proceed down Gay-Lussac Street, first on foot, then by bicycle. It is obvious that this street evokes "homosexuality," yet the memories of the violent demonstrations of 1968 are stronger. I arrived too late the morning of May 10th, after the battle, to look for injured friends. Anyway, I felt uncomfortable during the street fighting; I was inhibited in terms of physical confrontation with the police. Thus, here we can find a two fold matrix of the coarté effect: inhibition when faced with combat and when faced with homosexuality.

Yet, this inhibition has an evolution; since the background worlds here cease to be stacked one on the other as in a mirror. Instead, they create a processual chain at the meeting with the Ecologists, the dispute with Jospin and, in endless continuity, the memory of my ethnological friends: Cartry, Clastres, Adler etc., and of the first psychotic patient I had in therapy—who I took to visit them on a motorcycle, exactly the opposite side of Gay-Lussac

Street (Monsier le Prince Street), etc. And, I must add Lucien Sebag[10] and another dream that took place opposite the university classroom at Mutalité. In this dream, the theme of death and music was intermingled. In essence, it was an entire world of diverse life activities made up of creative machinic links.

It is the semiotic diversification with the grapheme game and the phoneme around A.D., as in a crossword puzzle, that allows me to articulate and differentiate the imaginary blockage that is provoked by the territorialized component of Mer. Nevertheless, a residual reterritorialization appears with the jealousy coarté effect. Throughout these various eras with Arlette Donati and A.D., though I was an avid believer in sexual liberation, I still became jealous whenever any of my partners took advantage of this liberation. This core of inhibition, which, with Arlette Donati, was present for a long time—causing me to look for her several times in my BMW, reappears in the ambivalence about Yasha and Gilles. Though, here, it is a neutral core, since accepted social behavior does not allow the problematic of jealousy in this situation.

A final analysis of the dream: beyond the fixing of native lands, the problematic of a desirous machine can start processual existential lines in motion. However, something continues to go wrong: a forgotten item, an inhibition, a lack of consistency, etc. Under these conditions, it is better not to be too abrupt and certainly not to forget the self-analysis of the slip of the tongue and of the forgotten item within the dream. This is the only way to conjure up a death fear, characterized both as essential and superficial, by the gesture of a dying father handing me a fifty-franc bill.

17

FOUR TRUTHS FOR PSYCHIATRY

Obviously, the stagnation in which psychiatry and psychological movements have been mired for a number of years is not independent of contemporary economic and social convolutions. The protest and counterculture movements of the '60s must have appeared, for those most intensely involved, to be the first fruits of profound transformations that would gradually win over the entire social fabric. But nothing like this has happened, although history may still have some surprises in store for us. In the meantime, it must be admitted that the repeated crises of the last few years vitally concern these movements. One can even wonder about whether they are one of their essential "objectives." Whatever were the hopes, the utopias, the innovative experiments of that period, only a hazy memory remains: touching to some, hateful and vengeful to others, and indifferent to most.

This does not mean, however, that the alternative undertakings and movements have been definitively swept out of the way or have lost all legitimacy. New generations have picked up the baton, with perhaps fewer dreams, more realism, less mythic and theoretic scaffolding... For my part, I remain convinced that the problems of that period, far from having been "surpassed," still influence the future of our societies. A choice must be made for a reorientation of human ends involving all kinds of reappropriations of individual and collective territories, to stemming the race towards a collective murderous and suicidal madness, whose indices and symptoms are amply visible in current events.

It is in this context that we should reevaluate the attempts to transform psychiatry in the past decades. Let us summarize the most salient: the first version of the movement for institutional therapy, under the impetus of people like Daumezon, Le Guillant, Bonnafé, etc., led to a humanization of the old psychiatric hospitals, with the beginnings of community healthcare in psychiatry, day clinics, protected workshops, home visits, etc. The second version of institutional psychotherapy, redefined by François Tosquelles, Jean Oury and Gt Psy, used psychoanalytical concepts and practices, different movements of alternatives to psychiatry, etc. Each of these carried with it a part of the truth, but none of them was in a position to confront the upheavals that were simultaneously occurring throughout society. Beyond their particular contributions—which I would be the last to underestimate—the question of a radical conversion of psychiatry, what in other registers could be called a change in paradigm, has always been avoided.

I am not, of course, in a position to set up an exhaustive cartography, but I would like to present some facts that constitute the necessary conditions for any progressive "boost" to this rather neglected domain. It appears to me that there are four levels of intervention, to which are indissolubly associated four truths, relating to:

1) the transformation of existing "heavy" facilities;

2) the strengthening of alternative experiments;

3) the mobilization of a wide range of social partnerships around these themes;

4) the development of new methods of analyzing unconscious subjectivity, on individual and collective levels.

We must stay clear of the dogmatic blindness and corporatist bickerings that have for so long hampered our reflections and practices. In this area, as in many others, one truth does not drive away another: there is no universal recipe; no single remedy can be applied in a single fashion. The first criterion is the possibility of involving social operators willing to be responsible at every level.

I will now try to show with a few examples how recent attempts to change psychiatry involved at least one of the "four truths," and how they fell short for not having engaged them all concurrently—which would have required the existence of collective arrangements capable of translating them into action.

In the years following World War II, what has been called the "first psychiatric revolution" led to noticeable improvements in the material and moral conditions of a number of French psychiatric hospitals. This would not have been possible without the conjunction of the following factors:

1) A strong current of progressive psychiatrists.

2) A powerful majority of psychiatric nurses who fought to change the conditions of mental asylum-institutions, for example with the creation of special training programs promoting active methods.

3) A nucleus of functionaries at the Ministry of Health who were working in the same directions.

Thus the particular conditions for intervening effectively on the first level of "heavy" facilities were in fact met. But none of the other three levels were engaged (that of alternatives, that of social mobilization, that of the analysis of subjectivity) even though they were often debated among the community hospitals that resulted in effect from this movement.

Community experiences in England, which developed in the wake of Maxwell Jones, then Ronald Laing, David Cooper and the Philadelphia Association, had a certain social intelligence and an undeniable social analytic sensibility in their favor. But they received no support from either the state or from what is traditionally called the left, so they were not able to gather strength to evolve.

If we now turn to the experience of La Borde, a clinic with about one hundred beds (over which Jean Oury has been the principal coordinator for some thirty years, and to which I remain principally attached) one finds a quite extraordinary institutional machinery, working as a "collective analyzer," which I consider tremendously interesting. Exterior support was no less wanting in this case, although in different modalities than those of the preceding examples. Let us just say that this clinic, although recognized by the social security system, has always been systematically marginalized from an economic point of view and, paradoxically, rather than improving since the arrival of the socialist government, its situation has only gotten worse. While some people treat it like a historical monument, it remains more vital than ever. It has been sustained by never flagging popular support, as the participation of more than a hundred French and international trainees and visiting practitioners attest to each year. And yet it remains isolated.

Still, this experiment could only have achieved its goal through a proliferating network of alternative initiatives. One question it implicitly raises concerns the role of hospitalization. Obviously it is urgent to put an end to all methods of incarceration. But this does not mean that it should be abandoned in every respect. For a number of "mental dissidents," reinsertion into what are called the normal structures of society is out of the question. In this regard, it is time to dispel the myth that returning patients to the family, or maintaining them there by force, or through guilt, is the solution. Other modalities of individual and collective life can be invented, and it is there that an immense space for research and experimentation opens up.

I could enumerate other examples that put the disharmony of the four levels of intervention into relief. But I will content myself with one illustration, involving Psychiatria Democratica and the work of Franco Basaglia, whose memory I here commemorate. This movement was the first to intensely explore the potentialities offered by fieldwork when it is associated with a mobilization of the left, public awareness and systematic pressure on public authorities.

Unfortunately, and for a long time this was a point of contention between my friend Franco Basaglia and myself, it was the analytical dimension that was toned down, sometimes even vehemently refused.

Why, you may ask, this insistence, like a leitmotif, on the fourth analytic dimension? Should it really be considered as one of the principle touchstones of our problem? Without expatiating at great length, I'd say that with it comes a healing of the leprosy of our psychiatric institutions and, beyond this, of the welfare system, with the hopeless serialization of individuals that it induces not only on its "users," but also on its therapeutic, technical and administrative "practitioners." Fostering large-scale institutional analyses would require permanent work on the subjectivity produced through all kinds of connections to aid, education, etc.

A certain type of subjectivity, which I would call capitalistic, is overtaking the whole planet: an equalized subjectivity, with standardized fantasies and massive consumption of infantilizing reassurances. It causes every kind of passivity, degeneration of democratic values, collective racist impulses… Today it is massively secreted by the media, community centers and alleged cultural institutions. It not only involves conscious ideological formations, but also collective unconscious emotions. Psychiatry and the various psychiatric and psychological domains have a special responsibility in relation to it, whether they underwrite its current forms, or try to turn it into non-alienating directions. Alternatives to psychiatry and psychoanalysis are important on that account. They will have no real impact unless they manage to ally themselves with other movements bent on changing subjectivity in various ways, i.e., through ecological, ethnic, feminist, antiracist and, more generally, through alternative practices that open up positive perspectives for the widening mass of the "marginal" and the unprotected.

But this implies at the same time that parties, groups, communities, collectives and individuals willing to work in that direction are capable of self-transforming, and stop tracing their organizations and their unconscious representations on repressive models. To do so, they would have to act not only as political and social instruments in relation to themselves and to the outside, but as collective analytical arrangements of these unconscious processes. Everything can be invented.

This is pretty much what we have been trying to do in the Alternative Network to Psychiatry. Since its creation in 1975 it has periodically organized international debates between the most diverse, most heterogeneous components of the psychiatric and psychological professions and alternative movements. Many other comparable efforts exist. I am thinking particularly of the encounters in mental ecology, organized by the Topia Group of Bologna, led by Franco Berardi. What is more than ever at stake is the right to singularity, to freedom of individual and collective creation away from technocratic conformism, postmodernist arrogance and the leveling of subjectivity in the wake of new technologies.

These are some of the elements I hope to bring into the debate. Now, in conclusion, permit me to make these comments.

It was certainly of the utmost importance to challenge the old legislation, and any backward step towards reinstating former asylum structures would be totally reactionary and absurd. If specific hospital rest-facilities must be reestablished—and I think this is absolutely necessary—they should be conceived as sites for evolving research and experimentation. Reimplanting them within general hospitals would obviously be counterindicated.

Only new forms of social mobilization will help mentalities to evolve and dissipate the menace of "anti-crazy" racism. In the final analysis initiative and decisions in this area do not belong to traditional political formations, tied up as they generally are in their bureaucratic choke-collar, but to the reinvention of a new type of social and alternative movement.

18

THE SCHIZOANALYSES

I needed your help to clarify my ideas. I noticed—and this is, incidentally, part of what I want to address here—that, in some situations, it was not possible to carry out such a clarification without the help of a *collective assemblage of enunciation*. Otherwise the ideas fall from your hands! As of quite some time now, I have been looking for a support polygon to define what has been running around in my head. I don't know if all of us here will constitute such a polygon. We will soon find out! We had started to put one together, Mony Elkaïm[1] and I, during previous discussions; only, it was in an episodic fashion, always "hurriedly," behind the scenes during meetings and symposia, where I was led to discuss systemist references in family therapy. But, until now, we hadn't really ever given ourselves the means to tie these questions to the critical work that I have undertaken, moreover, with Gilles Deleuze, on psychoanalytic theory and practice.

What I am proposing today, after some clearing of the ground, after something of a "tabula rasa," is to find out what still stands amid the psychoanalytic rubble, what deserves to be rethought through the use of other theoretical scaffoldings, if possible less reductionist than those of Freudians and Lacanians.

I obviously hope that this seminar will allow for the most wide-ranging and open debates. But I have to warn you straightaway that my positions will sometimes be "debatable" only with difficulty. Not that I intend to impose them! But they will venture onto a territory that is, let's say, solitary, where it will be a bit difficult for me to make myself understood in an exhaustive manner. It goes without saying that at issue here is neither pedagogy nor scientific confrontation, but exclusively the support for the work of each of us, of an assemblage of enunciation that should permit, if all goes well, to expand our respective processes of elucidation. With the hope that these will be subjected, along the way, to intersections, cross checks that will permit them to develop into a rhizome.

This seminar on "the *schizoanalyses*" will thus find its own scheme only if it itself begins functioning on a level that I would qualify as "meta-modelisation." Put in other words, if it allows us to better grasp our own assemblages of enunciation—although it would be better to say: the assemblages of enunciation to which we are adjacent. On this subject, I am eager to repeat that I have never conceived of schizoanalysis as a new special field that would be called to find a home in the psych. domain. Its goals should be, in my view, both more modest and bigger. More modest because, if it is to exist one day, it is because it already exists *a little bit everywhere*, in an embryonic form, under different modalities, and it has no need for an institutional foundation in due form. Bigger, inasmuch as it is cut out, in my view, to become a reading discipline of *other systems* of modelization. Not as a general model, but as a deciphering instrument of modelization pragmatics in numerous domains. One could object that the limit between a model and a meta-model does not always show up as a stable border. And that, in a sense, subjectivity is always more or less the work of meta-modelisation (in the view proposed here: *transference of modelization*, transversal passages between abstract machines and existential territories). The main thing is then a displacement of the analytic accent that consists in making it derive from systems of *utterance* and from preformed subjective *structures*, towards *assemblages of enunciation* capable of forging new reading coordinates and "bringing into being" new representations and proposals.

Schizoanalysis will thus be essentially off-center in relation to other professionalized psych. practices, with their corporations, societies, schools, didactic initiations, "pass," etc. Its provisional definition could be: *the analysis of the effect* (incidence) *of assemblages of enunciation on semiotic and subjective productions, in a given problematic context.* I will come back to these notions of "problematic context," scene, and "bringing into being." For now, I will be satisfied to point out that they can refer to things as different as a clinical picture, an unconscious fantasy, a daytime fantasy, an aesthetic production, a micropolitical fact... The key here is the idea of an *assemblage of enunciation,* and of an existential circumscription, which implies the deployment of intrinsic references—we could also say of a process of self-organization or singularization.

Why this return, like a leitmotiv, to *assemblages of enunciation*? In order to avoid getting bogged down, as much as possible, in the concept of the "Unconscious." In order not to reduce the facts of subjectivity to drives, affects, intra-subjective instances, and inter-subjective relations. Evidently, this sort of thing will have a place in schizoanalytic preoccupations, but only as a component and always in certain specific cases. We will observe, for instancee, that there are assemblages of enuciation not composed of semiological components, assemblages that do not have subjective components, others that do not have consciential components... The assemblage of enunciation will thus be led to "exceed" the problematic of the individuated subject, of the thinking monad consciously delimited, of the faculties of the soul (understanding, will...) in the way that they have traditionally been understood. I think it is important to underline straightaway that we will always be dealing with ensembles; at the beginning, equally material and/or semiotic, individual and/or collective, actively machinic and/or passively fluctuating.

The question then becomes that of the status of these components of assemblage, which find themselves thus "overlapping," between radically heterogeneous domains. I had said—I no longer remember where—that we would like to construct a science where we could mix dust cloths and napkins[2] with other even more different things; where we couldn't even group dust cloths and napkins together under the same rubric, but where we would be ready to accept with good grace that dust cloths become differentiated through singular becomings, along with a procession of contextual repercussions, where we could be dealing with a bar owner drying glasses with a dust cloth, as much as with the military launching a "clean-up" (*coup de torchon*) on a pocket of resistance. From a classical psychoanalytic perspective, we only take this sort of contextuality into account in terms of its signifying effects, and never as a referent generator of pragmatic effects in the given social and material institutional fields. It is this micropolitics of meaning that seems to me to have been turned upside down. The presumed analytic effect no longer resides in a derivation of semiologically interpretable chains, but in an—a-signifying—mutation of the "universal context," that is to say, of the constellation of the implicated registers of references. Collective and/or individual assemblages of enunciation are then not only full-blown objects of analytic investigation, but also equally privileged means of access to these objects, in such a way that the problematic of the enunciation transference starts, as a priority, on the problematic of imagos and structures allegedly constitutive of subjectivity. In a contingent manner, certain assemblages are put in the position of "analyzer"[3] of the formations of the unconscious. It is of little importance if these analyzers are conscious of their "mission" or invested by other authorities in order to occupy this position. An analytic assemblage, under these conditions, can size itself differently, depending on whether it is embodied:

— by an individual, Freud, for example, who invents psycho-analysis;

— by a sociologically delimited group, for example, a gang of youths that is "defined" by potentialities of a ghetto;

— by more diffuse social phenomena, such as mutations of collective sensibility or uncontrolled movements of opinion;

— by a pre-personal practice, a style, a creative mutation that engages an individual or a group without either him or it being aware of it.

(All of these scenarios, and many others capable of combining in multiple ways). Thus, the schizoanalytic approach will never limit itself to an interpretation of "given facts"; it will be interested, much more fundamentally, in the "giving" to assemblages that promote the concatenation of affects of meaning and pragmatic affects. As they also do not escape this general plasticity of assemblages, the "analyzers" don't appear as pre-established systems; they never claim to institute themselves as legitimate structures of enunciation, as is the case with typical therapy. Not only because there will not be any normalized schizoanalytic protocol, but a new fundamental rule, an "anti-rule rule" will impose a constant putting into question of analyzer assemblages, in close relation to their feedback effects on the analytic data.

All of this feedback, which is negative when it leads to a simple rebalancing of the assemblage, and positive when it generates processes of splitting, if not catastrophes, makes up the analytic material par excellence. How does an assemblage take the relay of another assemblage in order to "manage" a given situation? How can an analytic assemblage, or so-called analytic assemblage conceal another? How do several assemblages enter into relationship and what becomes of it? How can we explore, in a context that seems utterly blocked, the potentialities for constituting new assemblages? How can we "help," if need be, relations of production, of proliferation, the micropolitics of these new assemblages? This is the sort of question that schizoanalysis will be asked to raise. This work of subjectivity—in the sense that we work iron, or up and down the scales of the piano, or that we work through the fruitful moments of existence in the Proustian "Remembrance"—is here identified with the production of a referent, or, more precisely, with a *meta-modelization of trans-assemblage relations*. Far from corresponding with what we ordinarily understand as subjectivity, it no longer relates to the supposedly subtle and ineffable essence of a subject in search of a vertiginous and impossible accord with itself, with God as sole witness. Schizoanalytic subjectivity is set up at the intersection of sign fluxes and machinic fluxes, at the crossroads of facts of meaning, material and social facts, and, above all, of their transformations, resulting from their different modalities of assemblage. It is through the latter that it loses its aspect of human territoriality and is projected towards singularization processes that are both the most original and the most futuristic—animal, vegetables, cosmic becomings, immature becomings, multivalent gender, incorporeal becomings... By means of this subjectivity, without entirely ceasing to be a "thinking reed," man is currently adjacent to a reed "that thinks for him," to a machinic phylum that leads him well beyond his previous possibilities.

Archaic forms of enunciation rested mainly on speech and direct communication, whereas new assemblages increasingly resort to informative media fluxes that rest on increasingly machinic channels (the machines in question here are not exclusively of the technological order, they are also scientific, social, aesthetic, etc.), which explode the old individual and collective subjective territories from all sides. Whereas territorialized enunciation was logo-centric and implied a personalized mastery of the ensembles that it discursivized, deterritorialized enunciation, which can be seen as machino-centric, leaves it up to non-human memories and procedures in order to deal with semiotic complexes that, to a large extent, escape a direct consciential control.

But we won't content ourselves with such a simple dichotomy, which would run the risk of being far too reductive. In view of the preceding considerations, we are already naturally led to decline a variety of modalities of assemblages of enunciation, depending on which components of semiotization, subjectivation, and consciential-isation happen to prevail or not (this list being always likely to expand, depending on descriptive needs).

—non-semiotic assemblages

The stigmergic constructions of bees or termites offer us our first example due to the extremely elaborate forms that they end up developing, based on "modular coding" which appears to be neither semiotic, nor subjective or consciential. With the case of human enunciation, similar systems, such as endocrinal systems of regulation, can be led to play a decisive roll within assemblages whose semiotic components they, to some extent, suspend. In particular, I am thinking of the likely role of an endorphine-based self-addiction in the "hardening" of certain sado-masochistic situations, or in acute forms of mental anorexia.

—non-subjective semiotic assemblages

For instance, the psychosomatic clinical pictures related to the "character armor" studied by Wilhelm Reich. Subjective representations fall "to the side" of the somatic semiotisation.

—non-conscientized semiotic, subjective assemblages

For instance, assemblages pertaining to human ethology, which deal with processes of learning through unconscious stamps, delimitations of territory, behaviors of welcoming, parade, submission, hostility, etc. I imagine that a Lacanian who had the patience to follow me until now, would certainly object that everything that I'm talking about is well and good but has absolutely nothing to do with the Unconscious, the true psychoanalytic unconscious, that we could not conceive of outside of the snares of language… We all know that song! To this, I would respond that schizoanalytic assemblages have the most vital interest in reductionist structures of the oedipal triangle and symbolic castration sort, to which, in fact, a certain capitalization of subjectivity lead, in the context of what I would call capitalist subjectivity, except that this does not in any way exempt them from dealing with other productions of subjectivity in all the domains of psychopathology and anthropology, and with respecting their specific characters. In this sense, the claim of schizoanalysis, is really, I repeat myself, to set itself up as the meta-modelizing assemblage of all these heterogeneous domains that it will treat as so much "optional subject matter." Our point of departure will thus be the most extensive hypothesis, that of the existence, for man, of an unconscious domain that puts on an equal footing facts of meaning supported by structures of representation and language and systems on an equal footing—all very different from each other—of coding, modeling, tracing, imprinting… related to organic, social, economic, etc. components. Bringing the phenomena of subjectivation into play, that is, the establishment of lived territories, taken on as such in a relation of delimitation with an objectal world and alter egos, will only be occasional, optional. In other terms, neither the question of the subject, nor that of the linguistic signifier will necessarily be at the center of the problematics posed in this unconscious domain. The same holds for the question of the conscience. Various processes of conscientialisation following and/or superimposing themselves on each other can be brought into play here. In order to illustrate these sorts of connections (*branchements*) and disconnections (*débranchements*), a good example is provided by the driving of cars. It is not out of the ordinary, on the highway, for a person to start daydreaming in a pseudo-somnolent state? In reality, the subject is not sleeping; he is allowing many conscious systems to function at the same time, of which some are toned down and others suddenly become of primary importance. This is what happens when a road signal, an accident, or a passenger speaking up, makes the driver switch back to a state of hyper-vigilance. The assemblage of enunciation, in the enlarged sense I am giving it here, thus travels through several levels of machinic enslavement (*asservissement*) (to use an already old notion from cybernetics). Thus, instead of constantly returning to the same supposedly founding structures, to the same archetypes, to the same "mathemes," schizoanalytic meta-modelization will instead prefer to map (*cartographier*) the compositions of the unconscious, continent topics, in their connection to social formations, technology, arts, sciences, etc. Even when it will happen to bring to light some unconscious scenarios, based, for instance, on ego-organizing, per-sonological, conjugalist, familialist, or domestic formulas, it will never do it, I repeat, with the aim of defining a structural prototype.

Let's pause to consider some of the implications of the "split-off" (*décollage*) between the conscience and subjectivity in the manner in which we have started to consider it. I initially thought that it would be necessary to differentiate between:

— an absolute unconscious, at a molecular level, which would radically escape all representations and whose expressions would belong solely to the field of a-signifying figures;[4]

— a relative unconscious at a molar level, which would set itself up, on the contrary, in more or less stable representations. I then became afraid of falling prey, for my part, to a topical paralysis of psychic instances like the one that led Freud to separate the Unconscious and the Conscious (linked to the Pre-Conscious) into opposing sides and then, later, the Id and the Ego (with its attendant elements), or which led Lacan to erect a symbolic order as the framework of the Real and the Imaginary.

Already, upon first examination, the denomination "molecular unconscious" appears shaky. In fact, this type of assemblage is perfectly capable of putting up with the existence of consciential components. The molecular processes that are at work in a hysteric or obsessive neurosis are inseparable from a particular type of consciousness and even hyper-consciousness, with respect to the latter. An oneiric or a delirious assemblage, while operating from an a-signifying material—all of which doesn't prevent it from conveying as well images and signifying chains, but from them it only holds on to what it can treat as a-signifying figures[5]—themselves consist of modes of idiosyncrastic conscientialization. I don't think that we would have anything to gain from hoping to equip all of these instances with a single consciential essence that would be always self-identical. Gradually, we come to borderline-states of consciousness, with mystic experiences of rupture with the world, with catatonia, or even—why not—non-localizable organic tensions or more or less deep comas. And thus, all the instances of enunciation can be concurrently conscious and unconscious. It's a matter of intensity, of proportion, of reach. There is no consciousness or unconsciousness that isn't relative to incorporeal Universes of reference which authorize composite assemblages, superimpositions, slippages (*glissements*), and disjunctions. And we sense, that on their tangent, must exist an absolute conscience which could coincide exactly with our absolute consciousness, constitutive of a non-thetic presence to oneself, apart from any reference to alterity or society.

X: But is this absolute unconscious biological?

Félix Guattari: Yes, among other things!

J-C. P.: I was wondering if—with regard to this machinic molecular aspect you weren't returning to what you attributed to desire a few years ago? To something, really, thoroughly heterogeneous, chaotic, rhizomatic, etc.; whose digitalization—whose markings, if you like, by means of linguistic-type code—would release what Lacan calls the unconscious. That which allows him to say—to himself, but also to those who are working under him with psychotics—to say that "schizophrenia doesn't have an unconscious." Is it, in some sense, the same partition that is drawn between what is held in the folds of a signification or significance system and what isn't, i.e., everything else, the essential?

Félix Guattari: There is something in the way in which you formulated your question that bothers me a little. I'm not invested in reestablishing an opposition between the primary process and secondary elaboration, above all if this opposition has to be founded—as in the second Freudian topic (Id, Ego, Superego)—on the idea that the passage from the one to the other would correspond to a change of levels of the different modes of differentiation, with chaos on the side of the primary process and structuration on the side of the secondary. This is not—as, in fact, you emphasize—because we don't have a digitalized, binarized access to the molecular unconscious, that we, for all of that, sink together with into a world of irremediable disorder and entropy.

This brings me back to the issue of desire. Yes! It's true that I want to escape today from a number of misunderstandings of, let's say, the economic order, in the sense in which Freud understood it and which developed after *Anti-Oedipus* around ideas such as flux and break of flux (*coupure de flux*). In fact, we nevertheless stressed the deterritorialized machinic dimensions of desire, which escaped the habitual ensemblist coordinates (thus our insistence on paradoxical categories such as the Body Without Organs). But this way of presenting desire was perhaps not sufficiently demarcated from the idea of "flat," territorialized fluctuations, authorizing references to an economy in equilibrium, shut off in itself.

Moreover, this would be one of the principal objectives of this seminar to attempt to clarify how this category of deterritorialization can prevent us from transforming notions such as those of subjectivity, conscience, signification (*signifiance*)... into transcendental entities impermeable to concrete situations. The most abstract and the most radically incorporeal references are in direct connection with the real; they travel through the most contingent fluxes and territories. They are in no way safe from historical influences or cosmogenetic mutations. In short, the signifier does not transcend the libido. (We could, with respect to this, easily show how Lacan progressively substituted that one for this one). In some contexts, meaning can be massively opposed to material and signaletic fluxes that are conceived of as essentially passive. However, in other contexts, meaning can originate following a "machinic" of fluctuations that has broken loose (really or potentially) from the strata and homeostasis. It is this processual option, this refusal of a generalized economy of equivalences, this choice of the "clinamen," that led us to challenge fixed cartographies, the unvariables by right in the domain of subjectivity—even when they in fact appear in certain areas of assemblage, as is the case with oedipal triangulation in the field of capitalistic production.

We thus decided not to consider situations other than through the angle of crossroads of assemblages (*carrefours d'agencements*), which secrete, up to a certain point, their own coordinates of meta-modelization. Admittedly, a crossroads can impose connections, but it is not a fixed constraint; it can be bypassed, it can lose its connective power when some of its components lose their consistency. Let's try to illustrate this point. A singer loses her mother. The following week she also loses two octaves of her range; she starts to sing out of tune, her interpretive gifts seem to suddenly go to the dogs. This woman's singing was set up at the intersection of multiple assemblages of which the majority, of course, go beyond the domain (*circonscription*) of her person. The enunciation component that grafted itself onto her relationship with her mother underwent the trial of death. All of this is in no way synonymous, far from it, with her extinction. In fact, the unactual part of herself—the past that one can't return to—having taken first place over that part of herself open to possibilities, a representation of her mother, erratic and vaguely menacing is put into circulation. This image of death, sheltered from any reality test, brings about petrification. As Freud wrote, the subject clings to the lost object.[6] In this particular case, however, the only manifest consequence of this semiotic "contraction" seems to confine itself to the vocal part of the musical activity. It is conceivable that a more dogged exploration would have revealed other effects. But was such an investigation absolutely necessary? It's not clear, because in cases like these, we must always fear "inventing" new symptoms after the transference and the interpretation, either by exaggerating the elements of an etiological tableau which seems to "fit well" or, which often amounts to the same thing, when the subject himself brings you the suitable symptoms on a platter. In this case, it's a matter of keeping oneself clear of the temptation to root "the work of mourning" in a difficulty, for the libido, to find itself an object of substitution. Here as elsewhere, the description in terms of object, rather than in terms of assemblage of enunciation, presents the major disadvantage of prohibiting the shedding of light on fields of non-programmed possibilities. Where Freud saw only two options—either the slow and melancholy liquidation of the libido invested in the lost object, or, in the case of an extreme fixation, a "hallucinating psychosis of desire"[7]—we should be ready to welcome reorganizations of assemblage escaping without complex the curses of primary identification or the relation of "oral incorporation." And it is precisely what has happened with this singer who, if you allow me the expression, stood firm (*encaissé le coup*), conquering even, on this occasion, several new degrees of liberty and putting herself from now on in control of her superego in clearly a much more flexible manner. The loss of consistency of a component will not have been followed, this particular time, by a chain reaction of new inhibitions. It will instead have served as a sensitive plate, as a developer, as an alarm bell. But of what exactly? That is precisely the question! To which, actually, it is best not to answer too quickly. As there is perhaps no answer to it, strictly speaking. An a-signifying sign—the restriction on vocal performances—marks the halt of something without forbidding, as the context makes clear, that other things intervene. Great! This is already something! Certain paths marked out for a long time: singing, the moralizing surcoding of the mother, are experiencing a pragmatic transformation. Should these facts be considered liabilities and put down in record in the column of lacks and deficits: Nothing is less certain! But nothing is determined either! As a lot of things can depend on this inscription. It must be clear that all transferential induction, even the most subtle, the most roundabout, which would give us to assume the existence, behind this symptomatic manifestation, of a guilt of oedipal origin could have devastating effects or, at the very least, bring us back to the depressive tableau which is "normally" expected under such circumstances. It seems less risky to me to think about the material qualities of this component of expression, which perhaps allowed her to avoid further damage. Is it because of the presence of such a "luxurious" component that the song did not allow a preventative alarm to be raised and to suggest a bifurcation? From then on what was called to vegetate under the guise of inhibition was transformed into the beginning of a singularization process.

X: Do you think that, without the song, something else could have occurred?

Félix Guattari: Maybe she would have lost other types of octaves, in other sorts of registers! But nothing can be depended on in this domain. Everything here is a matter, I repeat, of the threshold of consistency, transformation quanta, of the possibility of concurrent effects. Some of the mother's facialist traits (*traits de visagéité*) broke free from her face, deterritorialized from the coordinates of the superego, in order to work on their own behalf, along other lines of possibilities, other universe constellations. Their surveillance frowns got stuck on the extremes of the scale where they found a sort of altar on which the sacrificial offerings would not be too costly. But perhaps this sort of description, which has more in common with the myths and the tales of the Gourmantche or the Warlpiri, is less secure than the framing, within "pre-fabricated" intra-psychic systems, of typified complexes and structuralized instances?

J-C. P.: Are you thinking about theories of hysteria?

Félix Guattari: Yes, of course! We could bring out the famous "pharyngeal lump," the "appearances and disappearances" of Kleinian objects, the rupture of identification consecutive to melancholic introjection and—why not?—the desintrication of the death drive.

J-C. P.: Ultimately, what you are saying is that you would like to leave open the possibility, not to interpret, but to articulate differently planes as seemingly far apart from each other as the concrete phonological voice, the musical voice as abstract fact and, for example, the family structure. This would involve venturing the hypothesis about completely different connections than those that we were able to imagine until now.

The category of deterritorialization should thus allow us to separate the problematic of consciousness—and, as a consequence, of the unconscious—from the representation of the ego and the unity of the person. The idea of a totalizing, indeed totalitarian, consciousness ("I am master of myself as of the universe")[8] takes part in a foundational myth of capitalistic subjectivity. In truth, there are only different processes of conscientializtation, resulting from the deterritorialization of existential territories which are themselves numerous and tangled up with each other. However, in their turn, these different instruments for forging a for-itself (*pour-soi*) and singling out a relation to the world distinct from the in-itself (*en-soi*) and alter egos, will not be able to acquire the consistency of an existential monad, unless they manage to express themselves on/through/by means of(?) a second dimension of deterritorialization that I would describe as energetic discursivation. Here we come to the following schema, which, to a certain degree, anticipates points that we will only address later.

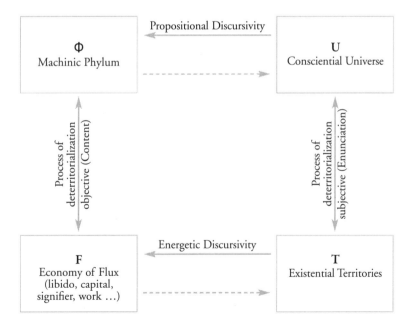

Four functers **F.T.Φ.U.**, through the means of their relations of reciprocal presupposition (indicated in abscissa) and of their relations of composition (indicated in ordinate) exhibit four domains:

—material and signalectic Flux

—existential Territories

—abstract machinic Phylum

—incorporeal Universes (qualified as consciential in this particular case)

By relying on these, we hope to succeed in creating a cartography of the configurations of subjectivity, of desire, instinctual energy, and of the different modalities of discourse and consciousness related to them, without further recourse to traditional systems of somatic infrastructure, instinctual basis, determinism founded on need and lack, behavioral conditioning, etc. To that end, entities pertaining to these four domains will not have a permanent identity. They will only support their own configurations through the relations that they maintain with them. They will be expected to change state and status according to the whole assemblage. In other terms, they will not be defined by a fixed topic, and the task of "managing" their modelization will be assigned to them. In order to be in the position of supporting the kind of crossing of orders that classical thought has always tried to keep separate, these functers must, moreover, authorize the setting up of composition laws between the two sets of categories, the actual and the virtual, the possible and the real. The crossing of their matrices is illustrated in Figure 2:

	Actual	Virtual
Possible	**Φ**: Phylum of the actual possible	**U**: Universe of the virtual possible
Real	**F**: Flux of the actual real	**T**: Territories of the virtual real

All the while keeping in mind considerations to come, we put forward, from the present moment, that the relations of inter-entitary presupposition coming into scope inscribe themselves according to the coordinates of objective and subjective deterritorialization, will not be able to maintain the Flux and the Territories of the real on an equal footing with the Phylum and the Universe of the possible—the latter two envelop and subsume the former, so much so that the real of the possible prevails over the possible of the real. In these conditions, the Phylum will constitute, in a way, the integrals of the Flows and the Universes, the integrals of the Territories. (Fig. 3).

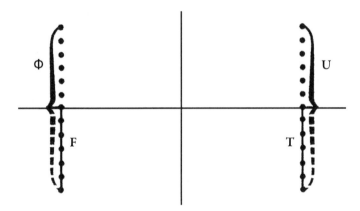

But haven't we thus secretly reestablished relations of transcendence between the possible and the real? Not really, insofar as, as we will soon establish, a synaptic game of extension of the assemblages in the sense of deterritorialization will leave open the possibility of a permutation of position of the constitutive entities of signifying realities and signified possibles.

Although it is always tricky to venture into the domain of Freudian filiations—the majority of psychoanalysts, for over fifty years now, having claimed authority from the work of Freud as if from a revealed text—it doesn't seem like a useless exercise to try to locate how the present attempt to refound the unconscious on deterritorialization takes its place within these filiations, and how it differs from them. Freud's first concern was to make psychology scientific by introducing *abstract quantities* into it.[9] It is this preoccupation that will disorganize the lawful ordering of the "faculties of the soul" of classical theories and bring about a deterritorialization of the psyche ending up in the promotion of an unconscious "scene," illocalisable within its ordinary phenomenological coordinates. However, while we could have expected that such an intrusion in the psychism would have had an essentially reductionist function, it was, conversely, the corollary of a genuine explosion of innovative interpretations of the discourse of hysteria, dreams, slips, wit, etc. It is a slight paradox to see thus coexisting mechanistic presuppositions directly inspired by the psychophysics of Fechner and the "psychophysicalism" of Helmholtz and Brüke, and an "abyssal" exploration whose adventurous character will have hardly an equivalent except with Dadaism and Surrealism. It all seems to indicate that the support that Freud took from the scientistic schemas of his epoch had given him self-confidence that allowed him to give free reign to his creative imagination. However the case, we certainly have to admit that his discovery of the processes of semiotic singularization of the unconscious —the famous "primary process"—would have quite a bit of difficulty in finding a home in the rigid associationist context that he was developing concurrently in the wake of his *Project for a Scientific Psychology* of 1895. Yet never did he cut off his connection with his initial neuronic models. (He will, for example, in the final edition of the *Traumdeutung* of 1929, hold onto his first reflexological professions of faith, with the consequence that the Unconscious and the Preconscious continue to find themselves sandwiched between perception and motricity).

The result of Freud's incessant comings and goings between an impenitent scientism and a lyric inventivity reminiscent of romanticism, is a series of reterritorializations carried out in reaction to the numerous projections of deterritorialization of the psyche. Here I will mention this phenomenon only with respect to a couple of concepts: that of the libido and that of the Unconscious.

The *libido* can be given two statuses: one of a processual energy that diverts heterogeneous systems far from their equilibrium, or that of a static energy working towards the stratification of psychic formations. Freud never succeeded in binding them together, even when he postulated the coexistence of an object libido and an Ego libido. We see things differently from our perspective; these two statuses cannot pertain to the hazards of an economic balance such as he proposed, but to fundamental micropolitical choices. The libido will thus find itself "denatured," deterritorialized; it will become a sort of abstract material of the possible. The generic choice will become either the deterritorialized option of the schizoanalysis of a *libido-phylum* (on the left axis in Figures 1 and 3) as integral of the transformational flows of desire (material and signaletic), either the reterritorialized option of a *libido-Flow* Freudianism, forming cysts first of all in the somatic part of drives (the thrust and the source, in contrast with the goal and the object), then put into psychogenetic stages in order to finally be left the prisoner of an intemporal face to face with an entropic death (Eros-Thanatos opposition).

For the *unconscious*, the generic choice will be: either to constitute itself as a *Universe* of reference of new (*inédit*) and unprecedented (*inouïs*) lines of alterity, of possibles and becomings (on the right axis of Figures 1 and 3), or to be a Territory-refuge for the repressed, held in check by the censor (in the Conscious-Preconscious system of the first topic) and by the Ego-Superego system (in the second topic).

Very early on, Freud left the first terrain to theoriticians like Jung who, by the way, hardly knew how to make use of it. On the other hand, he never stopped reterritorializing the Unconscious in different ways:

— on the spatial plane, as I just said, he circumscribed it by means of an instance which, in his second topic, that of the Id, finds itself emptied of all substance, reduced to an undifferentiated chaos.

— On a temporal plane, where with his discovery of the unexplored continent of infantile sexuality, he succeeded in the feat of conferring an historic dimension to the Unconscious discourse all the while removing from it the knowledge of the passing of time, and managed to outsmart the realist implications of the memory of the traumatisms of precocious seduction by territorializing them and by converting them into fantasmatic refrains (*ritournelles*), he lost all that he had gained, if I might say so, by reterritorializing the stages of libidinal maturation, and by periodizing a psychogenesis in a rigid fashion.

— Same reversal of situation with regard to the object of desire. At the time of the *Traumdeutung*, the object of desire appears in an ambiguous and rich manner. Like Albertine in Proust, "a many-headed goddess," (and probably a goddess of many genders as well), once again he escapes, to a certain extent, the binary and phallic capitalistic logics. For example, the Irma of the inaugural dream of the *Traumdeutung* is described as a "collective person" who gathers together a "generic image:"—the patient who is in question in the dream;—another woman that he would prefer to treat;—his own eldest daughter;—a child who is under his care at the hospital;—yet another woman;—finally, Madame Freud, in person ... Elsewhere, we will see that "localities are often treated as people." The object can then function as a "knot" of overdetermination, the "umbilic" of the dream, the "point at which it is linked to the unknown," and from which he makes lines of singularization proliferate. Deterritorialization will still gain some new ground through the exit of the libidinal object from its personological context in order to become "partial." From this point on, the door was open for other becoming: non human, animal, vegetable, cosmic, abstract machinic becomings... But the door was at once closed to all possible and imaginable ways, an exhaustive and typified list of the partial objects in question having been drawn up and made to serve as normative landmarks along the "obstacle course," which every subjectivity wishing to rise to the supreme stages of "oblative genitality" is supposed to get through, and as Freud's successors, with their "bad" and "good objects," and by moving from "object relations" to "transitional objects," then to objects "a," ended up turning the partial object into a general function stripped of all traits of singularity.

— The same goes for alterity, which Freud had nevertheless introduced as a requirement of truth in the most carefully guarded psychopathological pictures. In which it will also find itself reterritorialized by becoming prohibited from staying in the preoedipal relations supposedly fusional and structuralized into an initiatory complex of symbolic castration under the menacing eye of the Sphinx, and later transformed into the matheme "A" by Lacan.

To sum this up, the two "optional subject matters" of the Libido-Unconscious encounter/face-to-face could be represented in the following fashion:

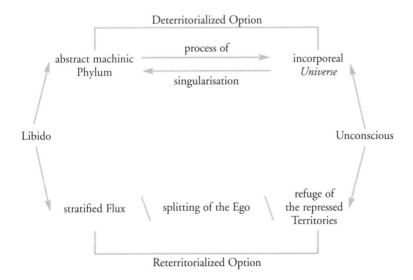

V

INTEGRATED WORLD

CAPITALISM

19

PLAN FOR THE PLANET

Nothing is less marginal than the problem of the marginal. It cuts across all times and places. Without getting to the marginal there can be no question of social transformation, of innovation, of revolutionary change. But why do Order, the Law and "Good Form" seem always to have to come out on top? Must we perhaps postulate the existence of a kind of semiotic entropy that is on the side of the dominant significations, and that is bound to rise in proportion as the fluxes turn back upon complete objects, closed territories, black holes that ensure a shut-in self-sufficiency and fix forever the hierarchization of social formations?

I do not trust metaphors from thermodynamics. There need not in theory be any need for a closed action/reaction circuit, a return to the original state. Both the laws of what calls itself the science of history and a-historical moral injunctions lack the micropolitical force that constitutes the true fabric of history. One must dismiss equally both terms of the alternative: free will *or* fate (whatever "dialectical" presentation one may offer of the latter!). One must rid oneself of all *a priori* values and norms: evaluation and transvaluation of the evolutive and involutive lines of the socius. There is no royal road to change, but there are many approach roads, starting

1) from the collective inflexion of the "preferential choices" inherent in the various components of an economico-ecologico-technologico-scientific rhizome.

2) from many possible "destinations," as they are semiotized by social forces of every sort and shape, marginal ones included.

Does this mean that a real revolution would be impossible today? No. Merely that a molar, visible, large-scale revolution—unless it is to be fascist/Stalinist—has become inseparable from the expansion and extension of molecular revolutions involving the economy of desire.

In other words: we must reject any one-way system of causality, any one-way street of history. The test of reality and truth, in this sphere, is part of a kind of inverse dialectic, exhausting the contradictions without ever resolving them, deriving from the false problems of the past, and from the dead-end situations of non-signifying residues, deterritorializing machinisms from which everything can start afresh, just when one thought that all was lost.

What tends to happen: the old stratified, totalitarian-totalized systems of the past, fixated on a transcendent reference-point, are losing their consistency. They can succeed in hanging onto their control of large social units only if

1) they concentrate their power;

2) they miniaturize their instruments of coercion.

Of the *n* possible courses that events may take, here are two extreme possibilities:

1) The consolidation and stabilization of an *integrated world capitalism*. This new type of capitalism results from transformations and mutual adjustments between monopoly capitalism and the various forms of State capitalism. Within a single world system, it integrates all the different elements of class and caste societies based on exploitation and social segregation. With its tentacles spreading all over the world, its centers of decision-making tend to develop a certain autonomy in relation to the national interests of the great powers, and to constitute a complicated network that can no longer be located in any one political area (networks of energy

complexes, military/industrial complexes and so on). The *modus operandi* of this new type of capitalism involves a constant reinforcement of control by the mass media.

2) A proliferation of *fringe groups, minorities and autonomist movements* (both new and established), leading to a flowering of particular desires (individual and/or collective) and the appearance of new forms of social grouping that will take over from the power-formations of the nation-States.

1. Stabilization of Integrated World Capitalism

Suppose the following things all happen:
— an increase in world population
— the gradual cutting-off of the flows of energy and raw materials
— the speeding-up of the concentration of machines and information systems

Then, in the framework of this first hypothesis, there could follow:

A RESHAPING OF CLASS ANTAGONISMS IN THE DEVELOPED COUNTRIES

— A relative reduction of the number of jobs in the sectors of industry on which the profit economy and State capitalism are based. Quite apart from the hazards of demand, the growth of jobs in the productive sector tends in practice to be limited by the world supply of energy and raw materials.

— An ever more marked integration of the more privileged sections of the working class into the ideology, lifestyle and interests of the petty bourgeoisie, while new social strata of great insecurity come into existence: immigrants, hyper-exploited women, casual workers, the unemployed, students without prospects, all those living on social security.

— Areas of under-development appearing within the great powers. The bankrupting of traditional economies and the failure to decentralize industry lead to regionalist demands and nationalist movements of an ever more radical nature.

— What determines the restructuring of the industrial map and the development of "peripheral capitalism" will be not so much the technological options involved as the socio-political problems (a calculation of the social "risks").

For some decades, the working classes and petty bourgeoisies of the imperialist metropolises "benefited"

1) from the existence of less integrated and less mechanized means of production than we have today, and

2) from the hyper-exploitation of the colonies.

Apart from the most skilled workers, those classes will have to be "brought to heel," to sacrifice their hopes of status, and lose some of the advantages they have gained. What is happening is not so much a race in which the great powers are competing for first place, as the creation of a new social segregation that will be the same all over the world. While high-level elites of workers, technologists and scientists are established in the poorest countries, there will still be large areas of extreme poverty in the richest.

The restructuring of capitalism in the established industrial powers thus involves a challenge to the most longstanding social achievements, to which the working classes cling tenaciously:

— all forms of social security, retirement pensions, family allowances and so on;

— collective bargaining, with government arbitration;

— government protection of important branches of the economy—State enterprises and nationalized enterprises, mixed enterprises and those with government subsidies, etc. From the standpoint of integrated capitalism, such protection is justified only in the case of sectors that make little or no profit (administration of the infrastructures, public services etc.). But in the dominant sectors, the managers of the multinationals expect to have complete freedom to decide such questions as the relocation of industries (at regional, national and continental level), and to make all decisions relating to technology, energy and so on.

The bureaucracies of the countries of Eastern Europe see the problem in different terms, but their discussions on profit-sharing, improved planning and so forth all have that same underlying objective of maximizing profits.

A RESHAPING OF THE INTERNATIONAL DIVISION OF LABOR

Nineteenth-century capitalism made real headway only to the extent that the geographical and social barriers of the *Ancien Régime*, with its legacy of feudalism, were brought down.

Today it seems that national barriers, national "franchises," and the class system, as stabilized and stratified in Europe in the past, especially in Europe around the Mediterranean, constitute a very real obstacle to the advance of twenty-first century capitalism and the birth of a new, worldwide, dominant class (forged out of the bourgeois aristocracies and the bureaucracies of West and East).

The present world crisis is directed, in the last analysis, to establishing a new method for the general economic and political subjugation of the collective labor force all over the world. The gradual fading out of traditional forms of State capitalism and their replacement by multinational powers and techno-structures (the deterritorialization of the centers of decision-making in relation to any particular country) is accompanied by

1) the relative advancement of a few Third World countries because of the permanent tension in the raw material market as a whole;

2) the absolute pauperization of hundreds of millions of people living in the countries that do not share in that economic take-off;

3) an intense exploitation of the countries and regions that lie between the super-rich and the super-poor.

Closer and closer relations between East and West, not only in economic terms, but also in policing the world: greater and greater cooperation between the technocrats, bureaucrats, armed forces etc. of the Eastern- and Western-bloc countries.

A change in the direction of the armaments race. It is not now so much a matter of preparing for the Third World War as

1) preserving a military—and therefore also a politico-economic—equilibrium among the super-powers;

2) of keeping a wide enough gap between them and the secondary powers;

3) of enforcing a certain type of centralist model in such spheres as those of the armed forces, the police, energy and technology inside each country.

It may well be that this last objective is what conditions the first two. For, since the traditional models of political centralism are threatened, it is becoming necessary for integrated world capitalism to overcome the apparent contradiction between:

— the relative reduction in the role of national governments in such sectors as energy, raw materials, the siting of industry, technological options, currency, etc.;

— the need to reestablish and territorialize the collective labor force upon a new sort of power formation.

The new, worldwide, bourgeois-bureaucratic aristocracy will continue to be based upon the hierarchy of international powers. But its tendency is not to be identified with any particular one of them. (Just as we had recently dispensed with the myth of the "200 families," so today we have to move away from that of the absolute primacy of German/American capitalism. The real target is far from being so concentrated. The most dangerous seats of capitalism are to be found in Eastern-bloc and Third World countries as well as in the West.)

The formula now being experimented with, that is to say the "German model" (paralleling the attempt to set up a "European arena"), is seeking to reconcile:

— the increasing integration of a workers' aristocracy that is becoming ever more detached from the proletariat of nations of the second rank;

— a strengthening of the repressive power of governments, especially in all the spheres connected with civil society;

— complete docility towards the decisions emanating from the centers of integrated world capitalism (with its multicentric, transnational, deterritorialized network).

In other words, it is a question of combining

— at the *local* level: an idiosyncratic reterritorialization of the labor force. (The mass media have a crucial part to play in molding individuals, and in creating a majority consensus in support of the established order);

— at the *European* level: "Community" responsibility for social control and repression;

— at the *world* level: a faultless adjustment to the new way in which capitalism now operates.

One could also take into consideration various other attempts by integrated world capitalism to restructure particular economic and social situations. For instance:

— the plan of an Inter-African force supported by France and the USA to counter Cuban and Russian intervention. The only tangible result of all this interference has been to reinforce the grip of world capitalism upon Africa.

— the ever greater role Brazil seems to be being called upon to play in Latin America.

Such examples make it clear that the role of "international

policemen" that had hitherto been played by the USA and USSR (remember Suez!) has now been taken over by international agencies which, though not easily identifiable, are no less implacable.

WORLDWIDE DEVELOPMENT OF A NEW FORM OF FASCISM

In some respects, it would be in the interests of integrated world capitalism to resort as little as possible to classical authoritarian solutions that demand the support and upkeep of political bureau-cracies and military castes, and the acceptance of formulas of compromise with traditional national structures—all of which could work against its own transnational and deterritorializing logic. It would be preferable to rely on more flexible systems of control, using miniaturized methods: far better to have mutual surveillance, collective preparedness, social workers, psychiatrists and a spellbinding TV than a repression dependent upon riot police! Better the voluntary participation of individuals in institu-tions than a burdensome bureaucracy that crushes all initiative.

But the long-term, general crisis that has for some years been paralysing the workings of the economy as a whole is leading to a collapse of the modern capitalist ideology that characterized the third quarter of the twentieth century.

The old class balance, the ways in which the State used to arbitrate among the various sub-wholes of the bourgeoisie, the political and juridical safeguards inherent in bourgeois democracy—all this has to be reassessed, as the super-managers of the Trilateral Commission have made clear. Integrated world capitalism can only hope to survive provided it can control the functioning:

1) of international relations and all major social changes (for instance the manipulation of the "carnation coup" of 1974 in Portugal, or what is now happening in Italy);

2) of the machinery of the State (including the machinery of justice—hence the importance of the current resistance among lawyers and magistrates);

3) of the machinery of trade unions, works committees etc. Contractual negotiations with workers would have to be considered henceforth as an integral part of the normal operation of every company, and the unions will have something of the same sort of function as a personnel department in ensuring good staff-management relations;

4) of all collective organizations—schools, universities and everything else that contributes to molding the collective work force;

5) of the workings of the press, the cinema, television and so on, and everything that contributes to molding familial and individual subjectivity. A protest in the mind of one person becomes a danger the moment there is any possibility of its contaminating others. It is therefore necessary to keep a close watch on all deviants and outsiders, even upon their unconscious reactions.

All this has not happened yet. Integrated world capitalism has so far proved quite incapable of offering any solution at all to the fundamental problems facing the world (demographic growth, ecological devastation, the need to define new goals for production, etc.). The answers it proposes to give to the problems of energy and raw materials have nothing to offer the vast mass of the world's population. Existing international bodies are clearly incapable of settling international disputes; in fact they seem to operate on the principle of setting up certain endemic military conflicts (the wan in the Middle East, Africa and so on) as safety valves. It hardly takes a hotheaded demagogue to point out that there is increasing anger and disillusionment with this form of "guardianship" of the interests of mankind; capitalism is well aware of this, and is trying to make what preparations it can to deal with protest and revolution.

However, the new totalitarian regime that the "experts" of the Trilateral Commission and the managers of integrated world capitalism are working to achieve cannot be identified purely and simply with national fascisms of the Hitler or Mussolini type. It will be everywhere and nowhere. It will contaminate whole areas of the world, but there will be zones of comparative freedom alongside zones of hyper-repression, and the borderline between the zones will remain fluid. This new regime will not act only through the instrumentality of governments, but through all the elements that contribute to the education of the work force, to the molding of every individual and the imposing of a particular lifestyle—in other words through a multitude of systems of semiotic subjugation operating in schools, commercial sport, the media, advertising and all the various techniques used to "help" people (social services, psychoanalysis on a large scale, cultural programs and so on).

2. A Proliferation of Marginal Groups

Integrated world capitalism does not plan any systematic and generalized crushing of the laboring masses, women, young people or minorities. In fact, the means of production upon which it depends require a certain flexibility in production relations and social relations, and a certain minimum ability to adjust to the new forms of feeling and the new types of human relationships appearing in so many places. (The "creative discoveries" of fringe groups are taken over by the mass media; there is a comparatively tolerant attitude to some forms of freedom of action; etc.) This being the case, a certain amount of protest, half-tolerated, half-encouraged and absorbed, can become an intrinsic part of the system.

Other forms of protest, on the other hand, are seen as far more dangerous, in as much as they threaten the essential relationships on which the system is based (respect for work, for the social hierarchy, for the government, for the religion of consumerism). It is impossible to make a clear-cut distinction between the fringe ideas that can be recuperated and those that lead down the slippery slope to authentic "molecular revolutions." The borderline remains fluid, and fluctuates both in time and place. The essential difference is whether, in the final analysis, a given phenomenon—however broad its implications—is one that remains on the margins of the socius, or whether it poses a fundamental threat to it. In this sense, what characterizes the "molecular" is that the lines of escape combine with the objective lines of deterritorialization of the system to create an irrepressible aspiration for new areas of freedom. (One example of such an escape line is the free radio stations. Technological development, and in particular the miniaturization of transmitters and the fact that they can be put together by amateurs, "encounters" a collective aspiration for some new means of expression.)

There are various factors to be taken into consideration, both in "objective" terms and in terms of new social behavior, in order to understand the possibilities for revolutionary change in the future:

1) Will integrated world capitalism manage to establish a social order accepted by the majority in which social segregation is intensified? Capital—in both West and East—is simply the *capital of power*, that is to say a mode of semiotizing, homogenizing and transmitting all the various forms of power. (Power over goods, land, work, over subordinates, "inferiors," neighbours, family and so on.) Only the emergence of new ways of relating to the world and the socius will make it possible to transform this "libidinal fixation" of individuals upon this system of capital and its various crystallizations of power. The capitalist system, in fact, can be maintained only so long as the vast majority of individuals do not merely share in it, but also give it their unconscious assent. The overthrow of modern capitalism, therefore, is not just a matter of

struggling against material enslavement and the visible forms of repression, but also, and above all, of creating a whole lot of alternative ways of doing things, of *functioning*.

2) Over the past decade, there has been a proliferation of "fighting fronts" of a quite different sort from those that have always marked the traditional workers' movement. (Among hitherto conformist workers, the unskilled who resent the jobs they are forced to do, the unemployed, exploited women, ecologists, members of nationalist groups, people in mental hospitals, homosexuals, the old, the young, etc.) Will their demands finally prove capable of being accommodated within the framework of protest acceptable to the system? Or will there be a gradual ramification of agents of molecular revolution beneath them all? (Movements that elude the dominant means of identification, that produce their own referential axes, that are interlinked by their own underground and transversal connections, and consequently undermine traditional production relations, traditional social and family systems, traditional attitudes to the body, to sex, to the universe.)

3) Will all these microrevolutions, these profound challenges to social relations, remain contained within restricted areas of the socius? Or will there be a new interconnectedness that links one with another, without thereby setting up any new hierarchy or segregation? In short, will all these microrevolutions end by producing a real revolution? Will they be capable of taking on board not only specific local problems but the management of the great economic units?

— In other words: are we going to get away from all the various utopias of nostalgia—getting back to our origins, to nature, to the transcendent? The objective lines of deterritorialization are irreversible. We have to come to terms with "progress" in science and technology, or we shall get nowhere, and the power of world capitalism will rally once more.

For instance, take the struggles for self-determination in Corsica and Brittany. It is obvious that these will intensify over the next few years. Is this just another case of nostalgia for the past? Surely what is involved here is the building-up of a new Corsica, a new Brittany and a new Sarcelles and a new Yvelines,[1] for that matter. It is a question of rewriting the past unashamedly into the web of a clear future. The demands of minorities, for instance, and nationalist demands as well, may contain within them a certain type of State power, of subjugation: in other words, they may be carriers of the capitalist virus.

What forms of resistance can be adopted by the most traditional groups now being disturbed by the way integrated world capitalism is developing? Will the trade unions and the classical parties of the left go on indefinitely letting themselves be manipulated and taken over by modern capitalism, or will they become profoundly transformed?

It is impossible to predict the forms of struggle and organization that the revolution now starting will adopt in future. It would seem at present that absolutely anything could happen. However, a few things seem clear—not as to what the questions will be, but what they most certainly will not be:

1) They will not be centered solely upon quantitative aims, but will be reexamining the whole purpose of work, and consequently also of leisure and of culture too. They will reconsider the environment, daily life, family life, relations between men and women, adults and children, the perception of time, the meaning of life.

2) They will not be centered solely upon those who are adult-male-white-skilled-industrial workers. (There will be no more of the myth of the revolutionaries in the Putilov factories[2] in 1917.) Production today can in no sense be identified with heavy industry. Essentially, it involves both machine-tools and computers, social services as well as science and technology. Production is inseparable from the education of the work force, starting with the "work" of

the smallest children. It also includes the unit of "maintenance," reproduction and education, that is the family, the burden of running which, in our present oppressive system, is borne in the main by women.

3) They will not be centered solely on a vanguard party considered to be the theorist of struggle, the source from which all "mass movements" will have to be defined. They will be centered on many different things. Their various components will certainly not be expected to harmonize totally, to speak the same stereotyped language: contradictions, and even irreducible antagonisms, may well exist among them. (As with the attitude women will inevitably have to movements dominated by men.) This sort of contradiction does not inhibit action, but merely indicates that a unique situation, a specific desire, is at issue.

4) They will not be seen solely in a national context. While closely concerned with the most down-to-earth everyday reality, they will also involve social totalities that extend beyond national boundaries in every sense. Nowadays, any program of struggle worked out solely in terms of a national framework is foredoomed to failure. Any party or political group, from the most reformist to the most revolutionary, that restricts itself to the aim of "the takeover of the political power of the State" condemns itself to impotence. (The solution of the Italian problem, for example, will be found neither by the socialists, nor the communists, nor the independents. It needs a movement of struggle to develop in at least four or five other countries in Europe.)

5) They will not be centered on a single body of theory. The various elements will, each at its own level, and following its own pace, develop their modes of semiotization in order to define themselves and direct their action. This brings us once again to the problem of getting rid of the opposition between productive and scientific or cultural work, between manual and intellectual work.

6) They will stop putting value in exchange in one compartment, value in use in another, and the values of desire in yet a third. Such compartmentalization is one of the most fundamental bases of the self-enclosed, hierarchical, power formations upon which capitalism and social segregation depend.

Social production, under the control of capitalist and technocratic "elites," is becoming ever more cut off from the interests and desires of individuals. This leads:

1) to a systematic over-valuing of industries that are endangering the very survival of the human race (the arms race, nuclear power and so on);

2) to an under-estimation of essential use values (world hunger, the preservation of the environment);

3) to the flattening-out and repression of the uniqueness of desires, in other words to losing the meaning in life.

This being so, we can no longer separate the prospect of revolutionary change from a collective assumption of responsibility for daily life and a full acceptance of desire at every level of society.

20

CAPITAL AS THE INTEGRAL

OF POWER FORMATIONS

Capital is not an abstract category: it is a semiotic operator at the service of specific social formations. Its function is to record, balance, regulate and overcode the power formations inherent to developed industrial societies, power relations and the fluxes that make up the planet's overall economic powers. One can find systems of capitalization of power in the most archaic societies. These powers can assume multiple forms: capital of prestige, capital of magical power embodied in an individual, a lineage, an ethnic group. But only, it seems, in the capitalist mode of production has a general procedure of semiotization of such a capitalization became autonomous. It developed according to the two following axes:

— a deterritorialization of the local modes of semiotization of powers, which become subjected to a general system of inscription and quantification of power;

— a reterritorialization of the latter system onto a hegemonic power formation: the bourgeoisie of the Nation-states.

Economic capital, expressed in monetary, accounting, stock-market or other languages, always rests in the final analysis on mechanisms of differential and dynamic evaluation of powers confronting each other on a concrete terrain. An exhaustive analysis of a capital, whatever its nature, would therefore have to take into account extremely diversified components, dealing with services that are more or less monetarized, for instance sexual or domestic (presents, acquired advantages, "secondary benefits," pocket money, lump sums, etc.) as well as to gigantic international transactions, which, in the guise of operations of credit, investment, industrial implantations, co-operations, etc., are in fact nothing else than economico-strategic confrontations. In this regard, any overemphasis on Capital as a general equivalent, or as currencies tied down to systems of fixed parity, etc., can only mask the real nature of capitalist processes of subjugation and subjection, which involve social and microsocial power relations, power slippages, advances and withdrawals of one social formation in relation to another, or collective attitudes of inflationistic anticipation meant to conjure any loss of ground, or also, of imperceptible take-overs which, ultimately, will only be revealed in broad daylight. The standards of reference have no other function than that of calculation or relative identification, transitory regulation. A genuine quantification of powers could only rest on modes of semiotization directly plugged in to power formations and productive arrangements [*agencements*] (material as well as semiotic) tied down to local social coordinates.

1. Machinic Labor and Human Labor

The value of labor sold on the capitalist market depends on a quantitative factor—work-time—and on a qualitative factor—the average qualification of labor. In this second aspect of machinic subjection,[1] it cannot be circumscribed in individual terms. First, because the qualification of a human performance is inseparable from a particular machinic environment. Second, because its competence always depends on a collective agency of formation and socialization. Marx frequently speaks of work as resulting from a "collective worker"; but for him, such an entity remains a statistical one: the "collective worker" is an abstract character resulting from a calculation based on "average social labor." This operation allows him to overcome individual differences in the calculation of the work-value, which thus finds itself indexed to univocal quantitative factors such as the work-time required for a production, and the amount of workers concerned. From there, this value can be broken down into two parts:

— a quantity corresponding to the labor that is necessary to the reproduction of labor;

— a quantity constitutive of surplus-value, which is identified with the extortion of surplus-labor by capitalism.[2]

Such a conception of surplus-value may correspond to an accounting practice of capitalism, but certainly not to the way it really functions, especially in modern industry. This notion of "collective worker" should not be reduced to an abstraction. Labor-power always manifests itself through concrete arrangements [*agencements*] of production, intimately combining social relations with the means of production, and human labor with the labor of the machine. Hence the schematic character of the organic composition of Capital, which Marx divides into constant capital (Capital tied down to means of production) and variable capital (Capital tied down to means of work), should be put into question.

Marx distinguishes the composition in value of Capital (constant and capital) from its technical composition by comparing the real mass of means of production engaged in the valorization of Capital and the objective quantity of work that is socially necessary for their implementation. One goes from a sign-value to material and social power relations. With the advances in mechanized labor, the capitalist mode of production ineluctably leads to a relative diminishment of variable capital in relation to the constant capital. From this, Marx deduces a law of tendential lowering of the profit rate, which would be a kind of historical destiny of capitalism. But in the real context of the arrangements of production, the Marxist mode of calculation of absolute surplus-value, based on the quantity of average social labor—a part of which would be, in some sense, stolen by capitalists—is far from obvious. This time factor, in fact, is only one among many parameters of exploitation. It is known today that the administration of the capital of knowledge, the degree of participation in the organization of labor, the corporate spirit, and collective discipline, etc., can also take on determining importance in the productivity of Capital. In this respect, the idea of a social average for an hourly output in a given sector doesn't make much sense. It is teams, workshops, and factories, wherever a local reduction of "productive entropy" appears for X reasons, which drive things forward, and actually direct this kind of average in a branch of industry or in a country, while collective worker resistance, organizational bureaucracy, etc., slow it down. In other words, it is complex arrangements—training, innovation, internal structures, union relations, etc.—which circumscribe the magnitude of capitalist zones of profit, and not a simple levy on work-time. Actually Marx himself had perfectly pinpointed the growing discrepancy between machinic, intellectual, and manual components of labor. In the *Grundrisse*, he had emphasized that the totality of knowledge tends to become an "immediate productive power." He then insisted on the absurdity and the transitional character of a measure of value based on work-time.

Let us note in passing the fragility of this parallel: indeed, if today it appears that the absolute rule of the measure of work-time is on the verge of vanishing, the same does not hold with the law of exchange-value. It is true that if capitalism seems to be able to do without the former, it is unimaginable that it could survive the disappearance of the latter, which could only be the result of revolutionary social transformations. Marx believed that the removal of the leisure-work opposition would coincide with the control by workers over surplus labor.[3] Unfortunately it is perfectly conceivable that it is capitalism itself which would loosen up the measure of work-time, and practice a politics of leisure and formation all the more "open" that would better colonize it (today how many workers, employees, and high-level staff spend their evenings and week-ends preparing for promotions!). The recasting of the quantification of value based on work-time won't be, as Marx assumed, the privilege of a classless society. And indeed, through modes of transportation, of urban, domestic, married life, through the media, the leisure industry and even the dream industry, it does seem that one cannot escape from the grip of Capital for one second.

One does not pay wages to a worker for the pure duration of "average social labor," but for putting the worker at one's disposal; one compensates the worker for a *power* that exceeds that which is exercised during the worker's presence in the factory. What counts here is filling a position, a power game between the workers and the social groups that control the arrangements of production and social formations. The capitalist does not extort a surplus of time, but a complex qualitative process. He doesn't buy labor-power but power over productive arrangements. Labor which is the most serial in appearance, for example, pressing a lever or keeping watch on a security blinker, always presupposes the prior formation of a semiotic capital with multiple components—knowledge of language, customs, rules and hierarchies, mastery of processes of increasing abstraction, itineraries, and interactions which are inherent to productive arrangements… Work is no longer, if it ever was, a mere ingredient, mere raw matter of production. In other words, the portion of machinic subjection entering into human labor is never quantifiable as such. On the other hand, subjective subjugation, the social alienation inherent in a work position or any other social function certainly is. That is in fact the function assigned to Capital.

The two problems concerning, on the one hand, work-value and its role in surplus-value, and on the other, the effect of the rise of productivity through increased mechanization over the profit rate, are irredeemably linked. Human time is increasingly replaced by *machinic time.*

As Marx says, it is no longer human labor which is made to fit mechanized labor. It does indeed seem that the assembly line and the various forms of Taylorism, in the most modern branches of the economy, are about to become far more dependent on general methods of social subjugation than on processes of subjection which are specific to productive forces.[4] This Taylorist alienation of work-time, these neo-archaic forms of subjugation to the work position, in principle, remain measurable in terms of a general equivalent. The control of average social labor, in theory, can always be incarnated in an exchange-value of powers (one could thus compare the formal alienation time of a Senegalese peasant to that of a civil servant in the Ministry of Finance or an IBM worker). But the real control of machinic times, from the subjection of human organs to productive arrangements, cannot legitimately be grounded on such a general equivalent. One can measure a time of work presence, a time of alienation, a time of incarceration in a factory or a prison; one cannot measure their consequences on an individual. One may quantify the apparent labor of a physicist in a laboratory, but not the productive value of the formulas that he elaborates. Marxist abstract value overcoded the whole of human labor, which was concretely assigned to the production of use-values. But the present movement of capitalism tends to turn all use-values into exchange-values; all productive labor is defined by mechanized labor. The poles of the exchange themselves have passed over to the side of mechanized labor; computers dialogue across continents, and dictate the terms of the exchanges to the managers. Automatized and computerized production no longer draws its consistency from a basic human factor, but from a machinic phylum that traverses, bypasses, disperses, miniaturizes, and co-opts all human activities.

These transformations do not imply that the new capitalism completely takes the place of the old one. There is rather coexistence, stratification, and hierarchalization of capitalisms at different levels, which involve:

— On the one hand, *traditional segmentary capitalisms*, territorialized onto Nation-states, and deriving their unity from a monetary and financial mode of semiotization.[5]

— And on the other, *a World-Wide Integrated Capitalism*, that no longer rests on the sole mode of semiotization of financial and monetary Capital, but more fundamentally, on a whole set of technico-scientific, macrosocial and microsocial, and mass media procedures of subjection.

The formula of Marxist surplus-value is essentially linked to segmentary capitalisms. It does not account for the double movement of globalization and miniaturization that characterizes the current evolution. For example, in the extreme case of an entirely automatized branch of industry, one cannot see what becomes of this surplus-value. If one rigorously stuck to Marxist equations, it should completely disappear, which is absurd. Should one then ascribe it solely to machinic labor? Why not? One could set forth a formula according to which a machinic surplus-value would correspond to surplus labor "required" from the machine, beyond its upkeep and replacement costs. But trying to rearrange the quantitativistic side of the problem would certainly not take us very far. In reality, in such a case—but also in all the intermediate cases of strong reduction of variable capital in relation to constant capital—the extraction of surplus-value for the most part evades the corporation and the immediate manager-employee relation, and refers back to the second formula of integrated capitalism.

The double equation posited by Marx, setting as equivalent "the real degree of exploitation of labor," the rate of surplus-value, and the time of surplus labor tied down to variable capital, cannot be accepted as such.

Capitalist exploitation tends to treat humans like machines and pay them like machines, in a purely quantitativistic mode. But exploitation, as we have seen, goes beyond that. Capitalists extract many other surplus-values, many other profits tied down as well to the standard of Capital. Capitalism is just as interested in the "social" as the exploited are. But while for it, the machinic precedes the social and must control it; for them, conversely, the machinic should be subservient to the social. What essentially separates humans from machines is the fact that humans don't let themselves be exploited passively. One may admit that, in the present conditions, exploitation concerns machinic arrangements at first—man and his faculties having become an integral part of these arrangements. From this absolute exploitation, secondly, social forces enter into a struggle for the dividing up of the *machinic product.* As the survival criterion of the worker has become relative—how indeed could we appreciate the "minimum subsistence," the portion of value corresponding to the labor that is necessary for the reproduction of labor?—all the questions of allotment of economic and social goods have essentially become political matters. But the concept of the political has to be broadened to include the whole of the micropolitical dimensions involving the various styles of living, experience, speaking, projecting the future, memorizing history, etc.

After pointing out that the subjugation of the worker only involves the quantitative factor of "average social labor" marginally, I have tried to "lift" the exploitation rate from the Marxist surplus-value rate. By doing this, I implicitly lifted it away from the profit rate, which in Marx is a close relative of the latter.[6]

This distinction is confirmed by the fact, which has become frequent in sectors subsidized by the State, that corporations "selling at a loss," despite a theoretically negative surplus-value, according to the Marxist formula, nevertheless generate considerable profits. Profit today may depend on factors which are not only outside the corporation, but also outside the nation, as the Third World is exploited "from a distance," by means of the international market of raw materials.

Let us note, lastly, that the alleged law of tendential lowering of the profit rate could not be sustained in the present politico-economic field. Transnational mechanisms have acquired so much importance that it is no longer conceivable to determine a local rate of surplus-value tied down to a local growth rate of mechanical labor in terms of constant capital.[7]

2. The Organic Composition of World-Wide Integrated Capitalism

Unlike what Marx thought, Capital was able to disengage itself from a formula that would have enclosed it in a blind mode of quantification of exchange values (that is, controlling the whole of the modes of circulation and production of use-values).[8] Capitalist valorization still has not caught the machinic cancer which, from the tendential lowering of the profit rate to crises of overproduction, should have led it to a dead end, and what is more, forced capitalism into total isolation. The semiotization of Capital now has more and more means to locate, quantify, and manipulate the concrete valorizations of power, and thereby not only survive but proliferate. Whatever appearance it may give itself, Capital is not rational: it is hegemonistic. It does not harmonize social formations; it enforces socioeconomic disparities. It is a power operation before being a profit operation. It cannot be deduced from a basic mechanism of profit, but imposes itself from above. Previously based on what Marx called "the total social Capital of a country,"[9] today it relies on a World-Wide Integrated Capital. Capital has always relied on a general movement of deterritorialization of all sectors of the economy, of science and technology, of mores, etc. Its semiotic existence is systematically grafted onto all the technical and social mutations, which it diagrammatizes and reterritorializes onto the dominant power formations. Even at the time when it seemed to be solely centered on an extraction of monetary profit from commercial, banking and financial activities, Capital—as the expression of the most dynamic capitalist classes—was already practicing a politics of destruction and restructuring: deterritorialization of the traditional peasantry, constitution of an urban working class, expropriation of the old commercial bourgeoisie and the old crafts, liquidation of the regional and separatist "archaisms," colonial expansionism, etc.[10]

It is therefore not sufficient here to evoke the politics of Capital. Capital as such is nothing but the political, social, and technico-scientific elements, related to each other. This general diagrammatic dimension appears more and more clearly with the growing role of State capitalism, as a relay to the globalization of Capital. Nation-States manipulate a multidimensional Capital: monetary masses, economic indices, quantities necessary to bring some social category "into line," fluxes of inhibition to keep people in place, etc. One witnesses a sort of collectivization of capitalism—whether it is circumscribed in a national framework or not. But this does not mean that it is about to degenerate. Through the continuous enrichment of its semiotic components,[11] beyond wage labor and monetarized goods, it takes control of a multitude of quanta of power which previously had remained contained in the local economy, both domestic and libidinal. Today, each particular operation of capitalist extraction of profit—in money and in social power—involves power formations across the board. Notions such as the capitalist corporation and the salaried position have become inseparable from the whole of the social fabric, which itself is directly produced and reproduced under the control of Capital. The very notion of the capitalist corporation should be broadened so as to include collective equipments, and the notion of work position, as well as most non-salaried activities. In a way, the housewife occupies a work position in her home, the child holds a work position at school, the consumer at the supermarket, and the television viewer in front of the screen... Machines in the factory seem to be working all by themselves, but in fact it is the whole of society that is adjacent to them. It would be quite arbitrary today to consider corporate salaries independently from the multiple systems of deferred wages, benefits, and social costs, which affect the reproduction of the collective labor-power more or less closely, move out of the monetary circuit of the corporation, and are taken on by multiple institutions and collective equipments. Let us add to all this an essential point about which more will be said: not only does capitalism exploit salaried workers beyond their work-time, during their "leisure" time, but moreover, it uses them as relay-points in order to exploit those who are subjugated in their own sphere of action: their subalterns, their unsalaried kin, wives, children, old people, dependents of all kinds.

We always come back to this central idea: through the wage system, capitalism aims above all at controlling *the whole of society*. And in a recurring way, it appears that in any circumstance, the play of exchange-values has always been dependent on social relations, and not the reverse. Mechanisms such as inflation illustrate the constant intrusion of the social in the economic. What is "normal" is inflation, and not price equilibrium, since the issue is to adjust power relations that are in permanent evolution (buying power, investment power, the various social formations' international exchange power). As economic surplus-value is irrevocably tied to surplus-values of power that have to do with labor, machines, and social spaces, the redefinition of Capital as the general mode of capitalization of the semioses of power (rather than as an abstract, universal quantity) therefore implies a redefinition of its technical composition. The latter no longer rests on two basic givens—living labor and labor crystallized in the means of production—but on at least four components, four set-ups which are irreducible to one another:

1) *The capitalist power formations*, through which Capital maintains order, guarantees property, social stratifications, and the allotment of material and social goods. (The value of a good, whichever it might be, being inseparable from the credibility of the repressive equipments of law and police... and also from the existence of a certain degree of popular consensus in favor of the established order.)

2) *The machinic arrangements* of productive forces, which constitute a fixed capital (machine, factory, transportation, storage of raw materials, capital of technico-scientific knowledge, techniques of machinic subjection and training, laboratories, etc.). This is the classic realm of productive forces.

3) *Collective labor-power and the whole of social relations which are subjugated by capitalist power*. Collective labor-power is no longer considered here in terms of machinic subjection, but of social alienation. It is subjugated to the bourgeoisies and the bureaucracies; at the same time, it is a factor of subjugation of other social categories (women, children, immigrants, sexual minorities, etc.). This is the realm of relations of production and social relations.

4) The network of equipments, apparatuses of State and para State power; the media. This network, both ramified on the microsocial and on the planetary scale, has become an essential element of Capital. It is through this network that it can extract

and integrate the sectorial capitalizations of power inherent to the three preceding components.

Capital, as the semiotic operator of all the power formations, thus deploys a deterritorialized surface of inscription on which these four components will evolve. But I will emphasize the fact that it is not just a stage where something would be *represented*, a sort of parliamentary theater where the various points of view would be confronted with one another. It will also be a directly *productive* activity, inasmuch as Capital participates in the ordering of machinic and social arrangements, and in an entire series of prospective operations concerning them. The specific diagrammatic functions of Capital—that is, functions of inscription which are not exclusively representational but operational—"add" something essential to what would be otherwise a mere accumulation of the various components mentioned above. The elevation of the level of semiotic abstraction corresponding to this level of diagrammatism may evoke what Bertrand Russell described in his theory of logical types, that is, that a fundamental discontinuity exists between a set and its components. But with Capital, discontinuity is not just logical but machinic, in the sense that it does not only emanate from fluxes of signs, but also from material and social fluxes. In fact, the reduction-ratio power of the diagrammatism proper to Capital is inseparable from the deterritorializing "dynamism" of the various concrete arrangements of capitalism. This makes reformist political perspectives grounded on intra- or inter-capitalist contradictions irrelevant, and this holds true to those that emphasize its humanization in response to the pressure of the masses. It is futile, for instance, to "play" multinational corporations off against national capitalism, or Germano-American Europe against the Europe of fatherlands, 'Western" liberalism against the social capitalism of the USSR, North against South, etc. Capital thrives on these contradictions; they are just so many tests promoting deterritorialization.

A revolutionary alternative, if such does exist, can certainly not be established on such bases.

3. Capital and the Functions of Subjective Alienation

The exercise of power by means of the semioses of Capital proceeds concurrently with a control from above of social segments, and by a constant subjugation of each individual's life. Even though its enunciation is individuated, there is nothing less individual than capitalist subjectivity. The overcoding by Capital of human activities, thoughts, and feelings makes all particularized modes of subjectivation equivalent and resonant with each other. Subjectivity, so to speak, is nationalized. Values of desire are reordered in an economy grounded on a systematic dependence of use-values in relation to exchange-values, to the point of making this opposition meaningless. Strolling "freely" down a street, or in the country, breathing fresh air, or singing a bit loudly have become quantifiable activities from a capitalistic point of view. Squares, natural parks, and free movement have a social and industrial cost. Ultimately, the subjects of capitalism—like the subjects of the king—only assume the portion of their existence that is accountable in terms of general equivalency, Capital, according to the expanded definition I am proposing here. The capitalist order claims that individuals should only live for an exchange system, a general translatability of all values so that their slightest desire is felt to be a-social, dangerous, and guilty.

Such an operation of subjugation, meant to cover the whole social field, while "targeting" accurately its minutest disparities, cannot be satisfied with exterior social control. The general market of values deployed by Capital will at once proceed from within and from without. It will not only be concerned with economically identifiable values, but also mental and affective values. It will be up to a multicentered network of collective equipments, State, para-State, and media apparatuses to make the junction between this "without" and this "within." The general translatability of the local modes of semiotization of power does not only obey central commands, but "semiotic condensators" which are adjacent to State power, or directly indentured to it. One essential function is to make sure that each individual assumes mechanisms of control, repression, and modelization of the dominant order.[12]

In the context of World-Wide Integrated Capitalism, one may hold that the central powers of Nation-States are at once everything and nothing. Nothing, or not much, with regard to real economic efficiency; everything, or almost everything, with regard to modelization and social control. The paradox is that, up to a point, the network of State apparatuses, equipments, and bureaucracies itself tends to escape State power. In fact, often it is the network that guides and manipulates the State by remote control, its actual interlocutors being "social partners," pressure groups, and lobbies. The reality of the State thus tends to coincide with the State and para-State structures which occupy a very ambiguous position in relations of production and class relations, since on the one hand they control real executive positions and effectively contribute to maintaining the dominant order, and on the other, they themselves are the object of capitalist exploitation, on the same basis as the various components of the working class.

Marx held that a schoolmaster was a productive worker since he prepared his pupils to work for the bosses.[13] But today's schoolmaster has multiplied infinitely. Through this capitalistic network, it generates training and sociability, to such a point that it would be quite arbitrary to break down the conglomerate of "collective arrangements" into autonomous spheres of material production, socius, and modes of semiotization and subjectivation.

The same ambiguity and the same ambivalence between production and repression which characterizes technocracies can be found among the working masses: workers "work" on themselves at the very time as they are working towards the production of consumption goods. In one way or another, all participate in the production of control and repression. In fact, as we saw before, one individual never stops shifting roles in the same day: exploited at the workshop or office, he in turn becomes the exploiter in his family or in the couple, etc. At all levels of the socius, one finds an inextricable mixture of vectors of alienation. For example, the workers and the unions of an advanced sector will passionately defend the position their industry occupies in the national economy, and will do so regardless of its consequences for pollution, or whether fighter jets will be used to strafe the African populations... Class borders, "fronts of struggle," have become blurred. Could one say that they have disappeared? No. But they have multiplied infinitely, and even when direct confrontations come forth, most often they take on an "exemplary character," their first aim being to draw the attention of the media, which in turn manipulates them at will.

At the root of the mechanisms that model the force of labor, at all the levels where ideology and affects keep overlapping, one discovers the machinic tentacles of capitalistic equipment. I would like to emphasize that they don't make up a network of ideological apparatuses, but rather a megamachine encompassing a multitude of scattered elements which concerns not just workers, but all those "involved in production," permanently and everywhere, women, children, the elderly, the marginals, etc. Today, for example, from birth through family, television and social services, a child is "set to work" and is engaged in a complex process of formation, with a view of adapting the child's various modes of semiosis to upcoming productive and social functions.

Today assessments of industrial maintenance in the management of enterprises are of paramount importance. Is it enough to say that the State is assuming the role of general "social mainte-nance"? To me, this would be completely insufficient. Both in the East and in the West, the State is directly hooked on the essential components of Capital—in this respect one has the right to speak of two modes of State capitalism, on condition that one simulta-neously modifies the definition of the organic composition of Capital and that of the State. The function of the network of Capitalist equipment (which includes, up to a point, the media, unions, associations, etc.) is to *make Capital homogeneous* with exchange values and the social Capital of power values. It manages collective attitudes, patterns of conduct, referents of every sort compatible with the "good behavior" of the system, as well as legal and financial means distributing the power of purchase and investment between the various social and industrial zones, or again, financing huge military-industrial complexes which serve as a backbone on an international scale.

It is essential to not isolate each of these domains into fool-proof categories. In each occasion, in the last analysis, we find the same Capital manipulated by socially dominant formations: Capi-tal of knowledge, of adaptation and submission of labor-power to the productive environment, and more generally the entire popu-lation to the urban-rural environment, the Capital of unconscious introjection of models of the system, the Capital of repressive and military force. All these ways of semiotizing power fully participate in the organic composition of contemporary Capital.

Thus the development of a general market of capitalist values, the proliferation of multicentered capitalist and State equipments that sustain it, far from contradicting powers centered on the Nation-States—which generally tend to reinforce it—in fact com-plement it. In reality, what is thereby capitalized is much more a power exerted as *the image of power* than a true power in the areas of production and of the economy. In the most diverse ways, the

State and its countless ramifications tend to recreate a minimum of coordinates and spare territories, in order to allow the masses to more or less artificially adjust their everyday life and social rapport. By contrast, the true axes of decisionality are elsewhere: they traverse and dodge the ancient and new modes of territorialization, being increasingly dependent on a system of capitalist networks integrated on a world scale.[14]

The spaces of contemporary capital no longer adhere to local turf, castes, ethical, religious corporative "precapitalist" traditions, and less and less to metropolises, industrial cities, to class relations and bureaucracies of segmented capitalism from the era of the Nation-States. Spaces are constructed on planetary as well as microsocial and physical scales. The feeling of "belonging to something" itself seems to result from the same sort of assembly-line as "life-design." It is easier to understand, under these conditions, why State power can no longer afford to sit on the throne of the social pyramid, legislating from a distance, but that it has to intervene endlessly in order to shape and recompose the social texture, constantly reshuffling its "formulas" of hierarchization, segregation, functional prescriptions, specific qualifications. Global Capitalism is moving forward in a dizzying race. It has to make use of everything and no longer affords the luxury of national traditions, legislative texts, or the independence, even formal, of institutions like magistracy, which might limit in any way its freedom.

4. Capital and the Functions of Machinic Enslavement

To the traditional systems of direct coercion, capitalist power keeps adding control mechanisms requiring, if not the complicity of each individual, at least its passive consent. But such an extension of the means of action is only possible inasmuch as they involve the inner springs of life and human action. Miniaturization of these means goes far beyond machinic techniques. It bears down on the basic functioning of the perceptive, sensorial, affective, cognitive, linguistic, etc., behaviors grafted to capitalist machinery, of which the "invisible" deterritorialized part is probably the most fearfully efficient. We cannot accept the theoretical explanations of subjugation of the masses in terms of ideological deceit or a collective masochistic passion. Capitalism seizes individuals from the inside. Alienation by means of images and ideas is only an aspect of a general system of enslavement of their fundamental modes of semiotization, both individual and collective. Individuals are "equipped" with modes of perception or normalization of desire just as they are with factories, schools, and territories. The expansion of the division of labor to planetary levels implies, on the part of global Capitalism, not only an attempt to integrate productive forces of every social category, but moreover a permanent recomposition, a reinvention of this collective workforce. The ideal of Capital is no longer to bother with individuals endowed with passions, capable of ambiguity, hesitation and refusal as well as enthusiasm, but exclusively human robots. It would rather deal with only two types: the salaried and the subsidized. Its aim is to erase, neutralize, if not suppress, any categorization founded on something other than its own axiomatic of power and its technological imperatives. When, at the close of the chain, it "rediscovers" men, women, children, the old, rich and poor, manual laborers, intellectuals, etc., it pretends to recreate them by itself, to redefine them according to its own criteria.

But, precisely because it intervenes on the most functional levels—sensorial, affective and practical—the capitalist machinic enslavement is liable to reverse its effects, and to lead to a new type of machinic surplus-value accurately perceived by Marx (expansion of alternatives for the human race; constant renewal of the horizon of desires and creativity).[15] Capitalism claims to seize the force of desires borne by the human race. It is by means of machinic enslavement that it settles in the heart of individuals. It is doubtlessly true, for example, that social and political integration of workers' elites is not only based on material interests, but also on their involvement, sometimes very profound, with their profession, their technology, their machines... More generally, it is clear that the machinic environment secreted by capitalism is far from being indifferent to the great masses of people, and this is not only due to the seduction of advertisement or the internalization by individuals of objects and ideas of the consumer society. Something of the machine seems to belong to the essence of human desire. The question is to know of which machine, and what it is for.

Machinic enslavement does not coincide with social subjugation. While enslavement involves full-fledged persons, easily manipulated subjective representations, machinic enslavement combines infrapersonal and infrasocial elements, because of a molecular economy of desire more difficult to "contain" within stratified social relations.[16] Directly involving perceptive functions, affects, unconscious behaviors, capitalism takes possession of labor-power and desire, which extends far beyond that of the working class, sociologically speaking. Accordingly, class relations tend to evolve differently. They are less bipolarized, and increasingly rely on complex strategies. The fate of the French working class, for example, does not solely depend upon its direct bosses, but also on those from the State, Europe, the Third World, multinationals, and in another area, immigrant workers, women's labor, precarious and provisional work, regional conflicts, etc.

The bourgeoisie's nature has changed. It is no longer as vigorously engaged, at least in its modernist parts, in defending the personal possession of means of production—either individual or collective. Today its problem is to collectively and globally control the basic network of machines and social equipment. Its power, not only monetary, but social, libidinal, cultural, etc., comes from there. It is on this terrain that it defends itself against expropriation. And, in this regard, it is necessary to recognize that it showed a surprising capacity for adaptation, renovation, in particular for regeneration in the social-capitalist regimes of the East. It loses ground on the side of private capitalism, but gains ground on the side of State capitalism, collective equipment, media, etc. Not only does it incorporate new sectors of the State, bureaucracy and apparatus, technocrats, experts, teachers, but, to one degree or another, it manages to contaminate the whole of the population.

What limits will the capitalist classes encounter in their enterprise of converting across the board all human activities into a unique semiotic equivalent? Up to what point is a revolutionary class struggle still conceivable in such a system of generalized contaminations? No doubt these limits are not to be found among traditional revolutionary movements. Revolution is not uniquely played out at the level of explicit political discourse, but also on a far more molecular plane, in mutations of desire, artistic and technico-scientific mutations, etc. In this dizzying course, capitalism is engaged in systematic control of everyone on this planet. Today, it is at the apex of its power, having integrated China, but perhaps at the same time, it is about to reach an extreme threshhold of fragility. Its system of generalized dependence may be such that the slightest hitch in its functioning may create effects of which it won't be the master.

21

CAPITALIST SYSTEMS, STRUCTURES AND PROCESSES

The question of capitalism may be considered from multiple angles, but economics and "the social" de facto constitute a necessary starting point.

From the first angle, capitalism may be defined as the general function of semiotization of a system of production, of circulation and distribution. Capitalism, the method of Capital, will then be considered as a procedure allowing merchandise, goods, activities and services to be valorized through indexing systems governed by a particular syntax apt to overcode and control. Such a "formalist" definition is possible, for despite the fact that it is inseparable from the technical and socioeconomic arrangements that it strives to direct, this semiotic system nonetheless possesses an intrinsic coherence. In this regard, the capitalistic modes of writing could be compared to mathematical structures whose axiomatic consistency is not affected by the applications that can be performed in extra-mathematical fields. I suggest that this first level be called *semiotic machine of capitalism or semiotic of capitalistic valorization*.

From the second angle, capitalism will rather appear as the generator of a particular type of social relations: segregational laws, customs, and practices here move to the first rank. The processes of economic writing may vary; what is primary is the conservation of a certain type of social order founded on the division of roles between those who monopolize power and those who are submitted to it, and this applies just as much in the areas of work and economic life as in those of lifestyle, knowledge, and culture. All of these divisions cross over with divisions of sexes, classes, ages, and races, and end up making up, in their final form, the concrete segments of the socius. This second level, for which I suggest the name of *system of segmentarity of capitalism or capitalistic segmentarity*, also seems to preserve its own system of "axiomatic" coherence, whichever its transformations or upheavals imposed by history may be.

Capitalism is coded, but not in the manner of a "tablet of the law." The social order that it governs evolves as much as its economic syntaxes do. In this realm, as in many others, the influences are not unilateral, and we are never faced with a one-way causality. There is no question here, then, of opposing this semiotic machine and that system of segmentarity. These two components always go together, and their distinction will only be pertinent insofar as it will allow one to shed light on their own interactions with a third fundamental level, which is that of production. Let us specify right away that the latter must not be identified with what Marxists call "relations of production," or "infrastructure economic relations." Some of that is true, but it is quite different for technical machines and desiring machines. The notion of productive component (or processual component) will include both material machinic forces, human labor, social relations and investments of desire, inasmuch as all develop potentially evolving and creative relations. (These productive relations will also be termed diagrammatic, as opposed to the representative and/or programmatic relations of the first two levels.)

Is it legitimate to keep speaking of capitalism as a general entity? Aren't the formal definitions that are proposed a priori condemned to obliterate its diversification in time and in space? Since Marx, a double-tiered question has been asked: that of the place of capitalism in history and the place of history in capitalism. The sole element of historical continuity which appears to be able to characterize the various vicissitudes of modern capitalism indeed seems to be this *processual character* of the technico-scientific transformations it rests on. One can "find" capitalism in all places and times as soon as one considers it from the point of view of the exploitation of the proletarian classes, or of the mobilization of means of economic semiotization which are favorable to the rise of big markets such as fiduciary currency, bills of exchange, shares, bonds, credit currency, etc. But the capitalisms of the last three centuries only really "took off" from the moment that science, industrial and commercial technology and the socius irreversibly linked their common fate together. And everything leads one to believe that in the absence of such a machinic nexus in constant mutation, the societies within which the contemporary capitalistic formulas proliferated would probably have been unable to overcome the traumas of the great crises and world wars, and would certainly have met the same end as some great civilizations: a sudden, "unexplainable" death, or an interminable agony.

A calculator, Capital has also become a prediction machine, the computer of the socius, the homing head[1] of innovative techniques. Its raw material, its basic nutrition is made up of human labor and machinic labor, or, to be more specific, of the power of the dominant groups over human labor and of the power of the machines set up by this human labor. In other terms, what Capital capitalizes is not just social power—for on that account, there would be no cause for differentiating it historically from the prior systems of exploitation but above all, *machinic power*. Let's say that with regard to the powers-that-be and potencies in general, it is at once a *mode of evaluation* and a *technical means of control*. All of its "mystery" lies in the fact that it is thus able to connect, within the same general system of equivalency, entities which at first sight seem radically heterogeneous: material and economic *goods*, individual and collective human *activities*, and technical, industrial and scientific *processes*. And the key of this mystery lies in the fact that it does not merely standardize, compare, order, and computerize these various areas, but that, in each operation, it extracts one and the same element, which might be called *machinic exploitation value* or *machinic surplus-value of the code*. It is through machinic valorization that capitalism infiltrates itself, not only within the material machines of economic production (crafts, manufacturing, industry...), but also within the immaterial machinisms at work at the heart of the most varied human activities (productive-unproductive, public-private, real-imaginary...). Hence a "latent" market of machinic values and values of desire is necessarily added to, and overdetermines, any "manifest" economic market of exchange-values.[2] It is from this double-market system that the essentially inegalitarian and manipulative character of any operation of exchange in a capitalist context stems, insofar as its function is always ultimately:

1) to connect heterogeneous domains and asymmetrical potencies and powers;

2) to control the social arrangements and the arrangements of desire, which are organized in such a way as to program what the modes of sensibility, tastes, and choices of each individual should be.

Fernand Braudel showed that this fundamentally inegalitarian character of the capitalist markets was much more visible, much less "dressed-up" in the era of world-economies centered around cities such as Venice, Antwerp, Genoa, or Amsterdam, than in the era of the contemporary world market. The capitalist proto-markets deployed themselves in concentric zones from metropolises which held all of the essential economic keys and recovered the greater part of surplus-values, while in their periphery, they tended towards a kind of "zero degree," due to the lethargy of the exchanges and the low level of the prices prevalent there.[3] Even today it is obvious that the exploitation of the Third World is not at all a matter of egalitarian exchanges, but rather of a kind of pillage "compensated" by the exportation of glass-ware, Coca Cola and luxury gadgets destined to a handful of autochthonous privileged ones. This does not prevent the "new economists" of the Chicago School, the "neo-liberals," from preaching the redeeming virtues of the capitalist market, in all places and in all situations.

Were one to listen to them, only the capitalist market would be able to guarantee an optimal arbitration between individual preferences with the least cost and constraint.[4] According to the proponents of this kind of theory, the inequality of exchanges ultimately would only stem from "imperfections" in the structures of the *cost of information* in society.[5] A little more effort with costs and everything will be all right. However, it is obvious that, whether it is well or poorly informed, the Third World does not "exchange" its labor and its wealth for cases of Coca Cola or even barrels of petrol. It is set upon and bled to death by the intrusion of the dominant economies. And the same holds, in other proportions however, in the Third and Fourth Worlds within the well-off countries.

This pseudo-egalitarian make up of "exchanges" on the world market is not only done so as to mask the procedures of social subjection.[6] It complements the techniques meant to integrate the collective subjectivity in view of obtaining optimal libidinal consent from it, and even an active submission to the relations of exploitation and segregation. Contrary to what the theorists of "public choice" claim, the growth of information—particularly of the mass media information directed by the system—can only accentuate the inegalitarian effects of these techniques of integration.

The project which aimed to "complete the theory of production and of the exchange of goods or merchant service with an equivalent theory somehow compatible with the functioning of political markets"[7] might have come from the best of intentions, but it was definitely incomplete, and it went wrong; economic, political, and institutional markets are one thing, machinic and libidinal markets are another.

And it is essentially on the side of the latter that one will be able to grasp the essential workings of social valorization and machinic creativity, in short, the essential workings of history. To achieve that goal, theories of the "political market," far from striving to become equivalent, "compatible" with those of the economic market, would be better advised to promote all at once a vision of the political, market economics, machinic values and values of desire which would be radically heterogeneous and antagonistic to that of the present system.

With regard to machinic value and values of desire, the pertinence of the distinction between goods and activities seems to dwindle. In a certain type of arrangement, human activities, which are duly controlled and piloted by capitalism, are transformed into machinic goods, while the evolution of other arrangements makes some productive goods lose their economic relevance, thereby having their "machinic virulence" devalued. In the first case, a power of activity (power assets) is transformed into a highly valorizable *machinic potency*; in the second case, a machinic potency (potency assets) swings over to the side of *formal powers*. Henceforth, a definition of Capital which would really take into account the factors of production and their evolutionary dynamic would invoke the association of economic modes of evaluation which had been divergent or contradictory until then: statistical evaluation of supply and demand by market *prices*; "objective" evaluation of *quantities of labor* incorporated by manufactured goods; "subjective" evaluation, of the marginalist type, of anticipated profits in economic transactions; accounting evaluation, integrating financial and fiscal components, and amortization data.

These formulas of evaluation, which economists generally present as excluding one another,[8] have in fact never ceased to be in contact—either by competing, or by complementing each other—in real economic history.[9] Thus there is no reason to qualify each one of them in a univocal manner. Their different forms of existence (commercial, industrial, financial, monopolistic, statist or bureaucratic valorization) in reality result from bringing one of their fundamental components to the fore, "selected" from one set of basic components, which has been reduced here to three terms—the *processes* of machinic production; the *structures* of social segmentarity; the dominant economic semiotic *systems*.

Starting with this minimal model—a necessary model, but barely sufficient, for one is never faced with simple components, but with clusters of components, which themselves are structured according to their own systems of priorities—let us examine at present the kind of generative chemistry of the arrangements of economic valorization resulting from the combination of priorities between these basic components. In the following table of capitalistic arrangements of valorization,

1) structures of social segmentarity will only be considered from the angle of the economic problematic of the state—the consequences of a centralized management of an important part of economic fluxes (discernable within the national accounting) on the stratification of segmentary relations;

2) systems of economic semiotization will only be considered from the angle of the problematic of the *market* (in the broad sense evoked above, of markets of goods, of men, of ideas, of phantasies…);

3) productive processes will not be specified otherwise.

SIX FORMULAS OF CAPITALISTIC AGENCEMENTS OF VALORIZATION

(THE PRIORITIES BETWEEN COMPONENTS ARE INDICATED BY ARROWS)

Order of Priorities	Examples
a) State > Production > Market	Asiatic mode of production[10] War economy of Nazi type
b) Market > Production > State	Commercial proto-capitalism World Economies centered on a network of cities[11]
c) Market > State > Production	Liberal capitalism
d) Production > State > Market	Monopolistic colonial economy
e) Production > Market > State	World Wide Integrated Capitalism
f) State > Market > Production	State capitalism (of the USSR type)

The object of this table, I must emphasize, is by no means to present a general typology of the historical forms of capitalism, but only to show that capitalism is not identified with one formula alone (for example that of market economy). One could complexify and refine it by introducing additional components, or by differentiating the components belonging to each cluster, whose partitions are not airtight (there is "machinic production" within the semiotic machinery of the market and within the state; there is "state power" at the heart of the most liberal economic syntaxes; besides they never stop playing a determining role in productive spheres). It is only suggested here in order to bring out—out of some correlations inherent to the second system of connection internal to each formula—certain affinities between systems apparently quite far from one another, but which go in the same direction (or the opposite direction) of history.

More generally:

1) the capacity for the arrangements to assume major historical upheavals (or, to paraphrase Ilya Prigogine's favorite formula, their capacity for piloting "processes far from historical equilibriums") will depend on the primacy of productive components;

2) their degree of resistance to change will depend on the primacy of the components of social segmentarities (axioms of clanic, ethnic, religious, urbanistic, caste or class stratification.);

3) their power of integration, their capacity to "colonize" not only economic life, but social life, libidinal life, in other words, their capacity to transform the socius, to subject it to the machinic phylum, will depend on the more or less innovative character of their semiotics of valorization (the fact that they would or would not be capable of adapting themselves, of enriching themselves through new procedures; their degree of "diagrammaticity"). The fact that the "direction of history" is related here to the evolutionary phylum of production does not necessarily have as a consequence, let it be noted, a finalization of history on transcendent objects. The existence of a "machinic direction" of history in no way prevents the latter from "going off in every direction." The *machinic phylum* inhabits and orients the *historical rhizome* of capitalism, but without ever mastering its fate, which continues to be played out equally with social segmentarity and the evolution of economic modes of valorization.

Let us take up these various formulas of priorities again:

1) MARKET PRIORITIES

— priority (b), for instance that of commercial proto-capitalism from the 13th to the 17th century, relegates the question of the state to the third place. (Questions of state came so far behind commercial interests, for the merchants of the United Dutch Provinces in the 17th century, that no one was really scandalized by the fact that these merchants were providing their Portuguese or French enemies with weapons.[12] It brings together a specific problem with the enlargement and the consolidation of capitalism to the whole of society; these start off with a kind of Baroque efflorescence of all productive, cultural and institutional spheres.

— priority (c), for instance that of the *"savage" liberalism of 19th century capitalism*, relegates the question of production to the third place. It brings together a specific historical problem with the constitution of territorialized states. Paradoxically, liberalism was always more preoccupied with the constitution of a state apparatus than with a generalized increase in production. The existence of a large market is not enough for it. A central regulation—as flexible as it might be is also absolutely necessary to it. The "remote control" of production from a proliferating market complements the interventions and arbitrations of territorialized states, without which the system would run up against its own limits. It would prove especially incapable of producing basic equipments (public equipments, collective equipments, military equipments, etc.).

2) STATE PRIORITIES:

— priority (a), for instance that of the *Asiatic mode of production*, or the *war economy of Nazi type* (forced labor, relatively secondary role of the monetary economy, incarnation of the omnipotence of the state in the Fuhrer or the Pharaoh, etc.), relegates the question of the market to the third place. It involves specific historical problems:

1) with the management of the accumulation of capital. Surplus-value must accumulate in priority out of state power and its military machine; the growth of the economic and social powers of the various aristocratic strata must be limited, because it would ultimately threaten the caste in power; it would lead to the constitution of social classes. In the case of the "Asiatic" empires, this regulation

can be effected by halting production,[13] by massive sacrificial consummation, sumptuary construction, luxury consumption, etc. In the case of the Nazi regimes, by internal exterminations and war.

2) with outside machinic intrusions, especially innovations in military techniques that the state cannot adopt in due time, due to their conservatism, to their reluctance of letting any creative initiative develop. (Certain Asiatic empires were liquidated in just a few years by nomadic war machines bearing military innovations.)

— priority (f), for instance that of *Soviet State capitalisms* (plans of the Stalinist type, etc.), whose affinities with the Asiatic mode of production have often been emphasized—the Chinese model, at least that of the Maoist period, with its methods of massive subjection of collective labor-power, maybe more closely related to formula (a) than to formula (f)—but relegates the question of production to the third place. It brings a specific historical problem to bear with the question of the instruments of economic semiotization, especially with the establishment of markets, involving not only economic values, but also values of creation, innovation, and desires. In this type of system, the deregulation of market systems, together with a hyper-stratification of social segmentarity, is correlative to an authoritarian management which can only subsist insofar as its sphere of influence is not overly exposed to outside influences, to the competition of other branches of the productive machinic phylum. Thus the Gulag is ultimately only tenable inasmuch as the Soviet economy continues to partially freeze innovative arrangements in advanced technological, scientific and cultural domains. This problematic is prolonged henceforth by that of demands connected to a democratization of the social-semiotic management apparatus of the system. (Example: the "self management" struggles of the Polish workers).

3) PRODUCTION PRIORITIES:

— priority (d), for instance that of *classical imperialist exploitation*, constitutes a form of accumulation which is adjacent to the great capitalist entities, without any notable machinic basis,[14] and disregarding the effects of disorganization on the colonized socius. The commercial monopoly of the periphery tends to favor tendencies to monopoly capitalism within metropolises, and to reinforce state powers. This brings together a specific historical question with the reconstitution of the devastated socius of the colonies, including the creation of the state in the most artificial forms.

— priority (c), for instance of *World-Wide Integrated Capitalism*, establishes itself "above" and "below" capitalist and pre-capitalist segmentary relations (that is, at a level which is at once world-wide and molecular), through semiotic means of evaluation and valorization of Capital which are entirely novel in their increased capacity to integrate machinically the whole of human activities and faculties. The specific historical question which is brought in here concerns the potential limits of this integrative potency. It is not obvious, indeed, that World-Wide Integrated Capitalism can indefinitely manage to innovate and retrieve techniques and subjectivities. It is once again appropriate to emphasize that World-Wide Integrated Capitalism is not a self-sufficient entity. Even though today it pretends to be "the highest stage of capitalism" (to take up an expression that Lenin applied to imperialism), after all, it is only one capitalistic formula among others. Besides, it adapts to the survival of large zones of archaic economy, it lives in symbiosis with liberal and colonial economies of the classical type, it coexists with economies of the Stalinist type … "Progressive" in the domain of technico-scientific mutations, it has become thoroughly conservative in the social domain (not for ideological reasons, but for functional reasons). Hence one may rightfully ask if one is not presented here with one of its unsurmountable contradictions. The capacities of adaptation and reconversion of the economic arrangements of enunciation of World-Wide Integrated Capitalism may perhaps arrive at their limit with the renewal of the capacity of resistance of all of the social layers which refuse its "one-dimensionalizing" finalities. To be sure, the internal contradictions of World-Wide Integrated Capitalism are not such that it must ineluctably succumb to them. But its illness might nonetheless be deadly: it results from the accumulation of all the lateral crises that it engenders. The potency of the productive process of World-Wide Integrated Capitalism seems inexorable, and its social effects, unavoidable; but it upsets so many things, bruises so many other modes of life and of social valorization, that it does not seem absurd to count on the development of new collective answers—new arrangements of enunciation, of evaluation and action, stemming from the most diverse horizons—finally being able to demote it. (The appearance of new popular war machines of the Nicaragua type, the self-management struggles of great magnitude in Eastern Europe, the struggles for self-valorization of work of the Italian style, the multitude of vectors of molecular revolution in all the spheres of society). I believe that it is only through this hypothesis that the objectives of a revolutionary transformation of society can be redefined.

22

MICROPHYSICS OF POWER /

MICROPOLITICS OF DESIRE

The following abbreviations are used to cite Michel Foucault's work. The original pagination is cited first, followed by the available English translation.

A.S. *L'Archéologie du savoir* (Paris: Gallimard, 1969); *The Archaeology of Knowledge*, trans. A.M. Sheridan Smith (New York: Pantheon Books, 1972).

H.F. *Histoire de la folie à l'âge classique* (Paris: Gallimard, 1976); *Madness and Civilization*, trans. Richard Howard (New York: Random House, 1973).

H.S. *Histoire de la sexualité,* Vol. 1. *La Volonté de savoir* (Paris: Gallimard, 1976), Vol. 2. *L'Usage des plaisirs* (Paris: Gallimard, 1984); *The History of Sexuality*, trans. Robert Hurley (New York: Random House, 1978); Vol. 2. *The Use of Pleasure*, trans. Robert Hurley (New York: Random House, 1985).

M.C. *Les Mots et les choses* (Paris: Gallimard, 1966); *The Order of Things* (New York: Random House, 1970).

M.F. Hubert Dreyfus and Paul Rabinow, Michel Foucault. *Un Parcours philosophique*, trans. Fabienne Durand Bogaert (Paris: Gallimard, 1984); *Michel Foucault: Beyond Structuralism and Hermeneutics* (Chicago: University of Chicago Press, 1983).

O.D. *L'Ordre du discours* (Paris: Gallimard, 1971); "The Discourse on Language," in *The Archaeology of Knowledge*.

P. "L'Oeil du pouvoir," in Jeremy Bentham, *Le Panoptique* (Paris: Belfond, 1977); "The Eye of Power," in *Power/Knowledge: Selected Interviews and Other Writings 1972–1977*, ed. C. Gordin (New York: Pantheon Books, 1980).

R.R. *Raymond Roussel* (Paris: Gallimard, 1963); *Death and the Labyrinth: The World of Raymond Roussel*, trans. Charles Ruas (New York: Doubleday and Co., 1986).

S.P. *Surveiller et punir* (Paris: Gallimard, 1975); *Discipline and Punish; The Birth of the Prison*, trans. Alan Sheridan (New York: Vintage Books, 1977).

Having had the privilege of seeing Michel Foucault take up my suggestion—expressed somewhat provocatively—that concepts were after all nothing but tools and that theories were equivalent to the boxes that contained them (their power scarcely able to surpass the services that they rendered in circumscribed fields, that is, at the time of historical sequences that were inevitably delimited), you ought not as a result be surprised in seeing me today rummaging through Foucault's conceptual tool shop so that I might borrow some of his own instruments and, if need be, alter them to suit my own purposes.

Moreover, I am convinced that it was precisely in this manner that Foucault intended that we make use of his contribution.

It is not by means of an exegetical practice that one could hope to keep alive the thought of a great thinker who has passed away. Rather, such a thought can only be kept alive through its renewal, by putting it back into action, reopening its questioning, and by preserving its distinct uncertainties—with all the risks that this entails for those who make the attempt.

I leave it to you to relate this initial banality to the somewhat tired genre of the posthumous homage! In one of his last essays, which dealt with the economy of power relations, Foucault entreated his reader not to be repelled by the banality of the facts that he mentioned: "the fact [that] they're banal does not mean they don't exist. What we have to do with banal facts is to discover—or try to discover—which specific and perhaps original problem is connected with them." (M.F. 299/210) In this way, I believe that what is quite exceptional and perhaps now ready to be discovered, in the manner which Foucault's thought is destined to survive him, is that this thought traces out, better than any other, the most urgent problematics of our societies. And to date, nothing has shown itself to be as elaborate as this thought, certainly not the already outmoded approaches of "postmodernisms" and "post-politicalisms," which in the face of these same problematics have all run aground.

The most crucial aspect of Foucault's intellectual development consists in having moved away from both a starting point that was leading him towards a hermeneutic interpretation of social discourse and from a final goal that would have entailed a closed structuralist reading of this same discourse. It is in *The Archaeology of Knowledge* that he supposedly carried out this two-fold conspiracy. Whereas in fact it is here that he explicitly freed himself from this perspective, initially employed in *Madness and Civilization*, by announcing that for him it was no longer a question of "interpreting discourse with a view to writing a history of the referent." Rather, his stated intention was to henceforth "substitute for the enigmatic treasure of 'things' anterior to discourse, the regular formation of objects that emerge only in discourse." (A.S. 64 67/47–49)

This refusal to make reference to the "foundation of things," as well as the renunciation of the profound depths of meaning, is parallel and symmetrical to the Deleuzian position that rejects the lofty objects [*objet des hauteurs*] as well as any transcendental position of representation. With Foucault and Deleuze, horizontalness—a certain *transversality* accompanied by a new principle of contiguity-discontinuity—is presented in opposition to the traditional vertical stance of thought. It should he noted that it was around this same turbulent period that oppressive hierarchies of power were being put into question. It was also a period marked by the discovery of new lived dimensions of spatiality, as seen, for example, in the somersaults of the astronauts, the innovative experiments in the field of dance and, in particular, the flourishing of the Japanese Buto.

Foucault's new program was now spelled out: to renounce the "question of origins,"[1] to leave for analysis "a blank, indifferent space, lacking in both interiority and promise" (AS. 54/39) without, however, falling into the trap of a flat reading of the signifier.

It was in this respect that during his inaugural talk in 1970 at the Collège de France, Foucault issued a kind of solemn warning:

"[d]iscourse thus nullifies itself, in reality, in placing itself at the disposal of the signifier." (O.D. 51/228)

Indeed, after a period of initial hesitation, Foucault came to consider as pernicious any structuralist endeavor to "treat discourse as groups of signs (signifying elements referring to contents or representations)." Instead, he wished to apprehend these discourses from the perspective of *"practices* that systematically form the objects of which they speak." "Of course," Foucault continues, "discourses are composed of signs; but what they do is more than use these signs to designate things. It is this *more* that renders them irreducible to language [*langue*] and to speech." (A.S. 66 67/49) [t.m.] In this way, Foucault left the ghetto of the signifier and the asserted will in order to take into account the productive dimension of the enunciation. But of what is this "more" (that is here in question) constituted? Is it a matter of a simple subjective illusion? Does this "more" go in search of an "already there," or a process that is being deployed? There is probably no universal answer to these questions. Each regional or global cartography, depending on whether it is inclined towards aesthetic or scientific ideological claims, defines its own field of pragmatic efficiency. And it is quite evident that a renunciation—of the sort proposed by Foucault—of the reductive myths that are generally in fashion in the human sciences would not be without its effect on the political and micropolitical stakes of, for example, the care giver cared for relationship, the role of specialists in psychology, the positions occupied by these specialists within the university, the preoccupations of the mass media, the hierarchies existing between the different levels of the state, and so forth. Having successfully devalued the imaginary component of the real, to the exclusive benefit of its symbolic component, the French structuralists of the sixties in effect established a kind of religious trinity comprised of the Symbolic, Real, and Imaginary—its missionaries and converts disseminating and preaching the new good tidings just about everywhere, attempting brutally, or sometimes quite subtly, to invalidate any view that did not mesh with their own hegemonic will. But we know quite well that no Trinity—whether it be of the overwhelming sort that is the Hegelian accomplishment, or that of a Charles Sanders Pierce, whose richness still remains largely unexplored—has been, nor will ever be, able to take into account, for example, the singular being of an ordinary sliver in desiring flesh. And upon a moment's reflection, we can very well understand why this is so: these trinities are constituted precisely as a way to conjure away the random ruptures or rare occurrences which Foucault has shown us to be the essential thread of any existential affirmation. "Rarity and affirmation; rarity in the last resort of affirmation— certainly not any continuous outpouring of meaning, and certainly not any monarchy of the signifier."[2] (O.D. 72/234) In a word, the reality of history and desire, the productions of the soul, body, and sex, do not pass through this kind of tripartition, which is ultimately quite simplistic.[3] These involve a completely other categorical reduction [démultipication catégorielle] of the semiotic components opening onto imaginary scenes or in the form of symbolic diagrams. Both the rupturing of the portmanteau concept of the signifier, as well as the critique of the Lacanian adage that only the signifier can represent the subject for another signifier, go hand in hand with the radical questioning of the philosophical tradition of the "founding subject." Foucault challenges the conception of the subject that supposedly "animates the empty forms of language with its objectives." (O.D. 49/227) [t.m] Instead, Foucault commits himself to describing the actual agents that engender the discursivity of social groups and institutions—which in turn leads him to the discovery of a vast domain of forms of collective production and technical modalities of the construction of subjectivity, virtually unrecognized until then. This is not to be understood in the sense of a causal determination, but rather as the *rarefaction* and/or *proliferation* of the semiotic components at the intersection from which they arise. Behind the obvious "logophilia" of the dominant culture, he analyses a profound "logophobia," a ferocious will to master and control "the great proliferation of discourses, in such a way as to relieve the richness of its most dangerous elements; as well as to organize its disorder so as to elude its most uncontrollable aspects" and a mute fear against the sudden appearance of statements, of events, and against "everything that could possibly be violent, discontinuous, querulous, disordered even and perilous in it, of the incessant, disorderly buzzing of discourse." (O.D. 52 53/228 29) [t.m]

We can distinguish two ways in which Foucault considers how the subjectivity which he explores eludes the reductionistic approaches that have taken root virtually everywhere:

1) that of a reterritorialization leading to an updating of subjectivity's institutional components of semiotization, and what charges it with history and factual contingency—it is at this level that it distinguishes itself from all variations of structuralism;

2) that of a deterritorialization that shows subjectivity to be, according to an expression put forth in *Discipline and Punish*, a creator of a "real, non corporeal soul." It is also implied in this humorous warning: "It would be wrong to say that the soul is an illusion, or an ideological effect. On the contrary, it exists, it has a reality, it is produced permanently around, on, within the body." (S.P.34/29) We are here in the register of an "incorporeal materialism" (O.D. 60/231) that is as far removed from the rigid forms of hermeneutical interpretations as it is from the lures of a certain currently fashionable "non materialism."

It is a matter, henceforth, of escaping from, by way of an analytic practice—what Foucault calls a "discourse as practice"—the agents of subjugation, whatever may be their level of institution. In an interview—that seems to constitute a kind of testament—with Hubert Dreyfus and Paul Rabinow, Foucault continues to assert that "we need to promote new forms of subjectivities by renouncing the type of individuality that was imposed upon us over several centuries." (M.F. 301 302) [my trans.] Furthermore, he takes care to list the conditions that permit an advancement towards a new economy of power relations. The struggles for the transformation of subjectivity, Foucault explains, are not ordinary forms of opposition to authority. Rather, they are characterized by the following aspects:

1) they are "transversal" (for Foucault this means that these struggles are to be understood as emerging from the particular context of the country in question);

2) they are opposed to all categories of power effects, and not just those that pertain to "visible" social struggles; for example, those effects that are exercised over people's bodies and their health;

3) they are immediate, in the sense that these struggles are aimed at the forms of power that are closest to those engaged in the struggle, and because they do not yield to any predetermined resolution, such as we find in the programs of political parties;

4) they put into question the status of the normalized individual and assert a fundamental right to difference (which is, moreover, not in the least incompatible with community choices);

5) they are opposed to the privileges of knowledge and their mystifying function;

6) they involve a refusal of the economic and ideological violence of the State, and of all its forms of scientific and administrative inquisition.

Across these various prescriptions, we see that the decoding of "the political technologies of the body," the "microphysics of power" (S.P. 31/26) and of the "discursive 'policy'" (O.D. 37/224), proposed by Foucault does not consist of a simple contemplative point of reference, but rather involves what I have called *micropolitics*, that is, a molecular analysis that allows us to move from forms of power to investments of desire.

When Foucault speaks of desire, which he does repeatedly in his work, he always means it in a sense that is far more restricted than the way Deleuze and I employ this term. We can, nevertheless, note that his quite distinct notion of power has, if I may say so, the effect of "pulling" this concept in the direction of desire. It is in this way that he deals with power as a matter that has to do with an investment and not with an "all or nothing" law. Throughout his entire life, Foucault refused to conceive of power as a reified entity. For him, relations of power and, by consequence, strategic struggles, never amount to being mere objective relations of force. Rather, these relations involve the processes of subjectification in their most essential and irreducible singularity. And within them, we will always find "the obstinacy of the will and the intransitivity of freedom." (M.F. 312 315) [my trans.]

As such, power is not exercised "simply as an obligation or a prohibition on those who 'do not have it'; it invests them, is transmitted by them and through them; it exerts pressure upon them, just as they themselves, in their struggle against it, resist the grip it has on them." (S.P. 31 32/27) To this I would add that despite our different points of view, let us say of our "framing of the field," it seems to me that our problematics of analytic singularity overlap.

But before settling on this point, I would like to make a more general remark regarding our shared dispute against Lacanian and related theories in order to underline the fact that our dispute was never accompanied by a neopositivist or Marxist negation of the problem of the unconscious. The *History of Sexuality* brought to the fore the decisive nature of the break that Freudianism carried out with respect to what Foucault called the "series composed of perversion-heredity degenerescence," that is, the solid nucleus of the technologies of sex at the turn of the last century. (H.S. vol. I. 157/118 119, 197 198/149 150) As Deleuze and myself are concerned, one must recall that we were rebelling against the attempt to reconstruct a particular form of analysis, namely, the Lacanian pretension of erecting a universal logic of the signifier that would account for not only the economy of subjectivity and of the affects but also of all the other discursive forms relating to art, knowledge, and power.

Let us now return to the feature that aligns us, perhaps more than any other, with Foucault, namely, a common refusal to expel those dimensions of singularity of the analytic object and its procedures of elucidation: "The theme of universal mediation," Foucault writes, "is yet another manner of eliding the reality of discourse. And this despite appearances. At first sight it would seem that, to discover the movement of a logos everywhere elevating singularities into concepts, finally enabling immediate consciousness to deploy all the rationality in the world, is certainly to place discourse at the center of speculation. But, in truth, this logos is really only another discourse already in operation, or rather, it is things and events themselves which insensibly become discourse in the unfolding of the essential secret." (O.D. 50 1/228) This return to singularity rests, in Foucault, on his very distinct conception of the statement as no longer representing a unity of the same sort as the sentence, the proposition, or the speech act. Consequently, the statement, for Foucault, no longer functions on the authority of a segment of a universal logos leveling out existential contingencies. Its proper domain is therefore no longer simply that of a relation of signification, articulating the relationship between signifier and signified, nor of the relation of the denotation of a referent. For it is also a capacity of *existential production* (which, to use my terminology, I call a *diagrammatic function*). In its mode of being singular, the Foucauldian statement is neither quite linguistic, nor exclusively material. It is, nevertheless, crucial that we be able to state whether or not we are dealing with a sentence, proposition, or speech act. "The statement is not therefore a structure... it is a function of existence that properly belongs to signs and on the basis of which one may then decide, through analysis or intuition, whether or not they 'make sense'..." (A.S. 115/86)

Is not this intersection between the semiotic function of meaning, the denotative function, and this pragmatic function of *mise en existence* precisely on that which all psychoanalytic experience turns—with its symptomatic indexes, witticisms, its lapses, its "dream navels" [*ombilics de rêve*], failed actions, its fantastical training and behavioralism clutching as it is onto its own existential repetition that is empty of meaning, or at the very least, empty in a pragmatic sense in the coordinates of dominant meanings? Whether he was traversing the "discourses" of collective instruments (for example, that of hospitals or prisons), the marking of bodies and of sexuality, the history of the emergence of the figures of reason and madness, or even the mechanical worlds of a Raymond Roussel (R.R. 120/93), Foucault's primary research was always concerned with the rifts of discourse, that is, the ruptures of meaning of ordinary language or of scientific discursivity. Foucault's objective was always that of carrying out a mapping of large groups of statements as a "series of intertwining lacunas and interplays of differences, distances, substitutions, and transformations." He never accepted as self evident the view that these groups of statements are to be characterized as "full, tightly packed, continuous, [and) geographically well-defined." (A.S. 52/37) [t.m.] When following Foucault on this terrain, one senses at times a connection with the dissident logic of the Freudian primary processes.[4] While this is true, Foucault's concept of singularity, whose importance I have already underlined, nevertheless differs profoundly from this logic in two ways.

First, one must never forget that Foucault undertook, indeed, in every way possible, to dismantle the false appearance of the individuation of subjectivity. I have already mentioned the subjugating function of social individuation—what Foucault calls "government of individualization"—which at once individualizes and totalizes (M.F. 302/212 13), and which, by means of a faceless gaze "transforms the whole social body into a field of perception: thousands of eyes posted everywhere, mobile attentions ever on the alert, a long, hierarchized network…"(S.P. 216/214) But this function is not necessarily exercised by a clearly defined rational social operator such as a caste in control of a state or by the executive administration of a political party. It may involve an *intentionality without subject* (H.S. vol. 1. 124 25/94 95) proceeding from "collective surfaces and inscriptions." (A.S. 56/41) Panoptic control, for example, leads to the subjectification of those who observe as much as those who are observed. It is an apparatus wherein no one has exclusive authority, and where "everyone is caught, those who exercise power just as much an those over whom it is exercised." (P. 156) In a more general way, we need to keep in mind that there exists no statement—in the Foucauldian sense—that would be free, neutral, and independent. Statements are always an integral part of an associated field; it is only because they are immersed in an enunciative field that they can emerge in their singularity. (A.S. 130/99)

This perspective also led Foucault to reconsider the status of the author at the level of the most basic procedures of the delimitation and control of discourse. For Foucault, the author is not to be identified with the speaking individual who has delivered or written a text, but as a "unifying principle of discourse"—which on my part, I have called a "collective assemblage of enunciation"— that gives this discourse its unity, its gesture, its meaning, as the seat of its coherence. (O.D. 28/221) [t.m.]

Secondly, the way Foucault positions the question of the existential singularities also constitutes a potential, but decisive, departure from the Freudian manner of approaching the forms of the unconscious, or "unthought" [*impensée*] to use a term inspired by the work of Blanchot. The individual as ruptured is no longer synonymous with singularity, and can no longer be conceived of as an irreducible point of escape from the systems of relations and representation. Even the cogito has lost its character of apodictic certainty to become, in a way, processual; it is now understood as "a ceaseless task constantly to be undertaken afresh." (MC. 335/324) Singularity is formed or undone according to the hold of the subjective strength of the collective and/or individual discursivity. Let us say, by way of returning to the context of our particular categories, that singularity has to do with a *process of singularization* in so far as it comes to exist as a collective assemblage of enunciation. With this aim in view, singularity can just as well embody itself through a collective discourse as it can lose itself in a serialized individuation. And even when it concerns an individual entity, it might very well continue to be a matter of processual multiplicities. This is not to say, however, that in becoming fragmented, precarious, and in freeing itself from its identitarian fetters a singularity is necessarily led to impoverish or weaken itself. On the contrary: it affirms itself. At least that is the orientation proposed by Foucault's micropolitics of the "analytic of finitude," breaking completely as it does with the analytic of representations issuing from the Kantian tradition. It would therefore be a serious misinterpretation to restrict his perspective to one type of global intervention of the subjectification of the social body. For Foucault's perspective is also, and above all, a micropolitics of existence and desire. Finitude, in this perspective, is not something that one resignedly endures as a loss, a deficiency, a mutilation, or castration. Rather, finitude entails existential affirmation and commitment. All the themes we might call Foucauldian existentialism converge on this pivotal point between semiotic representation and the pragmatics of "existentialization," and, in this way, places the micropolitics of desire alongside the micro-physics of power according to specific procedures. Each of these themes demands to be reinvented, one at a time, and case by case, in a process akin to artistic creation. Foucault's immense contribution lies in its exploration of the fundamentally political fields of subjectification, as well as the guiding light of a micropolitics that frees us from the pseudo-universals of Freudianism or the Lacanian mathemes of the unconscious. As a result of the methods he articulated, the lessons we can derive from his intellectual and personal development, as well as from the aesthetic character of his work, Foucault has left us with a number of invaluable instruments for an analytic cartography.

23

POSTMODERN DEADLOCK AND

POST-MEDIA TRANSITION

A certain conception of progress and modernity has gone bank-rupt. Its fall from grace has shaken collective confidence in the very idea of an emancipatory social practice. In a parallel fashion, a kind of glaciation has taken over social relations; hierarchies and segregations have hardened and destitution and unemployment today tend to be accepted as necessary evils. Unions are now clinging to the last institutional branches available to them and retreat into corporatist practices that lead them to adopt conservative attitudes that resemble those found in reactionary circles. The communist left is sinking irreparably into ossification and dogmatism, whereas the socialist parties, eager to come across as reliable technocratic partners, have renounced all progressive questioning of existing structures. No big surprise, then, that the ideologies that once claimed to serve as guides for reconstituting society on more just and egalitarian grounds, have lost their credibility.

Does it then follow that we are condemned to stand with tied arms before the rise of this new order of cruelty and cynicism that is on its way to overwhelm the planet with the firm intention of sticking around? This is, in fact, the regrettable conclusion at which numerous intellectuals and artists have arrived, especially those who claim some connection with the postmodernism vogue.

At least for the purposes of the present discussion, I will not discuss the launching, by the managers of contemporary art, of large promotional campaigns, that of "neo-expressionism," as it was tagged in Germany, "Bad Painting" or "New Painting" in the USA, "Trans-avant-garde" in Italy and, in France, "New Fauvism," etc. Otherwise, it would be too easy for me to show how post-modernism comes down to nothing more than the final spasms of modernism, that it is a reaction and, to a certain extent, a mirror of the formalist and reductionist abuses of the latter, from which it ultimately isn't really any different. No doubt some authentic painters will emerge from these schools; their personal talent will have protected them from the pernicious effects of this kind of fascination held up by means of publicity. But there will be no revival of the creative phylum that they had hoped to bring back.

Architectural postmodernism, insofar as it is better attached to the deeply reterritorializing tendencies of current capitalist subjectivity, seems to me, on the contrary, much less superficial and much more indicative of the place allotted to art by dominant power formations. Let me explain myself here. From time immemorial, historical misadventures aside, the capitalistic drive has always combined two fundamental components. One of these components is the destruction of social territories, collective identities, and traditional value systems. I qualify this as deterritorialization. The other component is the reconstitution—even through the most artificial means—of individuated personological frameworks, schemata of power, and models of submission which are, if not similar in form to those that the capitalistic drive destroyed, then at least homothetical to them, from a functional point of view. I consider this last component a movement of "reterritorialization." As deterritorializing revolutions, linked to scientific, technical, and artistic development, sweep away everything in their path, a compulsion toward subjective reterritorialization also begins. And this antagonism worsens that much more with the prodigious expansion of communicative and informatic machinisms, whether they focus their deterritorializing effects on human faculties such as memory, perception, understanding, or imagination, etc... A certain formula of anthropological functioning, a certain ancestral model of humanity thus finds itself, at heart, appropriated. And I think that it's for a lack of being able to face this prodigious mutation in an appropriate manner that collective subjectivity is giving in to the absurd wave of conservatism that we are currently seeing. As for knowing under what conditions it would be possible to lower the low-water levels of these baleful waters and what help might be given by the residual islets of liberating wills still emerging from this deluge, this is precisely the question underlying my proposal that we transition towards a post-mass media era. Without further extrapolating on this subject, it seems to me that this rocking motion that brought us to a dangerously retrograde subjective reterritorialization might spectacularly turn around the day when are asserted, in a sufficient manner, new emancipatory social practices and, above all, alternative assemblages of subjective production capable of connecting—on a mode different than that of conservative reterritorialization—to the molecular revolutions that work our era.

Let's now turn to our postmodern architects. For some of them, it isn't really in the figurative sense that one may speak of reterritorialization, for example, in the case of Léon Krier when he proposes, quite simply, to construct traditional towns, with their streets, their squares, their neighborhoods.[1] With Robert Venturi, the question is less about reterritorializing space than about cutting the bridges to time, refusing the drafts drawn on the future by modernists like Le Corbusier, as well as the backward-looking dreams of the Neo-Classicists. From now on, it is considered well and right that the present state of affairs is accepted as it is. Even better, Venturi will take on the most prosaic aspects, he will go into raptures about the "commercial strips," bordered by the "decorated sheds" that are tearing the urban fabric of the United States into shreds. He will go as far as to praise the kitsch decoration of prefabricated suburban lawns, which he will compare to the urns of Le Notre's flowerbeds.[2] When, in the domain of the plastic arts, young painters were required to submit to the masters of the market—because of which they saw themselves condemned to vegetate on the fringes—the most retrograde values of neo-liberalism were embraced one after another. It is true that painting, for the ruling classes, was never anything more than a "supplement to the soul," a currency of prestige, whereas architecture has always occupied a major place in the fabrication of territories of power, in the setting of its emblems, in the proclamation of its durability.

Are we not thus at the heart of what Jean-François Lyotard calls: the postmodern condition, one that, unlike this author, I understand as the paradigm of all submissions, of all compromises with the current status quo?[3] On the ground of the collapse of what he calls the great narratives of legitimation (for example, Enlightenment discourse or Hegel's discourse on the self-realization of Spirit, or that of Marxists on the emancipation of workers). Still according to Lyotard, one should be suspicious of the most vague impulses of concerted social action. All the agreed-on values, he explains to us, have become obsolete and suspect. Only the little narratives of legitimation, of "pragmatics of language particles," multiple and heterogeneous, whose performativity is necessarily limited in time and space, can still salvage some values of justice and liberty. Here Lyotard joins other theorists, such as Jean Baudrillard, for whom the social and the political have only ever been traps, "semblances" which it would be best to let go of as soon as possible. All social unrest then comes down to language games (one senses that the Lacanian signifier isn't far away), the only kitsch watchword that Lyotard—that former leader of the leftist magazine *Socialisme ou Barbarie*—succeeds in saving from the disaster, is the right of free access to computer memory and databases.

Be they painters, architects, or philosophers, the heroes of postmodernism have this in common; they all think that today's crises in artistic and social practices can no longer result in anything but a total refusal of all collective project-making of any importance. Let's cultivate our garden, and preferably in conformity with the practices and customs of our contemporaries. Don't make waves! Just make fashion, gauged by the art and opinion markets, screened through publicity campaigns and polls. As for ordinary sociality, a new principle of "sufficient communication" should ensure that its forces are kept in balance and provide for its ephemeral consistency. If we think about it, how far have we come since the era when the banners of French sociology read: "Social facts are not things!" And now, for the postmoderns, they are no more than erratic clouds of discourse floating within a signifying ether!

But where, by the way, did they get the idea that the socius can in this way be reduced to facts of languages and these, in turn, to binarisable or "digitalisable" signifying chains? On this point, the post-moderns have hardly come up with something new! They place themselves squarely in the tradition—itself downright modernist—of structuralism, whose influence on the human sciences seems doomed to be relayed, in the worst possible conditions, by Anglo-Saxon systemism. The secret link between all these doctrines comes, I believe, from their having been subterranean—marked by reductionist conceptions, spread immediately after the war by information theory and the first research into cybernetics. The references that these different doctrines ceaselessly borrowed from the new communicative and information technologies were so hurried and so badly managed, that they threw us far behind the phenomenological research that had preceded them.

It will be necessary to bring this back to a simple truth, but one heavy with consequence, i.e., to know that concrete social assemblages—which must not be confused with the "primary groups" of American sociology, which still belong to the field of the economy of opinion—put many things into question other than linguistic performance: ethnological and ecological dimensions, economic semiotic components, aesthetic, bodily, fantasmatic, irreducible to the semiology of language (*langue*), a multitude of incorporeal universes of reference which don't willingly fit into the coordinates of the dominant empiricist approach. Postmodern philosophers can flit around pragmatic research all they want, they remain faithful to a structuralist conception of speech and language that will never allow them to relate the subjective facts to the formations of the unconscious, to the aesthetic and micropolitical problematics. To put it plainly, I think that this philosophy is no philosophy; it's nothing more than an ambient frame of mind, a "condition" of opinion that only takes its truths from the current intellectual climate. Why, for instance, does it bother to elaborate a serious speculative back up of its thesis, relative to the flimsiness of the socius? Doesn't the current all-powerfulness of the mass media amply supplement the fact that any social link can stand in, without noticeable resistance, the desingularizing and infantilizing leveling of the capitalist production of signifiers? An old Lacanian adage, according to which "a signifier represents the subject for another signifier" could function as the motto of this new ethics of disengagement. Because, in fact, that is exactly what is happening! Only, there is nothing much to rejoice about, although the postmoderns are doing it. Instead, we should be concerned with figuring out how to get out from such a deadlock.

That the production of our signaletic raw materials is increasingly dependent on the intervention of machines does not imply that human freedom and creativity are inexorably condemned to alienation by mechanical procedures.[4] Nothing prohibits that, instead of the subject being under the control of the machine, that it is the machinic networks that are engaged in a kind of process of subjectivation. In other terms, nothing prohibits machinism and humanity from starting to have fruitful symbiotic relations. With respect to this, it will perhaps be necessary to establish a distinction between the aforementioned signaletic material and subjectivities' electives. By this, I understand all of the domains of decisionality brought into play by the assemblages of enunciation (collective and/or individual). Whereas signaletic materials are defined by logics of discursive ensemble whose relations can be referred to objects displaying themselves according to extrinsic coordinates (spatio-temporal-energic), the electives are defined by logics of auto-reference that take on features of existential intensity that refuse any sort of submission to the axioms of set theories. These logics, that I will also call logics of Bodies without Organs, or logics of existential territories, have in common that their objects are ontologically ambiguous: they are object-subject bifaces which can be neither discernabilized, nor discursivized as figures represented on the background of coordinates of representation. We can thus not apprehend them from the outside; we can do no more than accept them, take them on ourselves, through an existential transfer.

The "transversalist" function of these ambiguous objects, the one that affords them the possibility of traversing the districts of time and space, and of transgressing identitary assignations, is found in the heart of the Freudian cartography of the unconscious and also, although in a different sense, in the preoccupations of linguists concerned with enunciation.

The primary process, the identification, the transference, the partial objects, the "after the event" function of the fantasy, all these notions familiar to psychoanalysts, imply, in one way or another, the existence of an ubiquity and a recursivity—prospectivity of the entities that it calls into question. But by indirectly making the logic of the unconscious depend on the logic of dominant realities—interpretation seeing itself handed the task of rendering the first translatable in the terms of the second— Freud lost the specificity of his discovery, the fact that some semiotic segments, being brought to leave the context of their ordinary signifying "mission," could acquire a particular power of existential production (in the world of neurosis, perversion, psychosis, sublimation, etc...). The Lacanian tripartition of the Real, the Imaginary, and the Symbolic, far from sorting things out, only succeeded, from this point of view, in aggravating the compartmentalization of topical authorities in their relation to one another.

For their part, linguists who deal with theories of enunciation and speech acts have highlighted the fact that some linguistic segments, in addition to their well-known classical functions of signification and denotation, can also acquire a particular pragmatic efficiency by crystallizing the respective position of speaking subjects, or else by putting, de facto, certain situational frames, into place.[5] (The classic example is the president who declares: "the session is open," and in so doing, opens the session). But they too believe that they should limit the import of their discovery to their specific field, whereas, in truth, this third "existentializing" function, the very one that they stress, should, logically, also imply a definitive rupture of the structuralist corset in which they persist in constraining language.[6] It is not exclusively to index, within utterances, general subjective positions—those of deictics—or to position the contextualization of discourse, that language thus leaves itself; it is also and above all in order to crystallize pragmatic singularities, catalyze the most diverse processes of singularization (delimitation of perceptible territories, deployments of incorporeal universes of endo-reference...). It goes without saying that this pragmatic of the "bringing into being" is not the exclusive privilege of language; all the other semiotic components, all the other procedures of natural and machinic encoding are competing for it. It is thus not by legitimate right that the linguistic signifier occupies the royal position that capitalist subjectivation has given it, on the grounds that it provides essential support for its logic of generalized equivalence as well as its politics of capitalization of abstract values of power. Other semiotization machines are capable of "running" the world's affairs and, in this way, of deposing this symbolic-signifying imperium, in which the current hegemony of mass media powers are rooted, of its transcendent position with regard to the rhizomes woven by real and imaginary processes. But these regimes will certainly not come about through spontaneous generation. Rather, they are there to be constructed, within reach of our hands, at the intersection of new analytic, aesthetic, and social practices, practices that no postmodern spontaneity will bring us on a platter.

The emergence of these new practices of subjectivation of a post-media era will be greatly facilitated by a concerted reappropriation of communicational and information technology, assuming that they increasingly allow for:

1) The formation of innovative forms of dialogue and collective interactivity and, eventually, a reinvention of democracy;

2) By means of the miniaturization and the personalization of equipments, a resingularization of the machinic mediatized means of expression; we can presume, on this subject, that it is the connection, through networking, of banks of data which will offer us the most surprising views;

3) The multiplication to infinity of "existential operators," permitting access to mutant creative universes.

Let's remark, finally, that the multicentering and the subjective autonomization of the post-mediatic operators will not be correlative to their reclosing on themselves or to a postmodern-type disengagement. The coming post-mediatic revolution must be called on to take the relay (with incomparable efficiency) of minoritary groups which are the only ones, even today, that have become aware of the mortal risk, for humanity, of problems such as:

— the race to stockpile nuclear weapons

— world hunger

— irreversible ecological damage

— mass-mediatic pollution of collective subjectivity

This is at least what I hope for and what I allow myself to invite you to undertake. Unless this be our future, I wouldn't have much hope for the end of the present millennium!

24

ENTERING THE POST-MEDIA ERA

By what means can we hope to accelerate the arrival of what I have called the Post-Media Era? What theoretical and pragmatic conditions can facilitate an awareness of the "reactional" character of the present wave of conservatism, which I don't believe is a necessary evolution of developed societies?

If "organized minorities" are to become the laboratories of thought and experimentation for future forms of subjectivation, how can they structure themselves, and ally themselves with more traditional forms of organization (parties, unions, leftist groups) to avoid the isolation and repression that threatens them, while at the same time preserving their independence and specific traits? The same question holds true for the risks they run of being co-opted by the state.

Is it possible to envision a proliferation of "minority becomings" capable of diversifying the factors of subjective autonomy and economic self-management within the social field? Are they, in any case, compatible with modern systems of production and circulation that seem to call for ever more integration and concentration in their decision-making procedures?

Rethinking all the ways that subjectivity is produced requires redefining the unconscious from outside the confining frames of psychoanalysis. The unconscious should no longer be reducible solely in terms of intrapsychic entities or the linguistic signifier, since it must also engage diverse semiotic and pragmatic dimensions that have to do with a multiplicity of existential territories, machinic systems and incorporeal universes. I called it *schizoanalytic* to mark it off from the psychoanalytic unconscious—which, in my opinion, is far too anchored to personological ego formations, transference and identifications, not to mention the way it is irremediably ballasted by fixed and psychogenetic conceptions regarding instinctual objects. Yet I did not intend to tie it down exclusively to psychoses. Rather, I wished to open it to a maximum variety of schizzes, like love, childhood, art, etc. As opposed to Freudian complexes, schizoanalytic arrangements are the sites of both internal transformations and transferences between prepersonal levels (like those Freud describes in *The Psychopathology of Everyday Life*, for example) and the postpersonal levels that can be globally assigned to the media-driven world, extending the notion of media to every system of communication, displacement and exchange. From this perspective, the unconscious would become "transversalist," by virtue of the skill with which it traverses the most diverse orders derived from abstract and singular machines, while not clinging to any specific substance of expression, and resisting universals and structuralist mathemes.

Thus, the ego entity, responsible for the essence of the subject and for a person's real and imaginary actions, is only considered as the more or less transitory intersection of arrangements of enunciation varying in size, nature and duration. (Although not present literally, the same inspiration can be found in animist cartographies of subjectivity.)

Analysis must radically change attempts to solve tensions and conflicts that are already "programmed into" the individuated psyche through transference and interpretation. Rather, it will conceive of and transfer enunciations so as to surmount the ever-increasing societal discrepancies, between (a) representations and modes of perception and sensibility having to do with the body, sexuality, social, physical and ecological environments, and with diverse figures of alterity and finitude, shaped by technico-scientific mutations, particularly through information, electronics and images; and (b) social and institutional structures, juridical and regulatory systems, state apparatuses, moral, religious and esthetic norms, etc., which, behind an apparent continuity, are really threatened and sapped from the inside out by deterritorializing tensions from preceding molecular registers, causing every evolutionary process to stop short, to become more and more molar, to hold on to the most obsolete forms, even to the detriment of functional efficiency.

Unlike the transcendental subject of philosophical tradition (the-closed-in-on-itself monad that structuralists claim to have opened to alterity solely by virtue of the linguistic signifier), pragmatic enunciative arrangements escape in all directions. Their subjective formations, at the intersections of heterogeneous components, cannot be reduced to a single semiotic entity. For example, the nature of economic subjectivity cannot be equated to aesthetic subjectivity: the quality of the Oedipus complex of a well brought-up little boy from New York's Upper East Side is going to be entirely different from that of the initiation into the socius of a *pivete* from a Brazilian *favela*.

The elucidation of the internal composition of various "arrangements," and their reciprocal relationships imply two sorts of logic:

1) those relating to discursive ensembles that determine the relationships between fluxes and machinic systems endo-referring to different types of energetico-spatiotemporal coordinates;

2) those relating to non-discursive organless bodies that determine the relationships between existential territories and endo-referring incorporeal universes.

The introduction into analysis of concepts like endo-reference or auto-organization does not imply a departure from the ordinary fields of scientific rationality, but a break from scientistic causalism. For example, one considers that a schizoanalytic map is not "second" in relation to the existential territories it presents; one cannot even say, properly speaking, that they represent them, because it is the map that engenders the territories.

A related question: does not every esthetic production depend in one way or another on this kind of mapping, which doesn't need any theory of sublimated drives? As soon as unconscious subjectivity is envisaged from the perspective of the heterogeneity of its components, its multiform productivity, its micropolitical intentionality, its tension toward the future instead of its fixations on past stratifications, the focal point of analysis will be systematically displaced from statements and semiotic links toward enunciatory instances. Rather than the analysis of fixed discursive elements, one considers the constituent conditions of the "giver." There will be no point any more chasing nonsense and paradigmatic ramblings in order to pin them down, like butterflies, on interpretive or structuralist grids. Singularities of desire, those unnameable residues of meaning that psychoanalysts thought they could repertory as part-objects—for years they have gone into such arm-waving ecstasies—will no longer be accepted as the limits of analytical efficiency but will be considered as potential for processual boosts.

For instance, rather than putting emphasis on a symbolic castration lived as post-Oedipian submission, the emphasis will be put on "contingent choices" circumscribing and giving existential consistency to new pragmatic fields. Investigations must give special attention to the singular virtues of semiotic links that support such choices (*ritournelles*, facial features, becoming-animals, etc.). In parallel to their semiotic functions of signification and designation, they develop an existential function that catalyzes new universes of reference.

Behind the relative non-sense of failed statements, there is no longer a hidden meaning that schizoanalytical pragmatics will force out into the open, nor some latent drive that it will try to liberate. It will focus on unfolding innumerable incorporeal, indivisible materials that, as the experience of desire has taught us, are capable of carrying us far beyond ourselves and far beyond territorial encirclements, towards unexpected, unheard-of universes of possibility. Consequently, the active a-signifying processes of existential singularization will be substituted for the passive insignificance that is the preferred object of hermeneutics.

These high intensity, non-discursive materials, woven into subjective arrangements, only continue to exist by continually deterritorializing themselves into actual and virtual "projectuality," and reterritorializing within real and potential strata such that they can be considered as so many ethico-political options. Every site of desire or reason is within reach of our hands, our wills, our individual and collective choices... But, in the capitalistic order of things—that is to say the monotheistic, mono-energy-istic, mono-signifying, mono-libidinal, in short, a radically disenchanted order of things—nothing can evolve unless everything else remains in place. Subjective productions ("subjectivities") are obliged to submit to the axioms of equilibrium, equivalence, constancy, eternity... So, what's left for us to reach for? How can we hold on to a lust for life, for creation, or find a reason to die for other horizons?

When everything becomes equivalent to everything else, the only things that count are the ugly compulsions for the abstract accumulation of power over people for various kinds of bonds, and the pitiful exaltation of specular prestige. Under such gloomy conditions, singularity and finitude are necessarily considered scandalous, while "incarnation" and death are experienced as sins rather than part of the rhythms of life and the cosmos. I am not advocating a return to Oriental wisdom, which can carry with it the worst sorts of resignation. Nor a rejection of capitalism's great equivalents—energy, libido, information—without cautiously or carefully experimenting with alternatives. Even capital can be reconverted into a dependable instrument of economic writing. All it takes is reinventing its usage, not in a dogmatic and programmatic manner, but through the creation of other "existential chemistries," open to all the recompositions and transmutations of these "singularity salts" whose secret arts and analysis can deliver up.

Analysis again. But where? How? Well, everywhere possible. Where unskirtable contradictions come to the surface. Where disturbing breaches of meaning trip us up amidst daily banalities, impossible yet perfectly viable loves, all kinds of constructivist passions that mine the edifices of morbid rationality... It can be individual, for those who tend to lead their lives as if it were a work of art; dual in all possible ways, including, why not, a psychoanalytic couch, as long as it has been dusted off; multiple, through group, network, institutional, and collective practices; and finally, micropolitical by virtue of other social practices, other forms of auto-valorizations and militant actions, leading, through a systematic decentering of social desire, to soft subversions and imperceptible revolutions that will eventually change the face of the world, making it happier. Let's face it: it is long overdue.

25

UTOPIA TODAY

[I hate this kind of survey, so I am addressing this answer to you alone; do with it what you like.]

Utopia, today, is to believe that current societies will be able to continue along on their merry little way without major upheavals. Social modes of organization that prevail today on earth *are not holding up*, literally and figuratively. History is gripped by crazy parameters: demography, energy, the technological-scientific explosion, pollution, the arms race… The earth is deterritorializing itself at top speed. The true utopians are conservatives of all shapes and sizes who would like for this "to hold up all the same," to return to yesterday and the day before yesterday. What is terrifying is our lack of collective imagination in a world that has reached such a boiling point, our myopia before all the "molecular revolutions" which keep pulling the rug out from under us, at an accelerated pace.

I'm just back from Japan. In a few dozen years, a society of "machinic mutants" has come to light—for money *and for the best!* You ask how I see future cities, ideal cities? Somewhat like that. Always more creativity, machinic vitality in the domain of technology, sciences, arts, ways of life and of feeling.

In saying this, I know that I am rubbing the humanist sensibility of many of our friends the wrong way. It's true. I'm crazy about machines, concrete and abstract, and I have no doubt that a fabulous expansion will eventually break down all the conservatisms that "keep us in place" in this absurd and blind society.

You wanted utopia…

Bibliography

GUATTARI BY HIMSELF

1. "I Am an Idea-Thief." Translated by Chet Wiener. An interview conducted by Robert Maggiori, "Petites et grandes machines à inventer la vie," in *Libération*, June 28–29, 1980. Reprinted in Félix Guattari, *Les Années d'Hiver: 1980–85* (Paris: Bernard Barrault, 1986)—Ed.'s title.

2. "Institutional Intervention." Translated by Emily Wittman. Unpublished manuscript, 1980.

3. "So What." Translated by Chet Wiener. An interview conducted by Michel Butel, in *L'Autre Journal*, No. 6, June 12, 1985. Reprinted in Félix Guattari, *Les Années d'Hiver: 1980–85*, op. cit.—Ed.'s title.

4. "Everywhere at Once." Translated by Chet Wiener. An interview conducted by Michel Butel, ibid.—Ed.'s title.

WHY ITALY?

5. "An Open Letter to Some Italian Friends." Translated by Emily Wittman. Unpublished manuscript, September 1977.

6. "New Spaces of Liberty for Minoritarian Desire." Translated by Emily Wittman. Unpublished manuscript, September 1977.

7. "Minority and Terrorism." Translated by Emily Wittman. Dialogue between Maria-Antonietta Macciocchi and Félix Guattari held at the Namur Colloquium in May 1978. Published in *Minorités dans la pensée* (Paris: Payot, 1979). (Edited version).

8. "Like the Echo of a Collective Melancholia." First translated by Mark Polizzotti in "The German Issue" of *Semiotext(e)*, Vol. IV, No. 2, 1982, Sylvère Lotringer, ed. Published in *Les Temps Modernes*, Special issue on Germany, July–August 1979. Reprinted in Félix Guattari, *La Révolution moléculaire* (Paris: UGE 10/18, 1977).

9. "A New Alliance Is Possible." Translated by Arthur Evans and John Johnston. An interview conducted by Sylvère Lotringer, in *Impulse* (Toronto) 10, No. 2, Winter 1982.

MICRO-REVOLUTIONS

10. "The Adolescent Revolution." Translated by Chet Wiener. An interview conducted by Christian Poslianec, in *Sexpol*, 1979: "Des Madame-Dolto partout." Reprinted in Félix Guattari's *Les Années d'hiver*, op. cit.

11. "A Liberation of Desire." Interview conducted and translated by George Stambolian, in *Homosexuality and French Literature*, G. Stambolian and Elaine Marks, eds. (Ithaca: Cornell University Press, 1979).

12. "Machinic Junkies." Translated by Chet Wiener. An interview conducted by Jean-Francis Held, in *Les Nouvelles*, April 12–18, 1984. Reprinted in Félix Guattari, *Les Années d'hiver*, op. cit.

PSYCHOANALYSIS AND SCHIZOANALYSIS

13. "Lacan Was an Event in My Life." An interview conducted and translated by Charles J. Stivale. Fragment of "Pragmatic/Machinic: Discussion with Félix Guattari, 19 March 1985," in Charles J. Stivale, *The Two-fold Thought of Deleuze and Guattari: Intersections and Animations* (New York: Guilford, 1998). Reprinted with permission.

14. "Psychoanalysis Should Get a Grip on Life." Translated by Charles Dudas. An interview conducted by Michèle Costa-Magna et Jean Suyeux, in *Psychologies* 5, November 1983 and reprinted in *Les Années d'hiver*, op. cit.

15. "The Unconscious Is Turned Toward the Future." Translated by Jeanine Herman. An interview conducted by Numa Murard and Luc Rozensweig, in *Recherches*, 1980. Unpublished manuscript.—Ed.'s title.

16. "The Refrain of Being and Meaning: Analysis of a Dream About A. D." Translated by Jill Johnson. Published in *New Observations* 74, Feb/March 1980.

17. "Four Truths for Psychiatry." Translated by Chet Wiener. From a conference on Psychiatry and Institutions sponsored by the Italian Socialist Party, Rome, 1985. Published in *Les Années d'hiver*, op. cit.

18. "The Schizoanalyses." Translated by Emily Wittman. Presentation to the Félix Guattari Seminar, 9 December 1980. Published in *Chimères*, 50, Summer 2003.

INTEGRATED WORLD CAPITALISM

19. "Plan for the Planet." Translated by Rosemary Sheed. Notes for a lecture given at a conference organized by Jean-Pierre Faye in Namur, on June 3 and 4, 1979, on the theme of minority thinking.

20. "Capital as the Integral of Power Formations." Translated by Charles Wolfe and Sande Cohen. Published in the 10/18 UGE version of *La Révolution moléculaire*, op. cit.

21. "Capitalist Systems, Structures and Processes." Translated by Charles Wolfe. Written by Félix Guattari and Eric Alliez, 1983. Published in *Change International Deux*, 1984. Reprinted in *Les Années d'hiver*, op. cit.

22. "Microphysics of Power / Micropolitics of Desire." Translated by John Caruana. Conference paper presented in Milan at a colloquium devoted to the work of Michel Foucault. Published in *Les Années d'hiver*, op. cit.

23. "Postmodern Deadlock and Post-Media Transition." Translated by Emily Wittman. Excerpts from a paper Félix Guattari gave in Tokyo in November 1985 and in Paris on January 10, 1986 at the European University of Philosophy. Partially published in *La Quinzaine Littéraire*, No. 246, 1986.

24. "Entering the Post-Media Era." Translated by Chet Wiener. Unpublished manuscript.

25. "Utopia Today." Translated by Jeanine Herman. This is Guattari's response to a survey by *La Quinzaine Littéraire*, No. 53, 1983.

Notes

Introduction by Charles J. Stivale

1. Félix Guattari and Suely Ronik, *Molecular Revolution in Brazil*, trans. Karel Clapshow and Brian Holmes (Los Angeles: Semiotext(e), 2008), was originally published in Portuguese as *Micropolitica: Cartografias do Desejo* (Petrópolis: Vozes, 1986). Félix Guattari, *The Anti-Oedipus Papers*, ed. Stéphane Nadaud, trans. Kélina Gotman (New York: Semiotext(e), 2006); Franco "Bifo" Berardi, *Félix Guattari: Thought, Friendship, and Visionary Cartography*, ed. and trans. Giuseppina Mecchia and Charles J. Stivale (Basingstoke, UK: Palgrave, 2009).

2. To recall the original organization in *Soft Subversions* (1996): 1) a very brief section on Schizo-Culture (concepts and practice of molecular revolution); 2) a long section on "minority politics" (a mix of Guattari's writings on popular and political culture); 3) a brief section on Guattari's cinema (now moved to *Chaosophy*); 4) a section on "Beyond Marx and Freud," Guattari's development of schizoanalysis toward a wider understanding of global capitalism and psychoanalytical practice (now given two separate sections in *Soft Subversions*).

3. See Félix Guattari, *Les Années d'hiver: 1980–1985* (Paris: Bernard Barrault, 1986). On Guattari's biography (as well as Deleuze's), see François Dosse, *Gilles Deleuze, Félix Guattari. Biographie croisée* (Paris: La Découverte, 2007). With the term "winter years," Guattari designates the period not only of immense disappointment with the Socialist in power, but also a series of personal disappointments that lead to his severe depression (see Dosse, 497–510).

4. The tone of Guattari's essay becomes clearer in light of the specific political issues of repression. John Marks summarizes the important "Klaus Croissant affair" in terms of its impact on the relationship between Deleuze and Michel Foucault: "Along with Deleuze, Foucault had become involved in supporting the West German lawyer Klaus Croissant, who had defended the members of the *Rote Armee Faktion* (often known as the 'Baader-Meinhof gang') in 1975. Croissant sought asylum in France since he risked imprisonment in West Germany for allegedly seeking to provide

material assistance for the members of the gang, who eventually committed suicide in Stammheim prison in 1977. As he applied for asylum, the West German government began extradition proceedings, and he was imprisoned by the French authorities. Both opposed the extradition, but Foucault would not sign the petition originally circulated by Guattari and that Deleuze had signed, which referred to West Germany as a fascist state and appeared to support the activities of the RAF," in *Gilles Deleuze. Vitalism and Multiplicity* (London: Pluto Press, 1998), 109–110.

5. This phrase "new spaces of liberty" provides Guattari with the title of his collaborative book with Antonio Negri, *Les Nouveaux espaces de liberté* (Paris: Dominique Bedou, 1985), translated (in part) as *Communists Like Us*, trans. Michael Ryan (New York: Semiotext(e), 1990).

6. The exchanges to which Guattari refers corresponds, in fact, to student demonstrations [against State oppression] organized by the Autonomia Movement in Rome, Palermo, Naples, Florence, Torino and Bologna in early 1977, especially in March, following which Franco Berardi (Bifo) fled to avoid arrest. He was given a warm welcome by Guattari in Paris, and Bifo's account of these events appears in the essay, "Anatomy of Autonomy," *Italy: Autonomia. Semiotext(e)* 3.3 (1980): 148–170. Bifo describes this September Convention in Bologna as "the great opportunity—missed, however—for the Movement to overcome its purely negative, destructive connotations, and formulate a programmatic position for the autonomous organization of a real society against the State… Unfortunately, the Convention turned into a reunion against repression, and this greatly reduced the theoretical importance and the possibilities of this period… The gathering concluded without producing any direction for the future, any new program, and without advancing the Movement" (159–160).

7. See Gilles Deleuze and Félix Guattari, *A Thousand Plateaus*, trans. Brian Massumi (Minneapolis: University of Minnesota Press, 1987), especially plateaus 4 and 5.

8. *Germany in Autumn (Deutschland im Herbst)* was directed by a team of filmmakers including Volker Schlöndorf and Rainer Werner Fassbinder. Its online synopsis reads, in part: "*Germany in Autumn* does not have a plot per se; it mixes documentary footage, along with standard movie scenes, to give the audience the mood of Germany during the late 1970s. The movie covers the two-month time period during 1977 when a businessman was kidnapped, and later murdered, by the left-wing terrorists known as the RAF-*Rote Armee Fraktion* (Red Army Faction)" (see http://www.imdb.com/title/tt0077427/).

9. The phrase "la nouvelle alliance" is an implicit reference to the French title of the work by Ilya Prigogine and Isabelle Stengers, *La Nouvelle Alliance* (Paris: Gallimard, [1984], 1986), translated in part as *Order out of Chaos. Man's New Dialogue With Nature* (New York: Bantam, 1984).

10. See Charles J. Stivale, *The Two-Fold Thought of Deleuze and Guattari: Intersections and Animations* (New York: Guilford, 1998), 191–224. This text is also available online under the title "Pragmatic/Machinic": (see http://webpages.ursinus.edu/rrichter/stivale.html, and elsewhere).

11. In fact, these essays published separately in different journals initially formed a coherent whole in a privately published and circulated text, "Plan pour la planète," limited initially to Paris, and then in an Italian translation (by Franco "Bifo" Berardi, who also introduced the volume), *Piano sul pianeta. Capitale mondiale integrato e globalizzazione* (Verona: Ombre Corte, [1982] 1997). The order of this text's chapters—chapter 1, "Capital as the Integral of Power Formation," chapter 2, "Plan for the Planet," and chapter 3, "Capitalist Systems, Structures, and Processes"—differs slightly from the order of their publication in journals (the order followed in this volume).

12. Jean-François Lyotard, *The Postmodern Condition: A Report on Knowledge*, trans. Geoff Bennington and Brian Massumi (Minneapolis: University of Minnesota Press, 1984), originally published as *La Condition postmoderne: rapport sur le savoir* (Paris: Minuit, 1979).

1. I Am an Idea-Thief

1. *Libération*, May 17, 1980. [Ed.]

2. See *Autonomia: Post-Political Politics*. Sylvere Lotringer and Christian Marazzi, eds. Op. cit. p. 234–237. [Ed.]

3. Cossiga was the Christian Democratic Minister of the Interior. [Ed.]

4. Berlinger was the Italian Communist Party chief. [Ed.]

2. Institutional Intervention

1. Centre d'Etudes, de Recherches et de Formations Institutionnelles (The Center for Study, Research, and Institutional Formation).

2. Groupe de Travail de Psychologie et Sociologie Institutionnelle led by François Tosquelles from 1960 to 1965.

3. The UNEF: L'Union Nationale des Etudiants de France (National Union of French Students), founded in 1907; La Mutuelle Nationale des Etudiants de France (MNEF): The National Cooperative of French Students, founded in 1948.

4. Fédération des Groupes d'Etudes et de Recherches Institutionnelle (The Federation of Study Groups and Institutional Research).

5. The GET (Group for Therapeutic Education), run by Fernand Oury.

6. BAPU: Bureau d'Aide Psychologique Universitaire (University Office for Psychological Assistance).

7. This vulnerability was made visible through two types of reactions: Either the leaders of '68 thought they should return to the groupuscular ideologies and practices, even if it meant renewing them somewhat (*Gauche Prolétarienne, Nouvelle Résistance Populaire*, etc...), or they chose to obtain state grants: the Department of Education, publicly-funded research, city planning, etc... Although certain Maoists accused it of going down this path, the CERFI, descended from the FGERI, tried hard to escape this alternative.

8. "Recherche Universitaire," 1964.

9. L'École freudienne de Paris (EFP), a psychoanalytic association founded in 1964 by Jacques Lacan.

10. After dissolving the EFP in 1980, Lacan founded *La Cause freudienne*, another psychoanalytic organization.

11. C.M.P.P. (Centres médico-psycho-pédagogique) are medico-social establishments, created to tend to the psychological and physical needs of children and adolescents.

12. "Capital as the Integral of Power Formations," supra, p. 244.

3. So What

1. Jacques-Alain Miller, Lacan's son-in-law, is also his literary executor and guardian of the Lacanian legacy. The group from the rue d'Ulm, where the École Normale Superieure is located, used to publish a magazine called *Cahiers pour l'analyse*. [Ed.]

2. Le Pen, the leader of the French National Front, is a colorful demagogue and xenophobic figure of the Right, as Poujade was before him. [Ed.]

4. Everywhere at Once

1. Lucien Sebag, anthropologist and disciple of Lévi-Strauss, committed suicide in the late 1960s. [Ed.]

2. "The Communist Path" was a Trotskyite political organization. [Ed.]

3. Serge July (who later became the editor of *Libération*) and Alain Geismar were leaders of May '68. "La Gauche prolétarienne" was a Maoist group which advocated "popular tribunals." Cf. Supra, p. 66 [Ed.]

4. The University of Vincennes, on the outskirts of Paris, was a hotbed of '68 and later-day leftists. [Ed.]

5. Coluche, a hugely popular standup comedian, actor, filmmaker and one-time politician (he ran for President in 1981) subsequently died in a motorcycle accident. [Ed.]

8. Like the Echo of a Collective Melancholia

1. Aldo Moro, President of the Christian Democrats, was kidnapped by the Red Brigades and executed in Rome on March 16, 1978. [Ed.]

2. By the term "Guaranteeism" is meant all the victories achieved by traditional pro-letarian struggles on the level of wages, job security, working conditions, social services. Cf. *Autonomia: Post-Political Politics*, op. cit. [Ed.]

9. A New Alliance Is Possible

1. See *Italy: Autonomia: Post-Political Politics*, op. cit.

2. See *The German Issue, Semiotext(e)*, IV, 2, 1982. Sylvére Lotringer, ed.

10. The Adolescent Revolution

1. *Sexpol*, "the magazine of sexuality, politics," 1979.

2. Allusion to Jean Baudrillard's "The Implosion of the Social" in *In The Shadow of the Silent Majorities*, trans. Paul Foss, John Johnson, Paul Patton, New York: Semi-otext(e), (1978), 2007. [Ed.]

11. A Liberation of Desire

1. Cf. Félix Guattari, "The Poor Mans Couch," in *Chaosophy: Texts and Interviews 1972–1977* (New York, Semiotext(e), 2009).

12. Machinic Junkies

1. Cf. "La Borde: A Clinic Unlike Any Other" in Félix Guattari, *Chaosophy*, op. cit.

13. Lacan Was an Event in My Life

1. D.-A. Grisoni, "La philosophie comme enfer," *Magazine littéraire*, no. 196 (June 1983), p. 18.

2. Jean-Paul Aron, *Les Modernes*, Paris, Gallimard, 1984, p. 285. Touted as a collection of memoirs "to do away with the master-thinkers," this book contains several vicious attacks on various French intellectual figures.

3. See Gilles Deleuze and Félix Guattari, *Anti-Oedipus* (Minneapolis: University of Minnesota Press, trans. Robert Hurley, Mark Seem and Helen R. Lane, 1983) ch. 2: "Psychoanalysis and Familialism: The Holy Family," and *A Thousand Plateaus*, trans. Brian Massumi (Minneapolis: University of Minnesota Press, 1987) ch. 2: "One or Several Wolves?"

4. However, only two months later, in May 1985, Guattari would present an address in homage to Foucault at a Milan conference. See supra, "Microphysics of Power/Micropolitics of Desire," pp. 278–290.

14. Psychoanalysis Should Get a Grip on Life

1. Robert Castel, *Le Psychanalysme* (Paris: Maspero, 1973).

15. The Unconscious Is Turned Toward the Future

1. Félix Guattari, *L'Inconscient Machinique.* (Paris: Recherches, 1979).

2. The Alternative Psychiatric Network is an international collective that gathers together psychiatrists, nurses, and psychiatric patients for a radical transformation of the approach to mental illness.

16. The Refrain of Being and Meaning

1. A paper delivered at the Cerisy Colloquium: "Temps et devenir á partir de l'oeuvre de Prigogine," June 1983.

2. Félix Guattari, *Psychanalyse et Transversalité* (Paris: Maspero, 1972).

3. Ancient societies, notably the Australian aborigines, are used to considering oneiric performances not only as diachronic progressions, but also as dreams experienced collectively, playing a fundamental role in establishing relations of filiation, planning rituals and setting all other types of traditions. Cf. Barbara Glowczewski. "Paper on the dreams of the Walpiri" in *Chimères*, No. 1, Spring 1987.

4. A place where, even longer ago, I met daily with Lucien Sebag, Pierre Clastres and a whole group of students.

5. Secretary General of the Socialist Party at the time.

6. Mikhail Bakhtine, *The Dialogic Imagination* (University of Texas Press, 1981).

7. The rue Gay-Lussac, in the Latin District, was at the heart of the May '68 rebellion. [Ed.]

8. Arlette Donati, a psychiatrist at the La Borde clinic, was Guattari's companion at the time.

9. The assimilation of "Mer" (sea) and "*mére*" (mother) is a standard psychoanalytic pun. [Ed.]

10. Pierre Clastres and Lucien Sebag, both anthropologists and close friends of Félix Guattari's, died prematurely (Sebag committed suicide and Clastres died in a car accident). [Ed.]

18. The Schizoanalyses

1. Mony Elkaïm, a close associate of Félix Guattari, practices systemic psychotherapy in Brussels. He is the author of *Si tu m'aimes, ne m'aime pas*. (Paris: Le Seuil, 2001).

2. In French, this idiom makes use of the subtle semantic difference between "torchons" (*dust cloths*) and "serviettes" (*napkins*), hence there is an important play on words when Guattari refers to a military clean up with the term "*coup de torchon*." [Trans.]

3. It is not without a certain perplexity that I am again taking up this old term of "analyzer," a term that I introduced in the sixties and that was "recuperated"'(just like "institutional analysis," "transversality," etc.) by the Lourau, Lobrot, Lapassade movement, from a perspective that is far too psycho-sociological for my taste.

4. This formula of the unconscious could be brought together with "primary process" as Freud conceived of it during the *Traumdeutung* period.

5. It is the first Freud of the *Traumdeutung* as well who had admirably grasped the nature of this "against the grain" treatment of the dream's significations: "The dream speech thus has the structure of breccia, in which the larger pieces of various material are held together by a solidified cohesive medium." *The Interpretation of Dreams* (New York: The Modern Library, 1950, p. 286). "Everything in dreams which occurs as the apparent functioning of the critical faculty is to be regarded not as the intellectual performance of the dream-work, but as belonging to the substance of the dream-thoughts, and it has found its way from these, as a completed structure, into the manifest dream-content." (*Id.* p. 309) But this "against the grain" micropolitics doesn't exclusively belong to psychic life; we also find it at work in artistic creation. In particular, I'm thinking about the way in which a Georges Aperghis, in his "gestual music," only retains from semantic content what works towards his a-signifying compositions.

6. Sigmund Freud, "Morning and Melancholia," in *Collected Papers*, Volume 4, trans. Joan Riviere (London: The Hogarth Press, 1957), pp. 152-70. *Selected Papers of Karl Abraham, M.D., with an Introductory Memoir by Ernest Jones:* Translated by Douglas Bryan and Alix Strachey. (London: The Hogarth Press and the Institute of Psycho-Analysis. London, 1927.

7. "Hallucinatory wishful psychosis," Sigmund Freud, *Standard Edition* (London: Hogarth Press, London, 1957), T. XIV, pp. 233 and 234, which, for Freud, is identical to Meynert's hallucinatory confusion or "amentia."

8. Corneille, Pierre: "Cinna," Auguste's monologue.

9. "I am plagued by two ambitions: to see how the theory of mental functioning takes shape if quantitative considerations, a sort of economics of nerve-force, are introduced into it; and secondly, to abstract from psychopathology what may be of benefit to normal psychology." Letter to Fliess, May 25, 1895. Sigmund Freud, *The Origins of Psychoanalysis*, Marie Bonaparte, Anna Freud, and E. Kris, eds. (New York: Basic Books, 1954), pp. 119–120.

19. Plan for the Planet

1. Sarcelles and Yvelines are dormitory towns around Paris that presented a challenge for reconstruction.

2. The workers' centre of resistance in Petrograd.

20. Capital as the Integral of Power Formations

1. Subjection understood in its cybernetic sense.

2. Marx defined surplus-value in these terms: "I call *absolute surplus-value* the surplus-value produced by the simple extension of the work day, and *relative surplus-value* the surplus-value which proceeds from the reduction of necessary time and of the corresponding change in the relative magnitude of both aspects which make up the work day." Karl Marx, *Oeuvres*, Pléiade, vol 1. (Paris: Gallimard, p. 852).

The rate of surplus-value is represented in the following formula:

$$\frac{\text{relative}}{\text{surplus-value}} = \frac{\text{surplus-value}}{\text{variable cap.}} = \frac{\text{surplus-value}}{\text{work-power value}} = \frac{\text{surplus-work}}{\text{necessary work}}$$

Marx adds: "The first two formulas express as a relation of value what the third formula expresses as a relation of time spaces in which these values are produced."

3. "True wealth being the full productive power of every individual, the standard measure won't be expressed in labor-time, but in available time. To adapt labor-time as the measure of wealth is to found the latter on poverty; it implies that leisure only exists in and by opposition to overtime work; it amounts to reducing all of time to the sole temporality of labor in which the worker is degraded to the sole role of an instrument" (Marx, op. cit., v. 2, p. 308).

4. In a different register of ideas, one realizes that the present triumph of behaviorism in the U.S. doesn't result from the "progress of science," but from a more rigorous systematization of methods of social control.

5. The "mercantilist revolution" would seem to be the referent I am thinking of, in particular, the great book of Thomas Mun, *A Discourse of Trade from England into the East Indies* (1609, London, 1621), which, for Marx, represented "the conscious break of mercantilism with the system from which it came." Mun's book would became the "Gospel of mercantilism."

6. According to Marx, it is the relative and progressive diminishing of variable capital in relation to constant capital (because of machinery and concentration of factories) that introduced disequilibrium in the organic composition of the total capital of a given society. "The immediate consequence is that the rate of surplus-value expresses itself in a decreasing profit rate, where exploitation remains unchanged or even increases" (Marx, op. cit, v. 2, p. 1002).

7. A multinational, after negotiating with State power, will introduce a super-modern factory in an underdeveloped region. Then, later, due to political motives or some "social instability," or on account of complex merchandizing, it will decide to close the factory. It is impossible, in these cases, to assess the growth in fixed capital.

In another area, say in steel production, an ultra-modern branch of industry will be toned down or dismantled because of market problems or alleged technological choices, which only express fundamental options concerning the totality of economic and social development.

8. As a number of anthropologists have shown for archaic societies, apparent exchange is always relative to actual relations of force. Exchange is always instrumentalized by power. Cf. E. R. Leach, *Rethinking Anthropology* (London: Athlone Press, 1966).

9. Marx, op. cit., v. 1, p. 1122; v. 2, p. 1002.

10. This general movement of deterritorialization nonetheless allows archaic strata more or less territorialized to remain or, more frequently, gives them another breath by transforming their functions. In this sense, the actual "rebound" in the value of gold constitutes a surprising example. It seems to work concurrently in two opposing directions: on the one hand, as a semiotic black hole, economic stasis and inhibition; and an the other, as a diagrammatic operator of power: (1) for those who *proved capable* of inserting their semiotic intervention in "good places" and at "the right moments"; (2) for those capable of injecting abstract credit of power, at the "right time" within key economic sectors. On the diagrammatic function, semiotic block holes, etc., Cf. Félix Guattari, *L'Inconscient Machinique* (Paris: Editions Recherches, 1979).

11. Beyond gold, fiduciary money, credit money, stocks and propriety titles, etc., Capital today manifests itself through semiotic operations and manipulations of power of all kinds involving information and the media.

12. Such is the role, parallel to the administration, police, justice, IRS, stock-exchange, the military, etc., of schools, social services, unions, sports, media, etc.

13. Marx, op. cit., v.1, p.1002.

14. One finds a relative reterritorialization at this level: multinationals which are not at all reducible to the economic sub-grouping of the U.S. and are objectively cosmopolitan, are nonetheless headed in majority by U.S. citizens.

15. The dialectical mechanism of Marx at times led him to envision a quasi-spontaneous and involuntary generation of this type of transformation: "While the system of bourgeois economy develops bit by bit, its negation does as well as the ultimate extension of this system. Here we have in mind the process of instant production. If we consider bourgeois society as a whole, we see that the final result of social production is society itself, in other words, man himself in his social relations" (Marx, op. cit., v. 2, p. 311).

16. Such a proposition can only be heard if one conceives desire not as some undifferentiated energetic drive, but resulting from a highly elaborated assemblage of deterritorialized machinics.

21. Capitalist Systems, Structures and Processes

1. Oskar Lange compares the capitalist market to a "proto-computer." Quoted by Fernand Braudel, trans. Sian Reynolds, *Civilization and Capitalism*, Vol. II (New York: Harper Collins, 1985).

2. Cf. the distinction Braudel makes between "trade." essentially unequalitarian exchange, and "market," self-regulating market of price.

3. According to Fernand Braudel, the capitalist proto-markets were deployed in concentric zones starting from the metropolises which held economic keys allowing them to draw in most of the surplus value, while towards the peripheries they tended to a sort of zero point, because of the lethargy of exchanges and the low level of prices found there. But Braudel considers that each economy-world was necessarily based on a single-world. But perhaps he is a bit too systematic on this point. Could one not imagine urban and capitalist processes which are not developed according to a mono-centered model, but according to a multi-polar stock of "archipeligoes of towns"?

4. Cf. Henri Lepage, *Demain le capitalisme* (Paris: Livre de Poche), p. 419.

5. Vera Lutz, *Central Planning for the Market Economy* (London: Longmans, 1969).

6. Quantity of subjection of human activity, focused on the technico-semiotic machines of the system. Subjection is understood here in a cybernetic sense.

7. James Buchanan, cit. in Henri Lepage, op. cit., p. 38. Cf. the ravages made in Pinochet's Chile by Milton Friedman's "Chicago boys." (Jacqueline de Linares, *Le Matin de Paris*, Sept 11, 1980.)

8. On these modes of evaluation of Capital, cf. Alain Cotta, *Théorie générale du capital, de la croissance et des fluctuations* (Paris, 1967) and the entry "Capital" in the *Encyclopaedia Universalis*.

9. Examples of complementarity: the fact that the proto-capitalism of the 15th and 16th centuries, even though it was predominantly merchant and financial, became industrial in some circumstances (cf. The revival of Antwerp by industrialization, evoked by Fernand Braudel, op. cit., vol. 3, The Perspective of the World); and the fact that market economies, whatever their apparent "liberalism" may be, have always contained a dose of State intervention, or that "centralized" planification (for instance, the Stalinist Plans) has always preserved a minimum of the market economy, either within its sphere of influence, or in its relation to the world market.

10. For instance China in the 2nd and 3rd centuries A.D. Cf. Karl-August Wittfogel, *Oriental Despotism: A Comparative Study of Total Power* (New Haven, CT: Yale University Press, 1957).

11. For instance Venice, Antwerp, Genoa, Amsterdam, between the 13th and 17th centuries.

12. Cf. Fernand Braudel, op. cit., Vol. III.

13. Etienne Balazs, *Chinese Civilization and Bureaucracy*, trans. H. M. Wright (New Haven: Yale University Press, 1964).

14. And which doubtless even slows the development of productive machinisms within metropolises: cf. F. Sternberg, *Kapitalismus und Sozialismus vor dem Weltgericht* (1951): "The alliance between European imperialism and colonial feudalism [...] slowed down industrial development, and in general, the progressive development of the economy in colonial empires, in an extraordinary *way*." Cit. by Maximilien Rubel in K. Marx, op. cit., vol. 1, p. 1708.

22. Microphysics of Power / Micropolitics of Desire

1. See also the theme of the "labyrinth of origins" in the work of Raymond Roussel: R.R., p. 204.

2. O.D., p. 72. During that period, we were rebelling against what we called the "imperialism of the signifier." Was it just a slightly different image? Or, perhaps, that Foucault put more emphasis on the role played by the "classical age" in this hold of power of the signifier over power in general—whereas Deleuze and I emphasized the dimensions of the signifier as they related to more advanced capitalism?

3. For the production of the domains of objects, see O.D. 71/234; for that of events: O.D. 61/231; of the soul: S.P. 34/29; that of sex: H.S, vol. I. 151/114, etc.

4. If one is to take seriously the assertion that struggle is at the heart of power relations, then one must realize that the good old "logic of contradiction is no longer sufficient, far from it, for the unraveling of actual processes" (P. 30/164).

23. Postmodern Deadlock and Post-Media Transition

1. Léon Krier. "La reconstitution de la ville" in Rationale Architecture, 1978 and *L'après modernisme.* (Paris: Ed. de l'Equerre, 1981).

2. Robert Venturi, Denise Scott Brown, and Steven Izenour, *Learning from Las Vegas* (Cambridge, Mass.: MIT Press, 1977) and *Complexity and Contradiction in Architecture* (New York: The Museum of Modern Art Press, 1966). See also: Charles Jenks, *The Language of Post-Modern Architecture* (London: Academic Editions, 1977).

3. Lyotard, Jean-François, *The Postmodern Condition: A Report on Knowledge*, trans. Geoff Bennington and Brian Massumi (Minneapolis: University of Minnesota Press, 1984).

4. This theme has been updated since 1935 by Walter Benjamin, "The Work of Art in the Age of Mechanical Reproduction," in *Illuminations* (New York: Schocken Books, 1969).

5. Austin, Émile Benveniste, John Searle, Oswald Ducrot, Antoine Culioli, etc...

6. It also implies, without my exhausting this point, the exit from an entire dualistic ontological tradition that makes existence dependent on a law of everything or nothing: "to be or not to be." Through a provisionally indispensable return to animist thinking, the quality of being prevails over a "neutral" essentiality of a universally operational and thus exchangeable being, that we can describe as capitalistic facticity. Existence gains itself, loses itself, intensifies, crosses qualitative thresholds, because of its adherence to this or that incorporeal universe of endo-reference.

Index

abstract machine. *See* machine, abstract

abyss, 68

actors, calm perspectives of, 76

actual, 220

Adelaide (A.D.), 189, 194–95, 197

adolescence, 131–40; and anxiety, 135; becomings of, 131, 140; control of, 137; and normalization, 134; revolution, 133–34; wild dreams of, 65

aesthetic: cartography, 281; machines, 179, 209; mutations, 28; practices, 299; problematics, 296; production, 206 revolutions, 161; subjectivity, 303

affective: components, 181; level, 262; space, 78; values, 257

affects, 50, 72–73, 142, 206, 208, 259, 263, 286; cartography of, 45–46; of collective media, 109

Africa, 235

AIDS, 75

Algerian War, 39, 82, 94

alienation, 14, 97, 143, 152, 181, 248–49, 255, 259, 262, 297; dis-, 55

Alternative Psychiatric Network, 180, 203, 318 n.2

Althusser, Louis, 75, 179

analysis, 17, 38, 41–42, 67, 69–70, 82, 138, 177, 199–200, 280, 283, 286–87,

289–90, 299, 302–4, 306; disastrous capitalist, 116; and film, 106; and interpretation / intervention, 52–53; and Marxism, 113, 115; molecular, 284; nothing neutral in, 54; and politics, 32, 152; self-, 189, 197; specialization of, 43; and transversality, 46. *See also* institutional analysis; psychoanalysis; schizoanalysis; women's movement, analytic impact of

analytic systems, co-opting of, 37

anguish, 68

anorexia, 50, 159, 210

anticapitalist struggles, 110

Antigone (Sophocles), 106

Anti-Oedipus (Deleuze & Guattari), 146, 154, 166, 170, 214

Anti-Oedipus Papers, The (Guattari), 9

anxiety, 64, 69, 135–36

"a" object, 225

Aperghis, Georges, 181

a priori, 229

arborescence, 151

Archaeology of Knowledge, The (Foucault), 280

armed struggle, 108–9, 112, 119. *See also* terrorism; violence

arms race, 122, 234, 243, 307

Aron, Jean Paul, 166, 169

arrangement, 24, 26, 181, 303. *See also* enunciation; expression

art, 16–17, 28, 67, 69, 79, 212, 286, 291–92, 294–95, 302, 306–7

Artaud, 152–53, 161, 182

artifice, 148

artisanal production, no return to, 27

artistic: aspirations, 60; creation, 77, 114, 290; crises, 295; development, 292; mutations, 264; possibilities, 74

artists, 14, 60, 98, 291

Asada, Akira, 80

a-signification, 69, 75, 140, 207, 212, 217, 305

assemblages, 8, 26, 47–50, 52–53, 207–11, 213, 215–16, 220–21. *See also* enunciation

asylum, 200, 203

attention, concentration of, and subjective production, 75

author, 288

autonomist movements, 231

Autonomists (Italy), 32, 91, 117–19

Bach, 84

Bachelard, Gaston, 38

Bakhtin, Mikhail, 189

BAPU, 34, 38

barbarity, 76

Barre, Raymond, 72

Basaglia, Franco, 201–2

Basques, 78–79, 95

Baudrillard, Jean, 114, 178, 294, 317 n.2

Beat Generation, 149

Beckett, Samuel, 150–51, 179, 182, 189; as great analyst, 43

Beckett assemblage, 48

becoming, 131, 140, 207, 209, 223–24, 301

becoming-woman, 143, 148, 183

Berardi, Franco (Bifo), 9, 16, 203, 313 n.1, 314 n.6, 315 n.11

Berlinguer, Enrico, 32, 315 n.4

Bifo, 9, 16, 203, 313 n.1, 314 n.6, 315 n.11

Black Panthers, 103

body, 29, 31, 72, 75, 95, 115, 131–32, 140, 143–44, 155–56, 303; political technologies of, 284; repression of relation to, 143; struggle in relation to, 144; transformed relations to, 178; without organs, 214, 297, 303

Bonnafé, Lucien, 37, 199

Borges, 151

bourgeois: aristocracy, 233–34; culture, 65; democracy, 236; family, 64; fear, 125; institutions, 92; legality, 97; novel, 172; regimes, 108; society, 322 n.15; system, 110

bourgeoisie, 26, 97, 114–15, 231–32, 236, 244, 253, 255; changed nature of, 263–64

Braudel, Fernand, 160, 268

Brazil, 172, 174, 235

bureaucratic: aristocracy, 234; choke-collar, 203; Eros, 145; inertia, 56; institutions, 92; segregation, 29; socialism, 122, 143; society, 119; stratifications, 45; valorization, 271

Butel, Michel, 8

Cage, John, 70

Candide (Voltaire), 116

capital, 15–16, 244–64 *passim*, 265, 270, 274 276, 306; as computer of socius, 267; and human robots, 262; as power operation, 252; redefinition of, 255, 257

capitalism, 15, 71, 79, 94–97, 108, 110–11, 115–16, 122–23, 230–33, 246–64 *passim*, 265–77; anti-, 110, 116; complexities of, 272, 276; cruel segregative techniques of, 27; engaged in systematic control of everyone, 264; extensive exploits of, 254; international restructuring of, 96; irreversible transformations of, 76; overthrow of, 239; radically disenchanted order of, 305; seizes individuals from inside, 262; submissive children of, 31

Capitalism and Schizophrenia (Deleuze & Guattari), 37

capitalist: production, 47; virus, 241

Castel, Robert, 171

castration, 184, 211, 225, 289, 304

causality, 230, 266

Cause freudienne, 40

CERFI, 33, 58–59, 82

certainty, questioning of, 45

CET, 36

Chicago School, 269

child, work position of, 254, 259

childhood, 134; and anxiety, 136; control of, 132, 137; historical transformation of, 136; wild dreams of, 65

children: becomings of, 131, 140; productive shaping of, 75

Christian Democracy (Italy), 103, 118

CINEL, 58–61

cinema. *See* film

class: antagonism, 231; balance, 236; struggle, 26, 44, 100, 264; system, 233

Clastres, Pierre, 117, 196, 319 n.10

CMPP, 43

CNR, 58

Cocteau, Jean, 107

collective: attitudes, 260; dimensions, and personal factors, 69; discourse, 289; equipments, 36, 47–48, 97, 254, 257, 264, 274; identity, 292; inflexion, 229; labor, 47, 233–34, 254–55, 275; modes of semiotization, 42; production, 282; project-making, 295; sensibility, 208; worker, 245–47; workforce, 262

Coluche, 86–87, 317 n.5

Common Program (France), 92

communication, 74, 140, 179, 183, 209, 295, 302; vs assemblages of semiotization, 49; experiments with, 46; nonverbal systems of, 181; and power, 152; transversal, 10, 46, 99

Communist Party: in France, 34, 73, 92–93, 99; in Italy, 43, 92–93, 98, 102–3, 118

computers, 15, 49, 182, 241, 249, 267–68, 295

conscientialization, 210–11, 213, 219

consensus, 55; majoritarian, 11–12, 46, 98, 110, 235

conservatism, 17, 56, 71, 96, 110, 118, 125, 137, 275–76, 291, 293, 301, 307

control, 14, 28, 41, 48, 51, 54, 57, 106, 108, 132, 137, 231, 235–36, 243, 247–48, 257–59, 261, 263–65, 267–68, 288; from within and without, 257

Cooper, David, 200

co-option, 35–37, 44–45, 52, 57–58, 62, 96, 250, 301

cops, 31, 176. *See also* police

Corbusier, Le, 293

corporation, 250, 252, 254, 256. *See also* multinationals

Corydon (Gide), 146, 153

cosmos, 72

Cossiga, Francesco, 32, 315 n.3

counterculture movements, 198

couple: and individual, 137–38; married, 155

creation, 28, 146, 161, 203, 232, 275, 290, 305–6

creativity, 13, 17, 29, 32, 36, 42, 72, 74, 76, 160, 262, 270, 297, 307; and desire, 149; and sexuality, 148

Croissant, Klaus, 11, 59, 94, 313 n.4

cure, 54, 67

cybernetics, 64, 212, 295

Dada, 151, 167, 222

databases, 295, 299

Daumezon, Georges, 37, 199

David, Yasha, 185–86, 189–90, 192–93

decisionality, 261, 297

De Gaulle, Charles, 72, 139

Deleuze, Gilles, 7–10, 12, 14, 21, 23, 37, 42, 56, 82, 142, 145–46, 151–52, 154, 165–67, 169, 185, 189, 192–93, 204, 280, 285; course at Vincennes, 83; Guattari's work with, 82, 84; meeting with Guattari, 83

demonic, as mystery, 147

desire, 27, 31, 37, 80, 213–14, 216, 220, 223–24, 242–43, 266, 282, 284–85, 305; always outside, 155; analysis of economy of, 24; capital's reordering of, 257; collective, 96; and creativity, 149; decentering of, 17, 306; demonic as residue of, 147; economy of, 44, 61, 71, 230, 263; no boxes in, 131–32; escapes power, 156; expressions of, 25 and film, 112; Foucault on, 285; investments of, 45, 52; in Japan, 160; and liberation, 153; liberation of, 142, 157; literature of, 154; and machine, 263; machines of, 148; machinic dimensions of, 214; meaning of, 142; micropolitics of, 16, 284, 289–90; minoritarian, 11; mutations of, 264; normalization of, 262; and progress, 74; reactionary theories of, 40; representational attitudes toward, 145; and sexuality, 152; singularities of, 304; values of, 257, 268, 270; woman close to, 143

deterritorialization, 11, 23, 84, 116, 215, 219, 221–24, 233, 240, 244, 253, 256, 283, 292

diagrammaticity, 49, 253, 256, 266, 273, 286

Discipline and Punish (Foucault), 283

discourse, 24–25, 45, 50, 54–55, 140, 170, 179, 220, 222, 280–81, 283, 286–89, 294–95, 298; irreducible to language & speech, 281; prisoners of styles of, 56

distraction, 93

domination, 27, 32, 144

Donati, Arlette, 189–90, 193, 195, 197, 318 n.8

dope, 13, 70, 158–61

Dostoevsky, 153

dream analysis, 184–97

Dreyfus, Hubert, 283
Dr. Strangelove, 124
drugs. *See* dope

East and West, 12, 71, 78, 113, 120–21,
    123, 233–34, 239, 260; complicity
    between, 28
École freudienne, 10, 23, 40–41, 67, 170
ecological: devastation, 63, 123, 237, 300;
    dimensions, 296; movement, 117,
    125; niches, 29; practices, 202;
    sensitivity, 138
ecologists, 65, 95, 188, 192, 196, 240
ecology, 10, 12, 98; mental, 203
Eden, Eden, Eden (Guyotat), 141
electronic revolution, vs free circulation, 27
Elkaïm, Mony, 204
Encres, 58
endorphins, 159, 210
energy, 231, 233–34, 237, 305, 307
enunciation, 168, 208, 213, 219, 257, 281,
    298; analytic assembalges of, 42, 53;
    archaic forms of, 209; arrangements
    of, 179, 277, 302; assemblages of, 49,
    205–7, 210, 212, 216, 297; collective
    arrangements of, 24; collective assem-
    blages of, 10, 58, 204, 288–89;
    collective set-up of, 150; matrix of, 189
environment, 76, 95, 241, 243, 303;
    machinic, 48
Estaing, Giscard d', 11, 58, 94, 96
ethology, 133, 179–81, 210
existence: micropolitics of, 289; passion for,
    71; reinvention of singular, 77
existential: chemistry, 306; coordinates,
    reinvention of, 79; production, 286,

298; territory, 78, 161, 187, 191,
    196, 205, 219–20, 297, 302–4
exploitation, 92, 95, 97, 230, 232, 234,
    247, 251, 258, 267–69, 276
expression, 22, 62, 83, 96, 112, 141, 156,
    181, 239, 299, 302; collective
    arrangement of, 81; liberation of, 55;
    nonverbal, 140; possibilities of, 121;
    extrapersonal level of, 181. *See also*
    individual, supra and infra; prepersonal
    domain

faciality, 14, 181, 218
false problems, 35, 58, 230
family, 178; and mental patients, 201; and
    politics, 114; structure, dissolution of,
    48; therapy, 13, 52–53, 171, 173,
    180, 204
fantasy, 155–56
fascism, 94, 103, 108, 238; micro-, 60,
    152; neo-, 71
fashion, 16, 30, 295
Fassbinder, 107
Faulkner, 182
Faure, Edgar, 36
Fechner, Gustav, 222
Félix (Bifo), 9
FGERI, 34–36, 81–82, 84
film: and collective emotion, 106; and
    desire, 112
finitude, 289, 303, 305
Foucault, Michel, 16, 25, 82, 113, 166,
    169, 278–90; D&G's alignment with,
    286; on desire & power, 285; on
    discourse, 281, 287; on subjectivity,
    282–84

Fourquet, François, 81–82

Freud, Sigmund, 26, 31, 37, 86, 167–69, 182, 189, 208, 212, 214, 216, 221–23, 225, 298; 'complex' of, 24, 302; creativity of, 168–70, 222; inhibitory prestige of, 44; and Little Hans, 50–51; seriously questioned by D&G, 154; and subjective continent, 30

Freudianism, 40, 173, 223, 285, 290; D&G's criticisms of, 42

Freudian School, 10, 23, 40–41, 67, 170

Freudian theory, reactionary to desire, 40

Friedman, Milton, 76, 116

Gallard, Helena, 186, 189

Gallard, Jean, 186

Geismar, Alain, 83, 316 n.3

Genet, Jean, 147, 153

genetic engineering, 75

Germany, 11–12, 57, 61, 94, 98, 106–12 *passim*, 121, 125

Germany in Autumn (film), 12, 106–12 *passim*

Gide, Andre, 134, 146–47, 153, 167

GIP, 82

globalization, 250, 253

Godard, Jean-Luc, 79

Goethe, 147

good intentions, no return to, 27–28

Grisoni, D. A., 165

group, 48–49, 52, 55, 84, 154, 178–79; and faciality, 181; subject-, 179

Grundrisse (Marx), 247

G.T.Psy, 33, 37, 199

Guattari, Felix: as analyst, 67, 144, 175, 177; background of, 64–65; crazy for machines, 307; meeting with Deleuze,

83; work with Deleuze, 82, 84; dream analysis of, 184–97; gets driver's license, 192; Foucault's influence on, 16, 169; global political vision of, 15; hyper-optimism and hyperpessimism of, 28; as idea-thief, 23; importance of Lacan for, 166–67; and Italian issues, 60, 91–93; as militant, 33, 39, 59, 65, 177; as neither academic nor school affiliate, 40; neologisms of, 9, 21; as student at Sorbonne, 167; training of, 39–40

guiding, 47–48

Guillant, Germaine Le, 37, 199

guilt, 31, 44, 107, 111, 151, 201, 217

Guyotat, Pierre, 141

Helmholtz, 222

Heraclitus, 25

heterogeneous: components, 23, 43, 184, 191, 195, 203, 211, 268, 303–4; universes, 34

heterosexuality, 143, 148, 150, 154–55

hierarchization, 28, 57, 229, 250, 261

hierarchy, 41, 75, 116, 234, 238, 240

history: contemporary black hole of, 70; crazy parameters of, 307; different conception of, 178; essential workings of, 270; reality of, 282; true fabric of, 229–30

History of Sexuality (Foucault), 285

homogeneous axiomatics, 24–25

homosexuality, 141, 143, 146–50, 153, 155, 183; Oedipal, 146

hospitals, 38, 41, 56, 199–201, 203, 224, 240, 287

human: activity, co-option of, 250, 257, 261, 264, 268, 270, 276; collectivities, need for reappropriation of, 78–79; interaction, new conceptions of, 27, 238; life, industrial production for maintenance of, 75; and machine, 251, 297; race, expanded alternatives for, 262–63; relations, 238; robots, 262; species, survival of, 26, 243; time, replacement of, 249

humanism, 103; anti-, 105

hunger, 174, 243, 300

hysteria, 213, 218, 222

ideology, 178–80, 231, 236, 259

Illich, Ivan, 75

immigrants, 28, 60, 71, 95, 104, 111, 231, 255, 263

imperialism, 108, 276

Inconscient machinique, L' (Guattari), 21, 180

incorporeal: materialism, 283; universes, 187, 213, 220, 296, 299, 302–3, 305

individual: attention turned away from, 154; and capital fixation, 239; capitalism's internal seizure of, 262, 268; capital's constant subjugation of, 257; and collective, 198–99, 201–3, 206–7, 231, 262, 268, 289, 305; machines explode, 209; consciousness, 159; consent of, 261; control and repression of, 259; and couple, 137–38; as cut by capitalism, 31; cut off from production, 243; and faciality, 181; hopeless serialization of, 202; identity, dissolution of, 48; impoverishment of content in, 73; and machine, 26, 160; and machinic enslavement, 263; manufacture of infra

mechanisms of, 47; modelization of, 47, 258; molding of, 235, 237–38; mythic references of, 171–72; participation vs domination of, 236; passion of, short-circuited by network of dependence, 71; and politics, 114, 146; and prepersonal domain, 31; prepersonal engagements of, 208; production of, 74–75; regression in behavior of, 78; and schizoanalysis, 145; and societal integration, 133, 135; and society, 175; subjective arrangements without, 152; supra and infra elements of, 43. *See also* extrapersonal level; infrapersonal elements; prepersonal domain

individuality, 284

industrial: cities, spaces of, 261; cost, 257; deserts, 79; maintenance, 259–60; map, 232; powers, 111, 232; production, 75; society, 244; society, subjective stabilization of, 160; and totalitarian system, 97

industry, 231–32, 234, 241, 246–48, 250, 268; biological, 75; defended regardless of consequences, 259

infantilization, 46, 72, 74, 87, 137, 296

inflexion, 229

information, 30, 41, 82, 100, 109, 126, 156, 178, 180, 182, 231, 269, 295, 299, 303, 305

infrapersonal elements, 263. *See also* extrapersonal level; individual, supra and infra; prepersonal domain

innocence, 151

institutional analysis, 33–34, 58, 202; origins of, 37–38

Integrated World Capitalism, 14–15, 48, 61, 77, 123, 229–43 *passim*, 250, 253, 258, 276–77

interdisciplinarity: supplemented by collective analytic elaboration, 35; vs intradisciplinarity, 23

international relations, 78, 94–95, 122, 236

internet, 13

interpretation, 66, 280, 298, 302; deformed by psychoanalysis, 145; and intervention, 52–54

intervention: and directivity in groups, 55; and interpretation, 52–54

Iran, 77–78, 119–20, 172

Italy, 11–12, 59, 61, 91–93, 98, 102–5, 117–19, 236; Autonomists of, 32, 91, 117–19; collective intellectual work in, 118; Historical Compromise, 92; USA interfering with, 91

Japan, 79–80, 158–60, 307

jobs, 231

Jones, Maxwell, 200

journalists, calm perspectives of, 76

Joyce, James, 156–57, 172, 182

July, Serge, 83, 316 n.3

Jung, 182, 223

Kafka, Franz, 145–47, 151, 153, 156–57, 159, 182; Pompidou exhibit on, 186

Kao, Micheline, 189, 195–96

Karepelin, Emil, 134

Kerouac, Jack, 149

Klein, Melanie, 134

knowledge, 42, 52, 160, 247–48, 255, 260, 266, 284; inhibitory prestige of, 44; as

productive power, 247

Krier, Léon, 293

Kuhn, Thomas, 173

labor, 15, 60, 175, 245–64 *passim*, 266–67, 269–70, 275; collective, 47, 233–34, 254–55, 275; division of, 27, 233, 262; force, 235; and machine, 246; machinic, 250, 267; manual vs intellectual, 42, 247; reproduction of, 246, 251, 254. *See also* work, manual vs intellectual

La Borde clinic, 8, 33, 39–40, 58–59, 65, 83, 159, 200–201; Guattari's changed relation to, 84

Lacan, Jacques, 10, 13, 23, 25, 33, 35, 39–41, 65–67, 144, 166–69, 182, 212, 214–15, 225; inhibitory prestige of, 44; tripartition of, 282, 298

Lacanian theory, 25, 170, 210, 285–86, 290, 294, 296; reactionary to desire, 40

Lacanism, 40, 65, 82–83, 167; D&G's criticisms of, 42; D&G's demolition of, 84

Laing, Ronald, 200

language, 74, 211, 282, 294–96, 298–99; discourse irreducible to, 281

Lascaux, 72

left, 11, 33, 63, 91–95, 98–99, 102, 104, 108, 110, 114, 118, 125, 167, 178, 200–201, 241, 291, 301; conservatism of, 56, 71; imprisoned militants of, 94

leisure, 47, 97, 118, 241, 247–48, 254

Le Pen, Jean-Marie, 70–71, 73

Libération, 25

liberation, 27, 30, 92, 152, 154, 157; and desire, 153; sexual, 142, 152, 197

liberation movements, 58, 152; subjection of, 28

lines of escape, 55, 239

linguistics, 50

Linhart, Robert, 58

literature, 21, 28, 69, 115, 149–50, 153; deformed by psychoanalysis, 145; of desire, 154; as liberation of desire, 157. *See also* psychoanalytic, readings

Little Hans, 50–51

Lotringer, Sylvère, 12

Louis XV, 69

Lyotard, Jean-François, 15, 294

Macchiocchi, Maria-Antonietta, 12

machination, 183

machine, 24, 31, 145, 158, 178–80, 231; abstract, 14, 43, 183, 194, 205, 220, 224–25, 302; concrete, 23, 65; desiring-, 142, 166, 192, 266; development of concept of, 84; explodes old subjective territory, 209; Guattari crazy for, 307; hateful pleasure, 71; and human, 251, 297; and human desire, 263; and individual, 26; infernal, 107; and labor, 246; literary, 148–49; mega-, 161, 259; military, 63, 112, 122, 274; and new possibilities, 74; production, 71; and recreation of world, 74; repressive, 148; semiotic, 265–66; semiotization, 49; society adjacent to, 254; vs structure, 142; tools, 241; writing, 149

machinic, 53; arrangements, 24, 251, 255–56; cancer, 252; collective passion,

79; dope, 13, 158–61; enslavement, 212, 262–63; environment, 48, 181, 245, 263; expression, 299; function, 77; kernel, 53; labor, 250, 267; markets, 270; phylum, 15, 28, 74, 187, 209, 220, 250, 273, 275; power, 267; precedes social, 251; production, 271–72; relations, 181; soup, 29; subjection, 245, 248, 255; subjectivity, 13, 158, 160; systems, 72, 74, 140, 303; teleguidings, 48; tentacles of capital, 259; time, 249; vitality, 17, 307; work, 26

madness, suicidal, 199

Madness and Civilization (Foucault), 280

mad people, extraordinary expressions of, 149

Magazine littéraire, 165

Maggiori, Robert, 7

Mahler, Horst, 108

majoritarian consensus, 11–12, 46, 98, 110, 235

Marchais, Georges, 73

marginal, 147, 202, 229–30; movements, 96; people, 62–63, 99, 111

marginality, 57–58, 98, 101

market economy, 116

marriage, 155

Marx, Karl, 26, 37, 114, 245–49, 251–53, 258, 262, 266

Marxism, 10, 38, 105, 113–15, 173, 177

masochism, sado-, 142, 150, 154, 156, 159, 210, 262

masses, 11, 87, 92–93, 97–98, 108, 110, 115, 123, 238, 253, 256, 259, 261–63

masturbation, 51, 141

materialism, incorporeal, 283

May 1968, 11, 22, 34–36, 82–83, 87, 117, 139, 176, 193, 196

mechanosphere, 182

media, 11, 13, 36, 47–49, 60, 71–72, 76, 87, 93, 97–98, 104, 106–8, 110, 135–37, 140, 173, 202, 209, 231, 235, 238, 248, 250, 255, 258–60, 264, 269, 281, 296, 302; crushing power of, 46; importance of, 47; and political affects, 109; post-, 17, 293, 299–301; and violence, 111

media personalities, calm perspectives of, 76

melancholy, echo of collective, 110

mental health workers, 40

mental patients, and society, 201

Merleau-Ponty, Maurice, 38, 132

meta-modelization, 205, 209, 211–12, 215. *See also* modelization

micropolitics, 12, 15, 31, 54–55, 57, 114, 120, 137–38, 161, 175, 179–80, 206–7, 209, 223, 229, 251, 281, 284, 289, 296, 304, 306

militancy, 32

militant: personality, 31; practice, 26, 44, 77, 306

militantism, 34, 49, 64

militants, 35, 45, 60–61, 91, 93–94, 109

military complex, 121, 126, 207, 231, 234, 236–37, 260, 274–75

Miller, Jacques-Alain, 65

miniaturization, 49, 239, 250, 261, 299

Ministry of Health, 56, 200

minor: languages, 10, 21; literature, 146; the, 12; theorization, 45

minority, 95, 101, 155, 161, 231, 238, 241, 255, 300–301

misery, 63, 92

Mitterand, François, 46, 96

modelization, 47, 168, 205, 220, 258. See also meta-modelization

Modernes, Les (Aron), 166, 169

Mogadishu, 106, 111

molecular revolution, 10, 12, 17, 29–31, 36, 44, 57–58, 62, 76, 95–96, 115, 117, 126, 138, 230, 239–40, 277, 293, 307

Molecular Revolution in Brazil (Guattari and Rolnik), 9

molecular transformation, 14, 62, 177–78

Molloy (Beckett), 150

Monde Diplomatique, Le, 58

Moro, Aldo, 103, 110, 317 n.1

Movement 2nd June, 104

Movement 77, 32

Movement of 22 March, 35, 42

movements, 62, 96, 99, 102, 104, 117, 123, 125, 160, 175, 198–99, 240, 242; disastrous effect of armed struggle on, 119; and self-defeating struggle, 152. *See also* autonomist; counter-culture; ecological; liberation; marginal; nationalist; nationalitarian; peace; protest; psychiatry; psychology; revolutionary; society;subjective; women's; workers'; Youth Hostel

multinationals, 95, 233, 263, 321 n.1. See also corporation

music, 67

mutants, 161, 300, 307

mutation, 13, 15, 28–30, 44, 49, 60, 63, 76–77, 118, 132, 161, 178, 183, 207–8, 215, 253, 264, 267, 276, 293, 303, 306

Mutuelle Nationale des Etudiants de
France, 34, 38

National Front, 71
nationalist movements, 232
nationalitarian movements, 60, 95
nature, 148, 151; no return to, 27
Nausée, La (Sartre), 175
Negri, Antonio, 11, 31, 59, 61, 91, 93
neo-liberal, 75, 269, 294
neologisms, 9, 21
neurosis, 50–51, 65, 134, 171–72, 174,
    213, 298
normalization, 134, 262
north and south, 12, 42, 111, 123, 256
nostalgia, 240–41
nuclear threat, 117, 122, 124–26, 243, 300

object "a," 225
Odette, and Swann, 68
Oedipus complex, 134, 303
organization, 120, 137, 301, 307; auto-,
    303; catastrophic means of, 27, 55;
    creation rejects contemporary systems
    of, 28; problems of, 45; of resistance,
    95; rhizomic, 32; structures of, 55–56;
    transversal, 12
origins, 280
Orlando (Woolf), 148
Oury, Jean, 8, 33, 39, 64, 69, 81, 199–200

Pace, Lanfranco, 61
pacifism, 92, 124, 126
Pain, François, 60
painting, 14, 67, 72–73, 149, 183, 292,
    294–95

Pasolini, Pier Paolo, 103
peace movement, 117, 124, 126
perception, 49, 74, 155–56, 222, 241,
    262–63, 287–88, 293, 303; ap-, 43;
    manufacture of systems of, 47; modeling
    of, 136; mutations of, 132; structuring
    of, 75
personal factors, and collective dimensions, 69
personality, 134, 159
Philadelphia Association, 200
Piano sul pianeta (Guattari), 16, 315 n.11
Pierce, C. S., 195, 282
pill, 178
Piperno, Franco, 59, 61
poetry, 67, 72, 155–56
Poland, 117, 119–20, 122, 172
police, 57, 60–61, 63, 93–94, 97, 104,
    110, 123–24, 196, 234, 236, 255.
    See also cops
political struggle, 180
politicians, 46, 68, 87, 91, 114, 125
politics, 31, 57, 70, 116, 124, 137, 140,
    151; and analysis, 32, 152; connection
    of global and molecular interventions
    in, 29; of destruction and restructuring,
    253; end of, 113–14, 138, 178, 294;
    and individual, 114, 146; and media
    affects, 109; media representations of,
    72; micropolitical broadening of, 251;
    minoritarian, 9; as painting, 73;
    super-power, 14; and terrorism, 93;
    worst kind of, 104, 108
pollution, 259, 307
Pompidou Center, 186, 192
Portugal, 236
Postmodern Condition, The (Lyotard), 15

postmodernism, 16, 74, 203, 279, 291–300

power, 8–9, 15, 36–37, 46, 52, 62, 93,
    97–98, 100, 104, 107, 110, 114,
    116–17, 121, 126, 144, 152, 231,
    234, 239–43, 248, 252, 257, 261–65;
    267, 270, 272, 280, 284, 286, 292,
    294, 299, 305; appeal of, 98; desire
    escapes, 156; formations, 15–16, 156,
    234, 243–45, 253, 255–56, 292;
    Foucault on, 285, 288; as image of
    power, 260; investments of, 45; and
    knowledge, 247; and media, 109;
    microphysics of, 16, 284, 290;
    relations, 49, 57, 66, 92, 152, 181,
    244–46, 254, 279, 284; and represen-
    tation, 151; and society, 152; state,
    36, 93, 97, 100, 112, 115, 118, 241,
    255, 258, 261, 272, 274, 276, 321
    n.7; and writing, 151

prepersonal domain, 31, 208, 302. See also
    extrapersonal level; individual, supra
    and infra; infrapersonal elements

Prigogine, Ilya, 273

prisoners, 56, 94, 98–100, 107, 195, 223

prisons, 31, 41, 57–58, 82, 94, 98, 106,
    249, 287

production, 14–15, 27, 30, 63, 71, 77, 97,
    135, 208, 232, 237–38, 240–41, 243,
    247–49, 252, 255, 258–60, 263,
    265–66, 268, 270–71, 273–75, 282,
    286, 293, 297–98, 301; capitalist, 47,
    215, 244, 246; desire precedes, 142;
    industrial, 75; and repression, 258–59

professionalization, psycho-, 65

profit, 116, 231–33, 246–47, 249, 251–53

progress, 28, 74, 77, 240, 291

Project for a Scientific Psychology (Freud), 222

Proletarian Left, 83, 235, 316 n.3

protest, 238, 240; movements, 36

Proust, Marcel, 132, 146–47, 153, 156,
    179, 183, 224; as great analyst, 14, 182

Psychiatria Democratica, 201

psychiatric revolution, 200

psychiatrists, 176, 236; manipulative
    character of, 39; progressive, 200

psychiatry, 15, 36, 65, 97, 180; alternatives
    to, 202; bogged down by Secteur, 36;
    movements of, 198–203. *See also*
    Alternative Psychiatric Network

psychoanalysis, 12, 38, 41, 66, 168, 171,
    180, 208, 238; absurdity of hypotheses
    of, 173; alternatives to, 202; classical
    perspective of, 207; confines of, 301;
    D&G's critical work on, 204; defor-
    mations of, 144–45; familialism of,
    170; Guattari's changed relation to,
    84; and money/payment relation, 54,
    67; savage, 53; and schizoanalysis,
    166; vs schizoanalysis, 144–45

psychoanalysts, 31, 69, 174, 221, 298, 304;
    Argentinian, 41; and money/payment
    relation, 54

psychoanalytic: methods, 51; myth, 70;
    readings, 182. *See also* literature,
    deformed by psychoanalysis

psychologists, 69, 176; manipulative
    character of, 39; and new frames of
    reference, 173

psychology: scientism of, 222; stagnation of
    movements of, 198

Psychopathology of Everyday Life, The
    (Freud), 302

psychosis, 53, 65, 134, 146, 149, 174, 216, 298, 302

Psychothérapie Institutionelle, 38

psychotherapy. *See* therapy

psychotics, 48, 133, 149, 196, 214

puberty, 133–34, 136; and perception, 132

public opinion, 109

Quinzaine littéraire, La, 148

Rabinow, Paul, 283

radio, 46, 49, 57, 59–60, 93, 99–100, 119, 140, 239

Radio Alice, 42, 60

raw materials, 231, 233–34, 237, 252, 255, 267, 297

Reagan, Ronald, 72, 122, 125

reality, art reveals breaks in, 151

Recherches, 34, 58–59; "Encyclopedia of Homosexualities," 141

Red Army Faction (RAF), 62, 103–4, 107–8, 110

Red Brigades (RB), 11, 31, 62, 91, 93, 102–5, 108, 110, 118, 317 n.1

reference, 44, 70, 76, 204, 206–7, 240, 245; archaic, 158; auto-, 297; coordinates of, 142; endo-, 87, 299, 303; and ideology, 178–79; incorporeal, 215; and little boxes, 131; mythic systems of, 171–72, 174; new territories of, 79; subjective formations of, 13, 173; system of, 73; transcendent, 230; universes of, 25, 66, 190–91, 213, 223, 296, 299, 304

referent, 50, 151, 207, 209, 240, 260, 280, 286

refrain, 14, 69, 85, 181, 183, 224

Reich, Wilhelm, 210

religion, 172; collapse of, 12; increase of, 72; and political change, 119

representation, 16, 78, 143–44, 211, 280, 289, 297; desire precedes, 142; and power, 151

repression, 11, 46, 56, 59, 92–94, 96, 99–100, 104, 106, 111, 152, 154, 184, 235–36, 238, 240, 243, 258, 301; internationalization of, 91; and production, 258–59; state vs soft, 12, 98

Réseau Alternatif à la Psychiatrie. *See* Alternative Psychiatric Network

resistance, 241

responsibility, 175, 200, 243

reterritorialization, 159, 195, 197, 223–25, 235, 244, 253, 283, 292–93, 305

revolution, 28–29, 36, 63, 95–96, 108, 120, 161, 230, 237, 241, 264, 292, 300; imperceptible, 17, 306; micro-, 132, 240. *See also* molecular revolution

revolutionary: alternative, 257; change, 229, 239, 243; crises, 121; movements, 99, 101, 109–10, 264; processes, 27; social transformations, 247; struggle, 34, 264; transformation, 277

rhizome, 11, 56, 61, 114, 151, 205, 229, 273, 299

Rimbaud, 149

Rolnik, Suely, 9

Rousseau, Jean-Jacques, 84, 172

Russell, Bertrand, 256

sado-masochism, 142, 150, 154, 156, 159, 210, 262

Sand, George, 148
Sartre, Jean-Paul, 39, 153, 167, 175
Scalzone, Oreste, 61
schizoanalysis, 13, 25, 52, 65, 144–45,
    165–66, 168, 180, 205–9, 211–12,
    223, 302; definition of, 206; depar-
    ture point of, 54; givens vs giving of,
    208; vs psychoanalysis, 144–45
schizophrenia, 214
Schleyer, Hans Martin, 103, 106–7, 110
Schmidt, Carl, 123
science fiction, 48, 124, 126
scientific: authority, 14; development, 292;
    domains, 275; logic, 24; paradigms,
    173; possibilities, 74; processes, 268;
    progress, 28, 74; revolutions, 29, 161
Sebag, Lucien, 81, 197, 316 n.1, 319 n.10
Secteur, 36
segregation, 14, 29, 79, 97, 139, 176, 230,
    232, 239–40, 243, 261, 265, 269, 291
semiotic: abstraction, 256; capital, 248;
    complexes, 210; components, 253,
    283, 296, 299; condensators, 258;
    dimensions, 302; entity, 303; entropy,
    229; flows, 155; function of meaning,
    287; guiding, 47; links, 304; lozenges,
    69; machine, 265–66, 272; manage-
    ment, 77; scaffolding, 87; segments,
    298; systems, 271; track, 54
semiotics, 42, 135, 143, 145, 149–50, 182;
    trans-, 182–83
semiotization, 16, 55, 148–49, 195, 210,
    239, 242, 244, 250, 262, 265, 267,
    271, 275, 283; assemblages of, vs
    communication, 49; collective
    arrangement of, 68; collective modes

of, 42; and power, 245, 252, 258,
    260; social, 77; somatic, 210
serialization, 202
sexuality, 136–38, 142–44, 149–50, 153–56;
    and creativity, 148; and desire, 152;
    expression of, 141; trans-, 147. See
    also heterosexuality; homosexuality
sexual liberation, 152, 197; vs liberation of
desire, 142
Shakespeare, 70
signification, 69, 214–15, 286, 298, 304;
    dominant, 229
signifier, 168, 174, 211, 215, 280, 282,
    286, 294, 296, 299, 301, 303
signifying: chains, 182, 213, 295; effects,
    207; elements, 281
signs, 281, 287
Silicon Valley, 13, 160
singularity, 16, 23, 44–45, 53, 73, 86–87,
    161, 203, 225, 285–89, 299, 305–6
singularization, 78, 161, 206, 209, 217,
    222, 224, 289, 299, 305
social: change, 236; end of, 113–14, 138,
    178, 294; fabric, transformation of,
    198; formations, 32, 212, 229, 244–45,
    248, 252, 254; group, dissolution of,
    48; practice, 16, 71, 77, 131, 291, 293,
    295, 299, 306; preceded by machinic,
    251; relations, 11, 14, 29, 38, 44, 92,
    97, 183, 238, 240, 246, 254–55, 263,
    265–66, 291; resources, importance
    of, 47; struggles, 36, 95, 99, 108;
    territories, reinvention of, 79;
    transformation, 229
socialism, 27, 96, 113, 122, 138
Socialist Party (France), 99

Social Rehabilitation (Spain), 99

society: adjacenct to machine, 254; ancient, 318 n.3; archaic, 244; archaic vs contemporary, 133; and change, 120; and control, 137; and doping, 160; and individual, 175; integration of individual in, 133; machinic dope as preservation of, 158; and mental patients, 201; mutation in, 118; paranoia of, 154; past movements influence future of, 198; people who want to change, 70, 116; and power, 152; rejection of bureaucratic, 119; repression diffused into all pores of, 98; revolutionary change of, 277; revolution and responsibility in, 243; and subjective arrangements, 152; upheavals throughout, 199. *See also* industrial society

soft subversions, 17, 306

solidarity, 120

SOS Racism, 71

space, 27–28, 46–47, 58, 79, 132, 261, 280, 297

specialists, 45, 281

specialization, 43

speech, 42, 49, 209, 286, 296, 298; discourse irreducible to, 281; transformation of relation to, 47

speed, 27

Spitz, R. A., 181

Stammheim, 106–7

state power, 36, 93, 97, 100, 112, 118, 241, 255, 258, 261, 272, 274, 276, 321 n.7

structuralism, 74, 82, 168, 183, 280–81, 283, 295–96, 298, 302–4

struggles, 43–44, 55, 100, 109, 119–21, 145, 153, 241–42, 251, 259, 277, 284–85; armed, 108–9, 112, 119; self-defeating, 152. *See also* anticapitalist; armed; body; class; movements; political; revolutionary; social

stuttering, 50

subject-group, 179

subjectification, 285, 288–90

subjection, 245, 250, 269, 275; and collective media affects, 109; politics of, 54; vs subjugation, 181, 249

subjectivation, 24, 184, 194, 210–11, 257–58, 297, 299, 301; post-mythic devices of, 172–73

subjective: continent, emergence of, 30; facts, 170; formation, 13, 38, 73, 161, 173, 303; formation, mapping of, 73, 76; identity, 78; movements, 119–20; territory, exploded by machines, 209

subjective arrangements, non-individual, and society, 152

subjectivity, 15, 22, 43, 69, 71, 206–7, 209, 212, 215, 220, 283–84, 286–87, 302–5; analysis of, 199–200; ancient vs psychoanalytic probings of, 172; capitalistic, 202, 211, 219, 257, 292; collective, 66, 76–78, 117, 269, 293, 300; mutation in, 77; contemporary vs neolithic, 72; leveling of, 203; machinic, 13, 158, 160; and meta-modelization, 205; modelization of, 168; molding of, 237; not engendered by language & communication, 74; production of, 48, 74–77, 87, 135, 137, 174–75, 282, 301 subjectivization, 179

subjugation, 52, 181, 233, 238, 241, 245, 248–49, 251, 255, 257, 262–63, 283; vs subjection, 181, 249

Surrealism, 167, 222

Swann, 183 and Odette, 68

Taylorism, 249

technical development, 292

technology, 180, 203, 233–34, 240–41, 253, 263, 267, 307

techno-science, 76, 79, 140, 250, 253, 255, 264, 267, 276, 303, 307

television, 49, 75, 93, 136, 159, 236–37, 254, 259

territoriality, 47–48, 158, 209

territorialization, 181, 239, 250, 261

territory, 79, 210, 215, 229

terrorism, 12, 61–62, 93, 108–9; politics of, 93. *See also* armed struggle; violence

theater of cruelty, 73

therapy, 14, 33–34, 37–38, 50, 170, 196, 199, 208; family, 13, 52, 171, 173, 180, 204

thermo-dynamics, 229

Third World, 63, 73, 77, 96, 108, 111, 233–34, 252, 263; bled to death by dominant economies, 269

Thom, René, 183

Thousand Plateaus, A (Deleuze & Guattari), 12, 165–66

tool box, 113

tools: of communication and modelization, 47; conceptual, 9–10, 12, 21–22, 24, 113, 180, 279

Topia Group, 203

Tosquelles, François, 36–37, 199

totalitarian systems: delusions of, 63; and industrial society, 97

transference, 52, 145, 171, 205, 207, 216–17, 297–98, 302

transportation, 47–48, 248, 255

transversal, 10, 12, 205, 240, 284, 297, 302

transversality, 23, 35, 65, 83, 280; and analysis, 46

Traumdeutung (Freud), 222, 224

Trilateral Commission, 236, 238

Ulysses (Joyce), 156

unconscious, 13, 30–31, 37, 44, 47, 50, 53–55, 66, 125, 145, 178–80, 184, 187, 199, 202–3, 206–7, 210–12, 214, 219, 222–24, 237, 239, 285, 289–90, 296–98, 301–2, 304; capitalism thwarts potentialities of, 31; deformed by psychoanalysis, 144; elucidating formation of, 43; media and trans-portation effects on, 48; molecular, 213–14; multiple futurological components of, 183; not solely structured by signifiers, 182; and politics, 114, 152; as site of every possibility, 32

UNEF, 34

Union of Magistrates, 178

unions, 63, 71, 95–97, 110, 119–20, 178, 237, 241, 247, 259–60, 291, 301

universals, 10, 21–22, 24, 80, 199, 281, 290, 302

universe. *See* heterogeneous, universes;

incorporeal, universes; reference, universes of

utopia, 17, 307

valorization, 116, 118, 246, 252, 265, 268, 270–73, 276–77; auto-, 17, 118, 306

values, deployed by capital, 257

Van Gogh, Vincent, 161

Veil, Simone, 56

Venturi, Robert, 293–94

Vincennes, University of, 83, 316 n.4

violence, 61–62, 91–93, 103–5, 107–8, 284; effective forms of, 11, 92; legitimation of, 92–93; and media, 111. *See also* armed struggle; terrorism

Virilio, Paul, 27, 121, 178

virtual, 220

Voie Communiste, La, 34, 81, 83, 316 n.2

wage system, 97, 111, 248, 253–54

Walesa, Lech, 120

war machine, 23, 30, 117, 275, 277

wars, 124

Weekend (Godard), 79

welfare system, 122, 202

Westheimer, Ruth, 136

women, 11–12, 79, 92, 109, 133, 143–44, 152, 158, 195, 231, 238, 240, 242, 255, 259, 262–63; liberation of, 25, 43, 95, 99; and men, 138, 241. See also becoming-woman

women's movement, 99; analytic impact of, 43

Woolf, Virginia, 148

work, 241–42, 245–49, 254; manual vs intellectual, 118, 242. *See also* labor

worker, collective, 245–47

workers, 11, 14, 40, 42–43, 45, 60, 62, 78, 92, 98, 102, 104, 111, 136, 160, 173, 231–32, 235–37, 240–41, 246, 248, 254, 259, 263, 275, 294; work on themselves, 259

workers' movement, 55, 95, 111, 114–15, 240; and conservatism, 95–96; and normalization efforts, 98

work force, 97, 237–38, 241

working class, 102, 108, 115, 153, 231–32, 253, 258, 263

world: adolescent apprehension of, 132–33; at boiling point, 307; crisis, 16, 56, 77, 91, 96, 102, 121–23, 198, 233, 236–37, 252, 267, 277, 295; fascism contaminates, 238; flattened-out c onceptions of, 72; and havoc of capitalism, 76; new ways of relating to, 239; recreated with machines, 74; same segregation all over, 232; singling out relation to, 219; uniformization of relations to, 74

World Integrated Capitalism. *See* Integrated World Capitalism

World Wide Web, 13

writing: machine, 149; and power, 151

written text, 153

Youth Hostel movements, 39

ALSO FROM SEMIOTEXT(E)

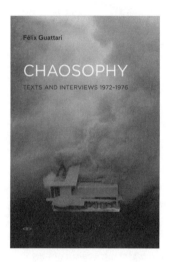

CHAOSOPHY, NEW EDITION
Texts and Interviews 1972–1977
Félix Guattari, edited by Sylvère Lotringer
Introduction by François Dosse

Chaosophy is an introduction to Félix Guattari's groundbreaking theories of "schizoanalysis": a process meant to replace Freudian interpretation with a more pragmatic, experimental, and collective approach rooted in reality. Unlike Freud, who utilized neuroses as his working model, Guattari adopted the model of schizophrenia—which he believed to be an extreme mental state induced by the capitalist system itself, and one that enforces neurosis as a way of maintaining normality. Guattari's post-Marxist vision of capitalism provides a new definition not only of mental illness, but also of the micropolitical means for its subversion.

6 x 9 • 336 pages • ISBN: 978-1-58435-060-6 • $17.95

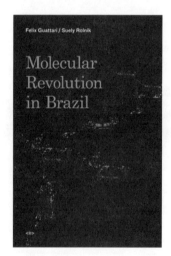

MOLECULAR REVOLUTION IN BRAZIL
Félix Guattari and Suely Rolnik

Following Brazil's first democratic election after two decades of military dictatorship, French philosopher Félix Guattari traveled through Brazil in 1982 with Brazilian psychoanalyst Suely Rolnik and discovered an exciting, new political vitality. In the infancy of its new republic, Brazil was moving against traditional hierarchies of control and totalitarian regimes and founding a revolution of ideas and politics. *Molecular Revolution in Brazil* documents the conversations, discussions, and debates that arose during the trip, including a dialogue between Guattari and Brazil's future President Luis Ignacia Lula da Silva, then a young gubernatorial candidate. Through these exchanges, Guattari cuts through to the shadowy practices of globalization gone awry and boldly charts a revolution in practice.

6 x 9 • 495 pages • ISBN: 978-1-58435-051-4 • $17.95

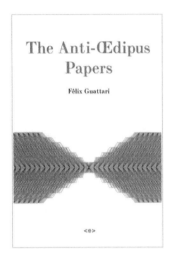

The Anti-Œdipus
Papers

Félix Guattari

<0>

THE ANTI-OEDIPUS PAPERS
Félix Guattari

Few people at the time believed, as Deleuze and Guattari wrote in the often-quoted opening sentence of Rhizome, that "the two of us wrote *Anti-Oedipus* together." They added, "Since each of us was several, that became quite a crowd." These notes, addressed to Deleuze by Guattari in preparation for *Anti-Oedipus*, and annotated by Deleuze, substantiate their claim, and finally expose the factory behind the theatre. They reveal Guattari as an inventive, highly analytical, mathematically-minded "conceptor," arguably one of the most prolific and enigmatic figures in philosophy and sociopolitical theory today. *The Anti-Oedipus Papers* (1969–1973) are supplemented by substantial journal entries in which Guattari describes his turbulent relationship with his analyst and teacher Jacques Lacan, his apprehensions about the publication of *Anti-Oedipus*, and accounts of his personal and professional life as a private analyst and codirector with Jean Oury of the experimental clinic Laborde (created in the 1950s).

6 x 9 • 439 pages • ISBN: 978-1-58435-031-6 • $17.95

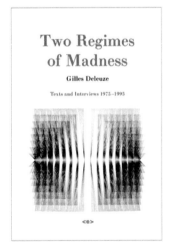

Two Regimes
of Madness

Gilles Deleuze

Texts and Interviews 1975-1995

<0>

TWO REGIMES OF MADNESS
Texts and Interviews 1975–1995
Gilles Deleuze, edited by David Lapoujade

Covering the last twenty years of Gilles Deleuze's life (1975–1995), the texts and interviews gathered in this volume complete those collected in *Desert Islands and Other Texts (1953–1974)*. This period saw the publication of his major works: *A Thousand Plateaus* (1980), *Cinema I: Image-Movement* (1983), *Cinema II: Image-Time* (1985), all leading through language, concept, and art to *What is Philosophy?* (1991). *Two Regimes of Madness* also documents Deleuze's increasing involvement with politics (with Toni Negri, for example, the Italian philosopher and professor accused of associating with the Red Brigades). Both volumes were conceived by the author himself and will be his last. Michel Foucault famously wrote: "One day, perhaps, this century will be Deleuzian." This book provides a prodigious entry into the work of the most important philosopher of our time.

6 x 9 • 424 pages • ISBN: 978-1-58435-062-0 • $19.95